THE
BYZANTINE
ART OF WAR

THE
BYZANTINE ART OF WAR

MICHAEL J. DECKER

WESTHOLME
Yardley

This book is dedicated to my wife Katy, Will, and Joy

Frontispiece: Sixth century relief showing Roman troops of the V Macedonian legion. (*Rheinisches Landesmuseum, Trier, Germany*)

©2013 Michael J. Decker

Maps by T. D. Dungan. ©2013 Westholme Publishing

Westholme Publishing, LLC

904 Edgewood Road

Yardley, Pennsylvania 19067

Visit our Web site at www.westholmepublishing.com

First Printing April 2013

10 9 8 7 6 5 4 3 2 1

ISBN: 978-1-59416-168-1

Also available as an eBook.

Printed in the United States of America.

CONTENTS

List of Maps

INTRODUCTION

On May 29, 1453, the twenty-one-year-old Ottoman Sultan Mehmed II led his 80,000-man army through the breach in the walls of the ancient capital of eastern Rome, Constantinople, where many of the 7,000 defenders lay dead. The dramatic assault, made possible by one of the earliest and most impressive displays of gunpowder artillery, punched through the hitherto impregnable fortifications, and led to the death of the last Byzantine emperor, Constantine XI Palaiologos, who perished in the assault; his body was never found. Greek legend holds that at the end of days, Constantine will return and rise from the floor of the great cathedral of Hagia Sophia in Istanbul to lead the Greek nation to final victory and the restoration of God's Roman Empire on earth—the Christian Byzantine state. In the spring of 1453, though, the noose that finally strangled the last vestiges of Greek independent political life from the Balkans was long in the tightening. Since 1356 the Ottoman Turks had made Edirne, in eastern Thrace, their capital and steadily strengthened their hold on the empire's former European lands. The Byzantines had been fatally weakened by the sacking of the capital of Constantinople two and half centuries prior in 1204 by the Christian crusaders from the West. This date marks the effective end of Byzantium as a major military and pan-Mediterranean power; after the sack of the capital, Latin warlords and their Venetian allies partitioned the empire while disparate Byzantine rulers regrouped and attempted to mount an effective resistance. Either date, 1204 or 1453, is arguably an appropriate one for marking the end of the Roman Empire. Although for centuries prior to either conquest the vast majority of the empire's inhabitants spoke Greek, and we refer to them as Byzantines, they called themselves Romans and viewed their empire as the state once ruled by Augustus or Trajan. After all, they were the direct inheritors of the Roman Empire's territory in the eastern Mediterranean, continued its administrative and legal framework without interruption, and, most important for our purposes, relied on the military apparatus that evolved from the old Roman legionary armies of antiquity.

The most striking thing about the Byzantine military, and Byzantine society at large, was its remarkable longevity. These medieval Romans, with their Greek speech and Christian faith, clung tenaciously to their culture in the face of constant internal and external pressures. Warfare, although never embraced by the majority of Byzantines as a virtue in the way that many western peoples viewed it, was nonetheless an essential component of the Byzantine experience. Foreign enemies were constantly at the door and they came from all directions, especially at the end of the empire's existence, when westerners threatened the shrinking borders of the state as much as did eastern and northern peoples. It is impossible to find anything like the *pax Romana* of the emperor Augustus and his successors, when Rome presided over one of the more tranquil periods of European history, having slaughtered most serious foes and bloodily dispatched of entire races in the process. However it was won, no parallel time of quietude ever descended on the Byzantine realm. Although the citizens of the empire probably fully expected a period of peace following the end of the brutal, apocalyptic struggle with Persia in the 620s, their hopes were sorely dashed when the ravenous armies of Arabia descended on the eastern provinces and rent them from the imperial grasp forever. In a matter of decades the Arab foes and bearers of the kernel of a new religion, Islam, were battering at the gates of Constantinople itself, and the empire had lost most of its territory to the Arabs or other invaders.

The survival of the embattled state and its much-reduced armed forces is one of the miracles of history. Far outclassed in terms of manpower and wealth and subjected to military challengers on multiple fronts, the Roman Empire of Byzantium nevertheless survived the assaults they received in the Dark Ages and emerged with a transformed state and society. The army, for which the bureaucracy and its tax system existed, both absorbed the blows of its enemies and dealt more shocks through rebellions and internal discord that marked the seventh through ninth centuries. Despite the upheavals, societal trauma, and the loss of so much territory and manpower, the Byzantine army adapted and fought on. By the time the Macedonian dynasty, the greatest of the medieval empire, came to power in the form of the usurper Basil I (867–86) the Byzantines were poised to embark on a two centuries-long program of expansion. Their reformed armies pushed the frontier into the borderlands of the caliph and reestablished Byzantium as the predominant power in the Mediterranean world. No state in European history absorbed such losses, survived, and revived to such prominence. At the center of this revival was the army, and the collective action of society, emperors, commanders, and soldiery make for one of the more compelling stories in world history.

In the pages that follow, I provide an overview of the basics of the medieval Roman army, including organization, logistics, armament, tactics, and strategy as well as delve into how these were employed. Although it is doubtful that the Byzantines ever thought of war in terms of grand strategy or professed military doctrines based on perceived universal experiences in war, one can clearly detect patterns to their approach to warfare with the benefit of hindsight. I call this the Byzantine Art of War.

THIS BOOK IS WRITTEN for a nonspecialist audience and students of military history and has been spurred by my own interest in the subject and by the enthusiasm for which my lectures on the topic at the University of South Florida have been received. In its crafting I am greatly indebted to the work of outstanding scholars the world over, especially John Haldon, who has pioneered much work on the Byzantine army, Timothy Dawson, Walter Kaegi, James Howard-Johnston, Taxiarches Kolias, Eric McGeer, Philip Rance, Dennis Sullivan, Warren Treadgold, and a host of other accomplished academics too numerous to mention. The reader wishing to know more will find the references necessary to pursue specific topics at their leisure— for this reason, and because I anticipate an audience whose primary language is English, I have endeavored to supply as many English-language secondary sources and translations as possible. I reference these in the notes. Original language sources may be found in the

Abbreviations and Bibliography. Finally, in an effort to produce a text as unencumbered as possible, I have limited diacritics in transliterating foreign-language names, terms, and sources and restricted the number of notes. I trust that those who wish to explore the subject further will find the bibliography an adequate gateway into a vast and growing body of literature on Byzantine warfare.

ONE

HISTORICAL OVERVIEW

EARLY PERIOD (FOURTH TO SEVENTH CENTURIES)

After six years of construction, the shining new capital city of Constantinople was consecrated on May 11, 330. By the time the city was completed, its founder, the emperor Constantine, was a hardy and hale emperor fifty-eight years old. Constantine had built a magnificent metropolis on the narrow straits that divided Europe from Asia and was the gateway into the vast hinterland of Anatolia and the Near East. Roman builders largely demolished and remodeled the old Greek fishing town on the site, Byzantium, into a city worthy of being capital of the greatest empire on earth. Thus, for many modern historians, the year 330 marks the beginning of the "Byzantine" or "East Roman" Empire. For their part, the Romans gathered on that spring day on the shores of the Bosphoros had no sense of a break with the past, rather they viewed with satisfaction the achievements and continued power of eternal Rome under their vigorous leader. The inhabitants of the Byzantine Empire called themselves Romans until the destruction of their state by the Ottoman Turks in the spring of 1453.

Constantine, like many of his successors, would find that the new capital was convenient for campaigns northward, across the Danube and against the Sarmatians and Goths. In 322, prior to his becoming sole emperor, Constantine attacked the Iranian Sarmatian tribes north

A view of Constantinople etched by Nicolas de Fer in 1696 clearly showing the city's commanding position along the Bosphorus, the straight connecting the Black Sea to the Mediterranean, a position coveted by various nations for centuries. (*Library of Congress*)

of the river and won a major victory, claiming the conquest of Sarmatia, *Sarmatia Devicta* on coins issued in 323–24. Both the Sarmatians and Germanic Goths provided troops to Licinius, the emperor in the east and the main rival of Constantine. In 332, Constantine ordered the old bridge of the emperor Trajan to be restored across the Danube, a symbolic act intended to convey to the neighboring peoples that the Romans would return to Dacia, which had been conquered by Trajan but abandoned by the emperor Aurelian during the period of near anarchy that braced much of the third century.

Constantine advanced with his Sarmatian allies against the tribal confederation that the Romans called Goths, a disparate mix of people of uncertain origin with a core Germanic element whose exact complexion and identity still remain open to debate. The Goths lived in a broad belt of territory across eastern Europe, namely present-day Romania eastward to the southern Ukraine and the Crimean steppe. Since the third century Gothic tribesmen had raided Roman territory

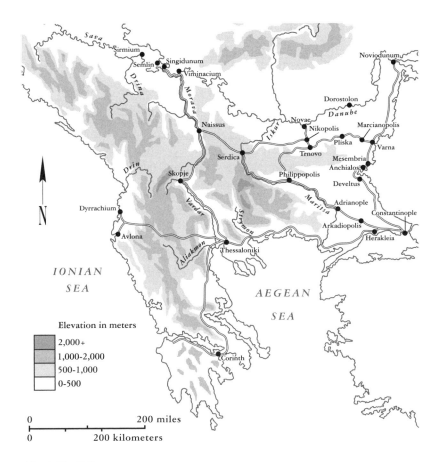

Map 1. The Balkans.

and from nearly the same period some served in the Roman army. Despite the Goths' considerable numbers and military capacity, Constantine's forces defeated those of their king Ariaric, whose people suffered tremendously from the war and the cold—one source states that 100,000 died. While exaggerated, the figure underscores the bloody contests between Romans and Goths along the northern frontier. The Gothic clans accepted Roman overlordship and remained at peace until the end of their rule. In the closing years of his reign, Constantine again campaigned against the Sarmatians, resettling thousands of them in Thrace, Scythia, Italy, and Macedonia.[1] So thorough

was the emperor's pacification of the Danubian frontier that no disturbances are known during the remainder of his rule.

Constantinople provided a valuable strategic location for wars in the
east, whence the emperor could march against the most serious
threat—the Persian Empire ruled by the Sasanian dynasty, whose
ascent to power a century prior had led to increasingly serious hostilities and major Roman setbacks, most notably the collapse of the
Roman eastern defenses in the 250s. For centuries, the Romans had
battled Iranian peoples in the east, first the Parthians, and then their
Sasanian successors. Even at its height the empire proved incapable of
digesting Mesopotamia—Hadrian disgorged the conquests of Trajan
and beat a hasty retreat and this in spite of the dominance of Roman
arms and the discomfiture of the Parthian enemy. These facts betray
the lack of a Roman answer for their eastern question: they could rarely
win decisive victory over the civilized power on their Syrian border and
in those rare instances when they did so, they seemed to prefer a
Parthian or Persian enemy to their own hegemony east of the Tigris
and Euphrates. The nadir of Roman power in the east came in 260
when the Roman emperor Valerian confidently advanced east to meet
the upstart Iranians in Roman Mesopotamia only to meet disaster at
the Battle of Edessa (modern Urfa in southeast Turkey) and fall prisoner to the mighty Sasanian "King of Kings" (Shahanshah) Shapur I
(ca. 240–ca. 270). The death of Shapur I around 270 led to internal
bickering among the Persians that allowed the Romans to seize the initiative. During his brief reign (282–83) the emperor Carus marched in
force through Assyria and down the Tigris to southern Mesopotamia
and the Sasanian capital of Ctesiphon (about 35 kilometers south of
modern Baghdad). This type of campaign, which saw the Roman army
march deep into Mesopotamia against the Sasanian capital, was to be
repeated several times in later centuries, and in each later excursion
there is a sense of déjà vu—once the Romans got there they did not
seem to know what to do about the place. Even if they did capture
Ctesiphon, as allegedly did Galerius in 298, they did not stay. Perhaps
it was the size of the city (really an agglomeration of settlements clus-
tered on the Tigris and along various canal branches), the stubbornness
of Persian defenses, or the difficulty of maneuver in a complex, conur-
bated landscape cluttered with canals. Perhaps it was the unmercifully
hot and pestilential land that stymied the Romans. Equally likely, the

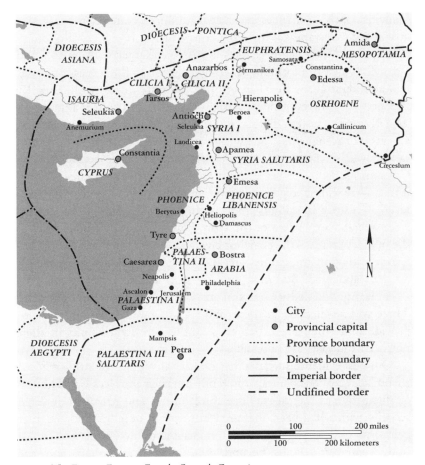

Map 2. The Eastern Frontier, Fourth–Seventh Centuries.

propaganda value of having reached Ctesiphon far outweighed the difficulties of capturing or administering an occupation. In July or August 283, the sudden death of Carus forced the Romans to withdraw under their new emperor, Numerian—one among many such failures. The youthful Numerian himself died in November 284, when the former duke (*dux*) of Moesia on the Danube, Diocles, assumed the imperial power and became Diocletian.

Diocletian stitched the Roman Empire whole after a half century (235–84) of military anarchy, economic trauma, and civil unrest. He made far-reaching changes in the civil administration, the military, and attempted to stabilize the economy. Although not revolutionary (Carinus had associated relatives in his rule as a fellow Augustus and Caesar), Diocletian formulated a bold solution to the succession crises and attendant chaos that had gripped the state in recent decades. By 293 he established a scheme based on the "rule of four" (Tetrarchy). The Tetrarchic system divided the empire into two zones governed by an emperor (Augustus) each with a subordinate (Caesar) who would take power once the senior emperors stepped aside voluntarily. As Constantine, among others, would prove, this system was effective only if men were willing to give up power, something that has occurred only rarely in history. In military matters, the most important changes were a considerable expansion of the army. During the tumultuous years of the military anarchy, the ceaseless civil and foreign wars had led to critical degrading of the empire's military forces. Diocletian inherited an army of about 389,000 men and, through a great conscription program, nearly doubled its size to somewhere over a half million men.[2] There was an increase in the proportion of cavalry units in order to provide more offensive capabilities and match horsed units of their northern and eastern opponents.

Our best evidence suggests that Diocletian and Constantine molded a Roman army considerably different from their predecessors. The aim of this program was to stabilize the frontiers and to ensure internal security which had been shattered in previous decades. Despite their bellicosity and propaganda, the Romans entertained no serious intention of annexing lands beyond their great river boundaries—the Rhine, Danube, Tigris, and Euphrates. But as the third century unfolded the policing of these permeable frontiers had become increasingly problematic, with multiple threats posed by barbarians who had become gradually more sophisticated and militarily capable. Roman frontier management with its frequent punitive raids, the infrequent large-scale invasion, and the complexities of trade and recruitment from among the tribes and neighbors who were often the target of aggression was both stimulated by and reacted to the shifting conditions of the vast borderlands. Diocletian's determination to keep the barbarians out is best viewed today in the massive fortifications of the east at places like Lejjun in Jordan and Resafa in Syria. In these places, rather standardized, large-scale legionary encampments embedded

An aerial photograph of the ruins of the massive Byzantine fortress at Resafa, Syria. (*Deutsches Archäologisches Institut*)

frontier troops in a line of defense. The troops that garrisoned these forts were called *limitanei*, border troops or frontier guardsmen who were regular soldiers and not, as some have speculated, a kind of militia. The frontier forces were strong enough to handle internal policing and local disturbances; in Syria the aggressors were often Bedouin tribal raiders. In the case of full-scale invasion, the frontier fortresses were meant to hold the line long enough for the arrival of the recently created mobile field army (*comitatus*) comprised of elite cavalry and infantry units initially drawn from loyal and seasoned legions, especially on the Danube frontier. The limitanei also formed part of the expeditionary armies on major campaigns, but without backing from the mobile imperial field army frontier garrisons lacked strategic initiative.[3] When the enemy arrived in force, as did the Persians at Nisibis in 337 and the Goths on the Danube in 376, they faced strongly manned hard points that they could not risk bypassing.

In 336 war broke out with Persia. Constantine sent east his nineteen-year-old son, the Caesar Constantius, to prepare for the brewing conflict. Constantius had mixed success while his father spent the year 337 preparing for landing a knockout blow against the Sasanians that he hoped would deliver peace to the Roman eastern flank. But the emperor was never to undertake the campaign. Constantine fell ill around Easter of 337 and traveled across the Marmara straits to take the hot waters at Helenopolis in Bithynia (modern Hersek). Sensing his end was near, he summoned his clergy and sought baptism, which had been postponed by the emperor following the common Christian belief of the day that the sacrament cleansed one of all sins committed to that point. On May 22, 337, the emperor died and with him hopes of punishing the Sasanians.

Constantine had divided the empire among his three sons: Constantine II, Constans I, and Constantius II. Constantine II ruled the territories in the far west including Spain, Gaul, and Britain. Constans II ruled the central portion including Italy and North Africa, while the east fell to Constantius (337–61). In addition, their cousins Dalmatius and Hannibalianus served as Caesars. It is difficult to conceive how Constantine envisioned such a brew of power sharing would work in practice, given that he had himself single-handedly overturned the Tetrarchy. In any case, the situation did not long survive him. In 337, Dalmatius and Hannibalianus were butchered along with other family members at the instigation of Constantius. Constantine II met his end in an ambush in Aquileia in 340 and his elder brother Constans in 350 fell victim to the rebel Magnentius. This dynastic strife distracted Constantius from his task of defending the eastern frontier against the Sasanians who had aggressively renewed the war.

Constantius proved a vigorous, if yeoman, commander. His loss of Amida (359) was a terrible blow to Roman prestige and underscored Persian might, but throughout his reign Constantius fought aggressively to defend Roman interests in the east. After the bloodletting of the succession was over, the young emperor faced a Persian siege of the city of Nisibis (today Nusaybin, Syria) on the upper Mesopotamian plain, an ancient city that was the linchpin of Roman defenses in the region. In either 337 or 338, the Persians battered the city in a grueling siege led by the young, vigorous King of Kings Shapur II (307–79) himself. Pitted against the shah was the local Syrian bishop of the city, Jacob of Nisibis, who organized the defenses and bolstered the morale of the citizens. Confronted over seventy days with a stubborn defense that confounded assaults using mobile towers and efforts to undermine the walls, Persian engineers dammed the local river Mygdonius and diverted it, unleashing the power of the pent-up waters against the city walls, one portion of which gave way beneath the rush of the torrent. The

Persians delayed their attack as the waters had turned the approach to the breach into a quagmire. The next morning, the Sasanians were shocked to find the breach filled with rubble to the height of the previous wall and defended by the soldiers and citizens of Nisibis, urged on by their omnipresent bishop. Shapur's last assault failed and the Persians were forced to decamp.

The rest of the war between Constantius and Shapur is muddled in our sources; it seems that there were numerous large-scale clashes—rare for the day—between the Romans and Persians, including two more major sieges of Nisibis and two encounters at the salient of Singara, in what is now western Iraq. Probably in the 340s, Singara fell to the Sasanians. In most of these battles, the Romans were bested, though in their assault on Nisibis in 346, the Persians failed to take the town. Their third attempt, in 350, saw the Sasanians mount a colossal four-month effort in which they once again flooded the plain around the city with waters diverted from the Mygdonius River. According to one account, they assaulted the city on boats—surely an amazing sight in what was once the midst of the desert steppe—but were repulsed by the valiant efforts of the defenders.[4] The war ground to a draw.

An uneasy calm settled between the two antagonists since internal rebellions against Constantius made it difficult to devote men and material to fighting the Sasanians. The emperor appointed his cousin Gallus to command of the eastern front in 351. The young Caesar, perhaps twenty-five at the time, was effective militarily but unpopular among the local elites at Antioch; he was executed in 354 for alleged treason. More than by Gallus's abilities, the Sasanians were largely restrained from offensive operations because of conflict on their own eastern front in Central Asia with the Chionites, a group of uncertain origin, but probably Iranian-speakers whom Shapur defeated and absorbed into his armies. Roman writers call the Chionites "Huns," but their ethnic makeup and way of life are unknown. Whatever the case, Shapur integrated large numbers of Chionites into his army and again turned his eye westward after peace negotiations broke down. By 359, the shah with his new Chionite troops under their king Grumbates probed Roman defenses along the Euphrates, bypassing Nisibis and seeking a passage across the flooded river. A high-level Roman deserter, who had fallen into debt and could not pay his taxes, the protector Antoninus, guided the Persians. Antoninus was well placed to be a spy, likely with wide-ranging access to imperial intelligence including the order of battle of the eastern armies and their logistical situation. His information was vital to Shapur, who on account of it attacked Amida, which fell after a bitter siege of seventy-three days of fighting vividly depicted by the Roman historian Ammianus Marcellinus, including a night attack by the Romans that nearly overwhelmed the Persian camp and the final herculean efforts of the Sasanians to carry their siege mounds to the walls.[5] Shapur sacked the city and deported its inhabitants to Khuzestan in what is now southwest Iran.

In the wake of the serious defeat, Constantius reshuffled his high command. More critically, he ordered his cousin Julian, the Caesar in the west, to dispatch Gallic troops to reinforce the east. Julian refused this order on the grounds that his troops were mutinous and declined to serve away from home. Instead, the Gallic legions proclaimed Julian emperor, whereupon they happily marched east to confront Constantius. Upon hearing the news of his cousin's rebellion, Constantius was apoplectic—his rage, coupled with the strain of years of campaigning and the heavy defeat at Amida—killed him, probably of an embolism, November 3, 361, in Cilicia. Julian, now uncontested, donned the imperial purple and immediately set about reversing what he saw as the pillars of the decadent house of Constantine: a devout pagan, Julian offered sacrifices personally to the old gods, ordered the temples reopened, and actively legislated against Christians. He was careful, however, to avoid outright persecution so as not to create more martyrs. Nevertheless, the animosity Christians held against the apostate emperor who had departed the true faith and had risen to power to destroy it knew no bounds—one Christian bishop dreamed that he saw a vision of the popular military saint, Merkourios, spearing the emperor.

Julian was an effective leader and, despite his rather frail frame and awkward manner, a fine soldier. Unlike most commanders, Julian personally fought in engagements, an act that won him widespread admiration among his soldiers, but betrayed a recklessness that would be his undoing. Perhaps his greatest strength was his zeal and devotion to the idea of Roman greatness as well as a personal identification with Alexander. Along with the desire to avenge recent defeats, these ideals drove the emperor to strike a decisive blow against the Persians, something that neither Constantine nor Constantius could do. A victory by the pagan emperor over the feared Sasanians would further undermine the Christian faith that Constantine and his sons had thrust upon the empire. In March 363 Julian left Antioch at the head of a large army that moved down the banks of the Euphrates, accompanied by a river supply fleet. Julian ordered the Roman client king of Armenia, Arsaces, to form a second invasion column and invade from the north. The emperor's forces made good speed and encountered only sporadic resistance on the way to Ctesiphon, which Roman forces reached in April. After defeating the garrison of Ctesiphon and sensing that the Persians were in his hands, Julian rebuffed Shapur's peace overtures, but he was unable to force his way into the Sasanian capital. Instead, as the weather grew hotter and Persian sabotage of the irrigation complex around the sprawling metropolis of Ctesiphon created a fetid quagmire, the Roman high command made the fateful decision to burn the supply fleet and strike inland.

Shapur II shadowed the Roman army as Julian moved northward along the banks of the Diyala River, then the Tigris on his way back to Syria. The Sasanians practiced scorched earth and launched constant harassing attacks that turned the march into a running battle across northern Mesoptamia. Exhausted, suffering from heat, thirst, and starvation, the Roman forces were ground down by desert combat. On June 26, the emperor fought in a major engagement against a large Persian force. Because of the searing heat he rushed to battle without his armor. A Sasanian cavalryman thrust him through with his spear and Julian died in his tent the same day.

The army elected Jovian emperor, the compromise choice selected not on merit but because he posed no threat to imperial elites. By this time, disaster threatened to overwhelm the entire Roman field army, caught as it was far from home and facing a potent enemy who was starving the Romans to death. Jovian proposed peace, and the terms that he accepted were devastating. Nisibis, the powerful Roman bridgehead and thorn in the side of the Persians, was unceremoniously handed over along with the territorial gains made long before by Diocletian. The strategic balance tipped toward the Sasanians but Jovian did not live long beyond the ink drying on the disastrous treaty; the emperor died in western Asia Minor in the winter of 364. His successor, Valentinian (364–75), chose his brother Valens (364–78) as co-emperor in March 364. Like many military men in the late antique empire, the brothers were Pannonians (a region on the central Danube) and among the last effective soldier-emperors of late antiquity. Valentinian assumed control of affairs in the west and Valens governed the eastern half of the state from Constantinople. In 364 the brothers divided the army into eastern and western forces and then left one another to stand on their own resources. Valens marched east and was in the central Anatolian city of Caesarea in Cappadocia when news came of the rebellion of Prokopios, a male relative of Julian and, as a member of the house of Constantine, a serious rival to the upstart emperor. Divisions among the conspirators led to the defeat and execution of Prokopios, who had Gothic military support.

With the east quiet for the moment, Valens turned his attention to punishing the Goths. In a three-year war he humbled the Gothic tribes north of the Danube. When the war wound down in 370 concessions on both sides led to relative quiet in the north for the next five years and established an equilibrium. Neither side could foresee the maelstrom that would destroy the Gothic polity and drive the tribes into a headlong collision with Rome.

Like many nomadic powers, the Huns appeared to have spontaneously generated in the vast steppe that swelled from the Black Sea to China. In the famous and oft-quoted fourth-century description of Ammianus Marcellinus, they were half-beasts who stitched together garments from the skins of field mice and who led a life of savagery forever on horseback. The truth is obscured and cannot be recovered; probably there was a much longer time horizon of Gothic-Hun contact and warfare than Ammianus leads us to believe.[6] Huns, whose ethnic origin is widely debated and uncertain, were most probably a mixed group of steppe warriors of Turkic language.[7] Nomad armies commonly integrate the conquered into their ranks and by the fifth century, the Huns included Chinese, Germanic, and Iranian elements along with the original Hun groups.

The Huns burst onto the European scene in 375 and smashed through the Gothic communities stretching from the Crimea to Transylvania, forcing the flight of many to the banks of the Danube where they sought to enter Roman territory as terrified refugees. Valens, who esteemed the Goths as good troops who had long provided serviceable recruits for Rome as well as formidable enemies, allowed the thousands of beleaguered people to cross the river. Once the Goths were out of immediate danger in Roman territory, the Romans struggled to maintain order and neglected to provide supplies to the mass of people whose precise numbers are unknown. When posing the question Ammianus, quoting the Roman poet Virgil, noted one might as well ask how many grains of sand were in the Libyan desert, so great was the host.[8]

Roman officials took advantage of the precarious state of the Goths and demanded high prices for food, exchanging dogs for children and treating their guests with contempt. After a riot in which Romans and Goths battled while Gothic and Roman leaders feasted at the city of Marcianople (today Devnya, Bulgaria) the Goths rose in revolt. They were led by Fritigern, the tribal head of a group of Goths known as the Tervingi. Other Goths from Roman army units in Thrace joined Fritigern, who disavowed the agreement with the Romans and began pillaging. A sharp encounter with local Roman troops ended in the Goths victorious and rampaging throughout Thrace.

By 377 Valens was alarmed—he ceased hostilities against Persia and prepared a strike against the Goths who ran amok in Thrace and Moesia. Gothic elements had formed themselves into a keen fighting force, well equipped with captured Roman arms and well provisioned. By 378, the Goths were hemmed in by troops from the western half of the empire under the emperor Gratian (367–83), son of Valentinian, who moved to assist his uncle Valens in the east. Though Gratian's advance forces advised Valens to wait for the full western field army to arrive before giving battle, the eastern emperor was impatient for a major victory that would bring glory and legitimacy to him and give the Romans a free hand to deal with their eastern question. Fritigern's army moved past Adrianople to the northeast and awaited reinforcements from the Greutungi Goths to whom he appealed as allies. Valens had been assured by his scouts that the Goths numbered only ten thousand, while the eastern field army was probably three times larger. Fritigern sued for peace, but Valens rebuffed his overtures and attacked the Gothic position on August 9, 378. Only the brief account of Ammianus survives, and due to the fact he was not an eyewitness and more concerned with the events surrounding the battle, we have only the faintest view of what happened that momentous day.[9]

The Greutungi made a sudden appearance in the nick of time to reinforce Fritigern's Tervingi. These reinforcements put the Goths close to numerical parity with the Romans. The Goths took up position on a hill, surrounding a wagon laager in which their families sheltered. The Gothic cavalry were away from the laager, burning the fields to hinder the Roman advance through the morning hours. The Romans arrived in mid-afternoon in the heat of the day in some disorder. Roman elite troops, too eager for battle, advanced before the rest of the army was fully ready and were easily repulsed, while the Roman cavalry on the left advanced to the laager beyond the support of their infantry where they were surrounded by the Gothic cavalry and infantry and routed. The Goths now attacked the Roman left flank and pressed the Roman ranks in a vice. By late afternoon the Roman infantry broke and fled and the slaughter was on. Valens himself was killed and his body never found. Adrianople was a disaster that rivaled Cannae in its significance, with two-thirds of the eastern army killed. The arrival of Gratian did little to halt the losses, as the young western emperor was reluctant to shed his own troops' blood in a risky confrontation with a menacing foe. Gratian recalled a disgraced senior commander, the Spaniard Theodosius, out of forced retirement and elevated him to Augustus. The western emperor provided some men and materiel for the unnerving task of staunching the open wound of the Gothic War.

Although many Goths attacked the Romans after Adrianople, some were induced to serve the empire. Increasingly, it was Gothic troops recruited into imperial service (labeled here as elsewhere by historians "Byzantines" or "East Romans" and later on "Greeks" due to the primary language of the empire) who formed the rank-and-file and officer corps of the eastern army. The Byzantines struggled to integrate their Gothic troops and failed to blend them fully into imperial society. The increasing "barbarization" of the army and officer corps, which endured for about a century from Adrianople, paralyzed the eastern state at a critical time and contributed to eastern passiveness and ineffectiveness against the Huns and other enemies. Fortunately, although there were some sporadic hostilities, the fifth century was generally quiet on the Persian front. This calm was due primarily to conditions within Sasanian Persia, whom the Hunnic Hephthalites had humbled when they killed the Sasanian Shah Peroz and captured his son, Kavad. Kavad ascended the throne in 488 and consolidated his authority against formidable internal enemies, then turned against Byzantium.

The war of 502–6 marked the first hostilities between the empires for sixty years. Along with Hephthalite troops, Kavad captured the major Byzantine fortress cities of Theodosiopolis, Martyropolis, and Amida while Arab auxiliaries under the fearsome Arab chief Nu'man pillaged Mesopotamia. Roman bungling and a divided command led to the war dragging on until 506.

By 527, Kavad (488–531) and the Sasanians once again waged war against the Romans. This time war erupted because of disputes over the Caucasus, coupled with the alleged refusal of the emperor Justin I (518–27) to adopt Kavad's son and heir, Kosrow (531–79). From 527–31, Byzantines and Persians fought along the fortified frontiers of Armenia and in a series of lightning raids executed by Mundhir, the Arab king and Sasanian proxy. Mundhir's opponent, the Roman-sponsored antagonist the Arab Harith, fought a series of bitter contests against the Persian Arabs. During these wars, both sides won and lost many battles. The general effectiveness (or ineffectiveness) of the soldiery and their commanders, along with strategic and logistical limitations, made these wars of attrition in which neither side could (or perhaps wished) to deal a knockout blow against the other. For all their propaganda and history of hostility, these ancient states appreciated the known and valued their ability to negotiate and manage their biggest enemies. When Kavad died in 531, Kosrow negotiated the "Endless Peace" out of necessity to deal with internal problems. Justinian (527–65) used the breathing room he gained to embark on recovering former Roman lands in the western Mediterranean. By the end of his reign he had recovered part of North Africa, southern Spain, and Italy.

The terrible consequences of all-out warfare between Byzantium and Persia unfolded in the first decades of the seventh century. When the emperor Maurice was assassinated in 602, his Sasanian counterpart, Kosrow II (590–628) (whom the Romans had helped regain his throne during a civil war of 590–91), warred against Byzantium, ostensibly to avenge the killing of Maurice. In complexion, Kosrow II's war was remarkably different than past encounters. While at first the Sasanians seem not to have intended to permanently occupy Byzantine lands, the total collapse of Roman resistance opened the possibility and the Sasanians quickly adapted their strategy.

The Roman-Persian War of 602–28 was an epochal struggle, which one historian has aptly called "the last great war of antiquity."[10] The two powers ceased sparring and now grappled for supremacy. The coup launched by the usurper Phokas (602–10) divided the Byzantine command and sparked resistance to the regime, which faced invasion from the east and internal rebellion. From the outset things went badly for the Romans; by 609–10 their defenses in Syria and Upper Mesopotamia collapsed, allowing Persian forces access to the Anatolian plateau and Syria, Palestine, and Egypt. These eastern provinces formed the rich, weakly defended underbelly of the Byzantine state where a combination of military defeat, religious dissension, and civil war made them low-hanging fruit plucked by Sasanian hands. In 609 the Byzantine governor of far-away Carthage in Byzantine North Africa equipped a fleet and land army in revolt against the emperor Phokas. In 610, the fleet arrived at Constantinople and deposed Phokas whereupon Heraclius, son of the African governor, ascended to the throne.

Heraclius's initial efforts against the Persians were disastrous. His heavy losses near Antioch in 613 led to the Sasanian conquest of Damascus in the same year, and in 614 the Persians sacked the holy city of Jerusalem, carrying away the "True Cross," the holiest of relics and a potent symbol of the discomfiture of the Byzantines and Christianity. By 619 Alexandria was betrayed to the Persians, and Egypt, the bread basket and most populous region in the empire, fell into Sasanian hands. Backed by the church and employing a highly religiously charged propaganda, Heraclius retrained and reformed the shattered Byzantine army. In 624, the emperor struck into Persian Armenia and Azerbaijan and sacked several cities there, then frightened off Kosrow with a bold strike against the shah and his army. When Kosrow fled, his army disintegrated and left the Byzantines to plunder extensively. In the following year, the Persians dispatched three armies against the Byzantines, but Heraclius outmaneuvered these forces and defeated them in turn. The year 626 brought the climax of the war. The Byzantines drew into alliance with the powerful Western Turk empire that lay astride the north and east of the Persian frontier. A two-pronged Roman-Turk offensive was a strategic nightmare for the Sasanians. For their part, the Persians allied with the new power north of the Danube, the nomadic Avar khaganate, and sought to envelop the Roman state. Persian troops ranged against the great city of Constantinople across the Bosphoros straits to the east, while Avar

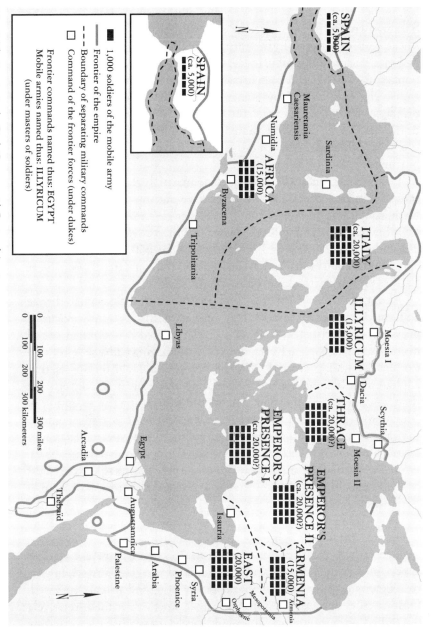

SPAIN
(ca. 5,000)

N →

Mauretania
Caesariensis

Numidia

Sardinia

AFRICA
(15,000)

Byzacena

Tripolitania

ITALY
(ca. 20,000)

ILLYRICUM
(15,000)

Moesia I

Dacia

THRACE
(ca. 20,000?)

Scythia

Moesia II

**EMPEROR'S
PRESENCE I**
(ca. 20,000?)

**EMPEROR'S
PRESENCE II**
(ca. 20,000?)

ARMENIA
(15,000)

Libyas

Egypt

Arcadia

Isauria

Armenia

Mesopotamia

Osrhoene

EAST
(20,000)

Syria

Phoenice

Arabia

Palestine

Augustamnica

Thebaid

N →

SPAIN
(ca. 5,000)

■ 1,000 soldiers of the mobile army
— Frontier of the empire
- - - Boundary of separating military commands
□ Command of the frontier forces (under dukes)

Frontier commands named thus: EGYPT
Mobile armies named thus: ILLYRICUM
(under masters of soldiers)

0   100   200   300 miles
0   100 200   300 kilometers

Map 3. The Empire in the Sixth Century with Regional Armies

troops besieged the city. The Persians' allies were to ferry across the Sasanian troops to complete the siege force, but the Byzantine fleet thwarted these efforts. In the meantime, the emperor Heraclius, who had made a colossal gamble in leaving his capital on its own to face the ponderous weight of Persian attack, renewed the offensive in the east. Buoyed by Turkic steppe nomads and Christian allies from among the principalities of the Caucasus, the emperor boldly drove into the heart of the Sasanian Empire. By January 627 the Romans ravaged the fertile heart of Persian Mesopotamia, scarring the land black with their burning.[11]

Inside the capital, disaffected elements of higher Persian society acted to salvage the state and staged a coup on February 23. The Shahanshah was first imprisoned, then executed after his son Kavad II was crowned. The young Kavad lasted less than a year and the Persians descended into dynastic and political chaos. By 630, the Sasanian generalissimo, Shahrvaraz, had taken control, but the fate of both Near Eastern empires was about to be sealed.

About the same year that Shahrvaraz ascended the Sasanian throne and the Romans continued their return to their recently regained provinces, a charismatic Arabian preacher named Muhammad seized his home city of Mecca. Born about 570 and having had a series of revelations beginning around 610, the best guess of historians is that Muhammad had been actively preaching and recruiting converts for the two decades prior to 630. The identity forged by the reception of Muhammad's message fostered a confident and aggressive spirit among the early community of believers who followed the nascent religion of Islam. The core of Muslim believers, the Companions (Arabic *sahabi*, pl. *sahaba*) carried the small body of new co-religionists to the conquest of the Arabian Peninsula and thence to Syria. The invasion of Roman Syria was a natural arena in which to expand; the Arabs of Mecca had extensive trade and property networks there, and the Romans were weak from decades of fighting.

The early Arab armies owed their success in part to Arab warfare experiences in the peninsula and in service of the great powers, in part to religious inspiration and apocalyptic vision, and in part to greed. Despite the decades of warfare, most areas remained relatively unscathed—their territories had only rarely, if ever, been traversed by armies or witnessed sustained sieges or battles, and their populous cities and numerous inhabitants promised rich pickings.

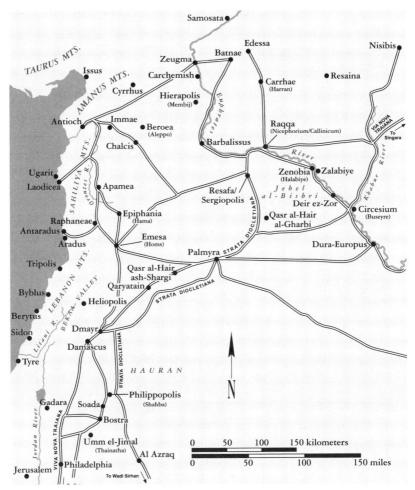

Map 4. Rome's Desert Frontier.

The first Arab attacks on Byzantine Syria had, in fact, preceded the concluding acts of the Persian War. The minor skirmish at Mu'ta, in what is today Jordan, ended in a Byzantine victory and was immortalized in Muslim memory as a heroic engagement in which several prominent early Arabian heroes became martyrs.[12] It was also a battle in which appears Khalid b. al-Walid, outstanding commander and critical leader of the great conquests. When the higher commanders were slain, leadership fell to Khalid, and he is credited with executing the withdrawal of the Muslim forces. As with all of the Muslim conquests, our sources are much later, often piecemeal, or even contradictory, and any reconstruction set forth is our best available interpretation.

When Muhammad died in 632, the Muslim community chose a caliph to be the spiritual and political head of the body. The Muslim invasion of Syria gathered momentum during the reign of Muhammad's successor, the caliph Abu Bakr (ca. 632–34). In 634, the Arab commander Amr b. al-As led a small Muslim army against Gaza, where he defeated the local Byzantine garrison. Probably in the same year, Khalid b. al-Walid led a raiding party from Iraq across the Syrian desert along the fringes of Roman occupation. Khalid's Muslims attacked the Ghassanid Arabs on the Christian holy feast of Easter. The Ghassanids were Arab Christian allies of the Byzantines and march wardens of the empire's desert frontiers. Khalid's attack on the Ghassanids led to the surrender of the important nearby city of Damascus, whose citizens capitulated and agreed to pay tax in exchange for Muslim protection.[13]

In summer of 634, the Arabs again encountered Byzantine forces, this time at Ajnadayn.[14] We have no contemporary information regarding the battle, but we know that the Muslims were once more victorious. The remnants of the Byzantine forces withdrew to Damascus and there faced a Muslim siege. The relief forces that Heraclius sent from his command center of Homs were defeated en route. The details provided of the Muslim siege of Damascus reflect later traditions which claim that one half of the city surrendered peacefully while the other half was stormed. Such incongruities in the sources allow us to only sketch the events of the conquest. What is generally agreed is that Heraclius mobilized a sizable force and marched them south to relieve Muslim pressure on Damascus and to end the Arab threat. It is doubtful at this time that the Byzantines understood that they were dealing with a new religious movement, nor could they recognize any difference between the Muslim Arabs and other Arab groups, of whom the Romans were often disdainful. Clearly by 635–36 the Byzantine high command comprehended that provincial forces had failed utterly in containing the threat and that decisive action was needed.

In 636 Heraclius, now old and ailing, dispatched a large army, variously estimated at 15,000–20,000 strong. They assembled in the Golan Heights, in the traditional pasturelands of their Ghassanid Arab allies. The Muslims prepared to meet the enemy field army with a force that seems to have been slightly larger and was commanded by prominent believers, including Abu Ubayda, Khalid b. al-Walid, Amr b. al-As, and Yazid b. Abi Sufyan, the brother of the future caliph Mu'awiya. No contemporary accounts of the subsequent Battle of Yarmuk survive; therefore, reconstructing the course of individual battles or campaigns cannot be done with confidence.[15] Though the details are opaque, the outcome of the conflict is clear—the Arab army won a crushing victory that ejected Heraclius and the Byzantines from Syria. Roman forces regrouped behind the Taurus Mountains on the Anatolian plateau as they had done during the dark years of the recent Sasanian wars. The emperor must have looked on his forces with a mix of emotions as he recalled the days spent in the highlands drilling his warriors to battle readiness before their epic encounter with the Persians more than a decade previously. But the emperor, now a sexagenarian, and his empire were exhausted by the decades-long war with Persia. Men and resources were strained to the limit and morale was catastrophically low. The imperial authorities were neither nimble enough nor capable enough to resist the determined and skilled Muslim advance. City after city fell.

The rich land of Syria was not the only prize sought by the Muslims. In 639 Amr b. al-As led a raid across the Sinai to Pelusium, the gateway to Egypt, which fell in early 640. Muslim reinforcements spearheaded a full-scale invasion of Egypt. The key fortress of Babylon on the Nile (near modern Cairo) fell in 640, and Alexandria surrendered the following year. By 647 the Muslims were on the offensive against Byzantine North Africa, where they crushed the local commander Gregory at Sbeitla in a battle that broke the backbone of Byzantine resistance. The first Arab civil war (656–61) that ended with the establishment of Mu'awiya ibn Abi Sufyan (661–80) as caliph afforded the Romans in Africa some breathing space in which to regroup. Despite the promising start, Africa did not fall easily—the conquest would not be complete until the Byzantines were driven from Carthage in 698.

DARK AGES AND MIDDLE PERIOD (SEVENTH TO TWELFTH CENTURIES)

Further east, Heraclius and his successors managed to withdraw the remnants of their shattered armies to Anatolia where the strategic triage included settling soldiers in the countryside in scattered garrisons and holding the line along the Taurus. This highland frontier

(Map 4), roughly the same that Heraclius had managed to maintain in the dark days of the Persian War, was constantly pressured by the new Umayyad caliphate. On numerous occasions Muslim flying columns penetrated the plateau, and from an early date raids became a regular feature of life in the uplands of Byzantine Anatolia. Like the later English *chevauchées* of the Hundred Years' War, Muslim raids were generally fast-moving plundering forays that aimed to keep the empire off-balance and weaken its social and economic fabric. However, once Mu'awiya constituted a Muslim fleet, the Mediterranean became a battleground where the empire fought for its life as the Islamic tide rose to the capital itself. The caliph launched a vast expeditionary army against Constantinople and established an operational base in the Sea of Marmara in 674. This sustained series of attacks were only defeated in 678 by determined defenders aided by the early use of a new weapon: "Greek fire", a naptha-based incendiary (see Chapter 8). In 717 the Muslims renewed their efforts to destroy the Byzantine state with a massive attack on the capital and once more they suffered heavy losses and defeat. Such was the weakness of the Byzantine army that the victorious emperor, Leo III (717–41), made no effort to go on the offensive.

Although they could not know it at the time, the empire had faced the worst of the storm. Yet the disruption of these military encounters was total. Cities shrank and virtually disappeared. The money economy faltered to near collapse. Literary society and high culture declined. Never before had an empire absorbed such unremitting punishment at the hands of an enemy, lost so much territory, and remained intact. Over the dark decades at the end of the seventh and beginning of the eighth century, the Byzantines adapted themselves to the new situation: they were much poorer in money and men than their enemy. The collapse of cities and the fiscal structure forced extreme economies on the army. The exact complexion of these changes remains in debate, but it seems that troops were settled in the countryside and provided with the barest of wages. Initially five regional army commands (Maps 4 and 5) were constituted from the remnants of the armies settled in the district—thus the billeting lands of the old Army of the East (Anatole) came to be called the Anatolik. These regional commands were called *thema*, a word of unknown origin. The thematic army was both qualitatively and quantitatively the inferior of its late Roman predecessor.

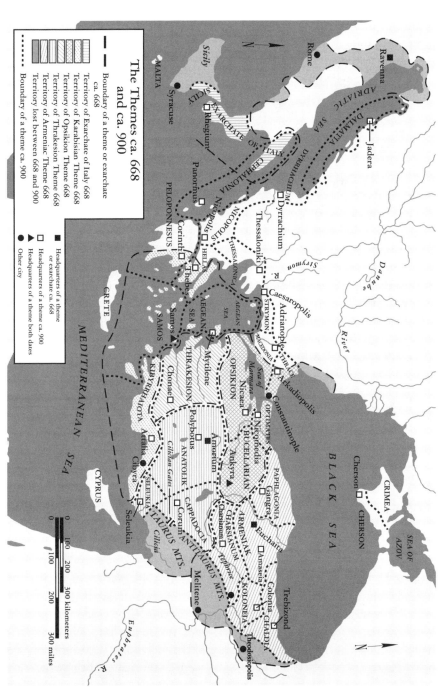

Map 5. The Themes ca. 668 and ca. 900

Equipment and training suffered, but the army remained a profession-al fighting force with recognizable units and regular drill. The Dark Age thematic army was a defensive force led by commanders who rarely risked pitched battle. Instead, Byzantine commanders preferred to harass and wear out enemies who already had to traverse great dis-tances from their bases in Syria to reach the populated places of the plateau. The low intensity conflict of raid and counter-raid, punctuat-ed by the occasional large-scale imperial or Arab expedition, became the norm from the later seventh through the ninth century. During this period, the frontier dwellers on the Anatolian plateau of Byzantium developed a military caste of families whose fortunes were linked to war. By 750, the eastern Roman state was recovering somewhat demo-graphically and economically—the first glimmers of a revival may be seen during the reign of Constantine V (741–75) who survived a bit-ter revolt by several themes. Around 743, Constantine formed a perma-nent body of professional cavalry regiments (*tagmata*) stationed in and near the capital where they could quickly muster to the emperor's aid. The tagmata provided a more professional, loyal, and disciplined core on campaign than the provincial armies of the themes. After decades of fitful defense, in 745 Constantine led the tagmata and thematic troops against the caliphate while the latter was hobbled by the Third Civil War.[16]

In 750, the fall of the Umayyad dynasty in the Third Civil War pro-vided some respite to the Byzantines who nonetheless remained weak-ened by internal political and religious dissent. The new Islamic state, the 'Abbasid dynasty, based itself in Iraq, and though ideologically still committed to *jihad* the 'Abbasids favored persistent raiding rather than the massive assaults that had failed the Umayyads and contributed to their downfall. It would be wrong to view the 'Abbasids as less aggres-sive than their predecessors, however. When the opportunity arose, 'Abbasid commanders were keen to polish their jihad credentials in warring against the Romans, and some invasions, like that of 838, pen-etrated the heart of the empire and could have laid the groundwork for outright conquests that political realities otherwise forestalled. For each large invasion and investment of Byzantine cities, there were scores of minor raids and spates of violence across the long, sinuous frontier. There, in the mountain passes and the high dusty hill country of Anatolia, endemic warfare and the weakened state led to the rise of the *akritai,* the border lords immortalized in the medieval Greek epic *Digenis Akritis* (*Two-blooded Border Lord*) which demonstrates the intimacy, respect, and violence of frontier elite warrior castes of the eighth through tenth centuries.

More than the caliphate itself, 'Abbasid border emirates mustered large forces for full-scale attacks. One of these expeditions provides modern historians blessed with hindsight a turning point in the Byzantine-Arab wars. In 863, Amr al-Aqta, the emir of Melitene (modern Malatya in eastern Turkey), and Ja'far, probably the emir of Tarsos, invaded the empire. Ja'far's troops advanced through the eastern Byzantine region of Cappadocia where they were defeated at a place called Bishop's Meadow, apparently by the emperor Michael III and the forces of the imperial tagmata. The second Arab raiding column, led by Amr al-Aqta, continued its raid, capturing Amisos (Samsun) on the Black Sea. The Byzantine commander-in-chief (*domestikos ton scholon*) Petronas, using elements of the thematic armies and the imperial tagmata, surrounded al-Aqta in the mountains of Anatolia near the banks of the Lalakaon River where, on September 3, the Byzantines dealt a devastating defeat to the army of Melitene and its Paulician allies, the latter a sect of Christian heretics in eastern Anatolia.[17] The victory at Lalakaon marked the end of massive Arab raids to the heart of Anatolia and opened the way for the Byzantine destruction of the Paulician homeland in eastern Asia Minor. It also proved that the Byzantine army of the Amorion dynasty (811–67) could match Arab armies in the field; thus by the end of Michael III's reign in 867, the Byzantines were on the offensive in the east, a drive they would sustain for more than a century.

While the Byzantines sought to maintain the core of the state— Anatolia and Constantinople and its hinterland—the losses in the provinces mounted. In Italy, by 750 the Byzantines had lost most of their territory to the Lombards, save some possessions in the south. Over a seventy-five-year period, beginning in 826, Sicily fell to the North African Muslims. Crete fell to Muslim raiders around 827 and became a raiding emirate founded on piracy. Perhaps the worst disaster to befall the army and state occurred not on the Arab front, but at the hands of the Bulgars, whose power challenged the empire in the north. Over the course of the seventh and eighth centuries, the former Balkan provinces had been mostly lost by the empire to Slavic tribes

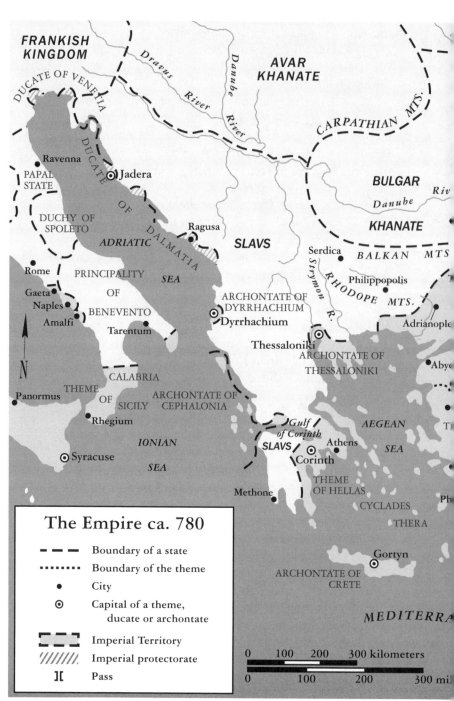

Map 6. The Empire ca. 780.

SLAVS

MAGYARS

KHAZAR
KHANATE

SEA OF
AZOV

GOTHS

er

Cherson ◉ ARCHONTATE
OF CHERSON

● Pliska

ABASGIA

B L A C K   S E A

● Anchialos
THEME OF
THRACE

Sinope

Arkadiopolis
◉

Euchaïta
◉

Constantinople
●

Claudiopolis ●

Amaseia

OPTIMATES

*Sea of
Marmara*

ARMENIAK

Nicaea ◉ ●Malagina   BUCELLARIAN

Theodosiopolis ●

dus

Mt. Olympus

THEME

OPSIKION THEME

Ankyra
◉

Charianon ●

Camachum

Nacolea ●

THEME

ARMENIA

● Pergamum

Amorium
◉

Halys   R.

Caesarea

CAPPADOCIA

ANTITAURUS MTS.

Amida

THRAKESION

ANATOLIK

Nazianzus ●

● Sardis

THEME

TAURUS MTS.

● Ephesus

Ikonion ●

Germanikeia ●

● Samosata

Chonae
◉

THEME

Cilician Gates

MESOPOTAMIA

hoenix

CILICIA ●Anazarbos
●Mopsuestia

Rhodes
●

Attalia
◉

Adana ●

CIBYRRHAEOT

Tarsos

● Antioch

Euphrates River

THEME

Seleucia ●

SYRIA

ARCHONTATE OF

◉

CYPRUS   Constantia

ABBASID

CALIPHATE

ANEAN   SEA

N

iles

and the nascent Bulgarian khanate. The Bulgar khanate subjugated many of the Slavic tribes across the Danube and by the ninth century emerged as a major foe. In the spring of 811, the emperor Nikephoros I (802–11) led a large army of professionals and conscripts north across the Danube where the Bulgar khan Krum (ca. 802–14) sued for peace. Nikephoros brushed him aside and on July 20, 811, burned and pillaged the Bulgar capital of Pliska. The emperor then withdrew south, but Krum trapped the imperial forces in a mountain pass. In a dawn attack, the Bulgars killed Nikephoros and mortally wounded his son and designated successor. Krum's forces routed the Roman army and seized the imperial treasury, and along with the emperor perished "an infinite number of soldiers so that the flower of Christendom was destroyed"; the Bulgar khan made a drinking vessel from the emperor's skull.[18] As a result of his victory Krum expanded his power to the south into Byzantine Thrace and set the stage for further conflict. Michael I (811–13) campaigned against the Bulgars but in June 813 after failed peace negotiations, Krum routed the Byzantines near Adrianople (modern Edirne) and pushed to the walls of Constantinople itself, where the new emperor, Leo V (813–20), attempted to assassinate the khan. Frustrated by his inability to breach the massive defenses of the capital, Krum withdrew; on the way he devastated Thrace and captured the major city of Adrianople. Only Krum's death the following year saved the Byzantines further humiliation.

Recruitment and maintenance of paid professionals expanded during the era of the Macedonian dynasty (867–1022), a period that marks the apogee of medieval Byzantine military power. Political fragmentation in the caliphate and improved economic and demographic conditions inside the empire allowed the Byzantines to regain much of their lost Balkan territories from Slavic tribes and to hold at bay their bellicose Bulgar neighbors. Wars against the latter were frequent and bitter. Under their ambitious and capable Symeon (893–927)—who betrayed his imperial designs by adopting the title of *tsar* (Caesar)— the Bulgars responded to a trade dispute with an invasion of Thrace where they successfully captured Adrianople. In the spring of 896, the Byzantines sent the combined eastern and western thematic armies and tagmata against Symeon, who inflicted a heavy defeat on them at the fortress of Bulgarophygon. Unappeased by being installed within the Byzantine hierarchy, Symeon warred against the Romans who allied with nomadic Pechenegs and the Serbs and sent an army under the *domestikos* (marshal) Leo Phokas, an easterner from a prominent military family. Romanos Lekapenos, the future Byzantine emperor, commanded the Byzantine fleet that was to ferry the Pechenegs across the river. At Acheloos (Anchialos), Symeon intercepted Leo's forces before his allies could join him and dealt him a decisive defeat—the historian Leo the Deacon commented that the piles of bleached bones of the Roman fallen could be seen in his own day, seventy-five years after the battle.[19] Symeon pressed his advantage and moved south, where Leo Phokas confronted him with hastily raised forces. In the autumn in Thrace not far from the Byzantine capital, Symeon again swept Leo's forces from the field. He broke off his war against the Romans to punish his rebellious Serbian vassal, and wars against the Serbs and Croats occupied the tsar until the end of his life in 927, when his son Peter made peace.

If the wars with the Bulgars demonstrate a certain Roman military futility, they underscore the capabilities of the enemies of New Rome, who were sophisticated, organized, and aggressive. They also demonstrate why the Byzantines preferred proxy warfare and negotiations to full-blown confrontations that were chancy even when the balance of forces seemed to favor the empire. Finally, these conflicts, in which the Byzantines were bloodied as often as victorious, proved the resilience of the Roman army, which could not be destroyed in any one "decisive" battle any more than could their Bulgar or Arab neighbors.

By the tenth century, the Arab attackers who had taught many harsh lessons to the Byzantines were themselves weakening. Byzantine commanders increasingly took the fight to the Muslim states on their borders. This eastern push coincided with the ascendance of powerful military clans in Anatolia, especially the families of Phokas, Skleros, and others like them who won their spurs fighting the Arabs and rose in the imperial hierarchy until they occupied the highest military commands. The prestige, salaries, and access to power the military provided fueled the war effort in the east, which offered plunder and honor. Once the weakness of their neighbors was exposed, the Byzantines were deliberate in their advance. In 934, the Byzantines captured Melitene, the heart of one of the two major Arab emirates on their eastern flank. The *domestikos ton scholon*, Nikephoros Phokas captured

Crete from the Arabs in 961. Two years later, Nikephoros seized the imperial throne and continued to lead armies in person. In 965 he destroyed the raiding emirate of Tarsos and Byzantine armies advanced into Syria. In the Balkans the military successes also mounted. In 970 the Byzantines under Bardas Phokas confronted near Arkadiopolis (modern Lüleburgaz in European Turkey) a Kievan Rus' prince Sviatoslav I (ca. 942–72), who refused to leave Bulgaria. The following year, the emperor John Tzimiskes (969–76) arrived across the Danube with his eastern field forces, which crushed the Rus' at Dorostolon.

The army of the Macedonian era relied increasingly on professional mercenaries. Though apparently eager to serve, the thematic troops were progressively called on to commute their services to cash payments so that the emperor and his generals could recruit paid professionals. These standing forces included not only Greek elements, but also more and more foreign contingents. Especially well-known were the Scandinavian Rus' recruited into the famed Varangian Guard of Basil II (976–1025), but the army continued to be dominated by troops recruited from Anatolia until the eleventh century. The reign of Basil marks another pivotal point in Byzantine military history, for he largely sidelined the eastern military families who challenged his rule on two occasions and who had come near to dethroning him. The eastern campaigns were largely suspended in favor of Basil's project against Bulgaria. Basil II's Bulgarian struggle was war as the Byzantines were best able to wage it—a long, patient trial by fire. The strategy of incremental advance and attrition, rather than master strokes of large pitched battle, proved that Basil adhered to the Byzantine preference for the avoidance of decisive combat in favor of longer term, but ultimately less risky approaches to warfare. By the time the Bulgarian war ended in 1018, the frontier of the Roman Empire lay on the Danube. The price for the attention the emperor paid to the Balkans was the alienation of a large swathe of the eastern military families and their marginalization within the command structure. Along with them probably also went large bodies of experienced, able troops. By the time of the last Macedonian leader, the aged empress Theodora (1055–56), Roman arms were running down. The emperor Constantine IX (1042–55) famously commuted the military service of thousands of Caucasian Iberian thematic troops into cash payments to the treasury, which he wasted on a lavish court.[20]

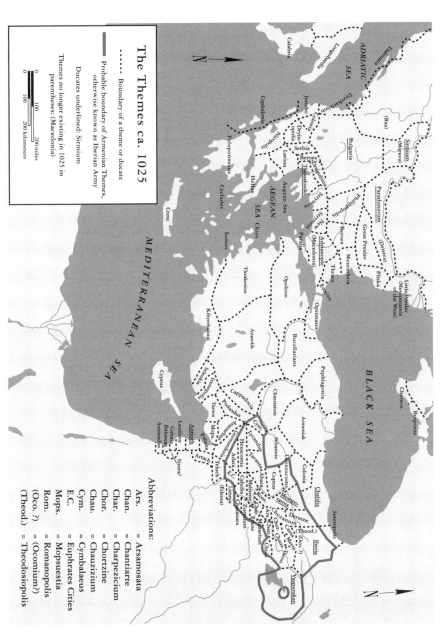

Map 7. The Themes ca. 1025.

Over the course of the eleventh century, Turkish tribes moved from the Aral Sea region into Persia and South Russia. A group of these, the Uz confederation, invaded the recently incorporated Bulgarian provinces along the Danube. Constantine X (1059–67) allegedly could muster only 150 men to oppose them. In the east in 1068, the Seljuk Turks under Sultan Alp Arslan (1064–72) seized the large city of Ani in Byzantine Armenia. The new emperor, Romanos IV Diogenes (1068–71), was among the last of the Anatolian military families to hold power. He tried to repair the thematic armies, but ultimately was forced to rely on professional mercenaries drawn from the empire and abroad. His position insecure, Romanos IV sought to land a hammer blow against the Seljuks and thus to stabilize the empire's rich eastern flank. In the summer of 1071, the emperor led to the east what some consider the largest army the Byzantines ever mustered, a polyglot force of Uz, Pecheneg, Norman, Greek, Iberian, and Armenian soldiers. In mid-August, on the road to the town of Mantzikert (today Malazgirt) by Lake Van in eastern Anatolia, the army met the outnumbered forces of the Seljuks under Alp Arslan. Romanos divided his forces and sent those under a Norman adventurer Roussel de Balleul and the Byzantine commander Joseph Tarchaneiotes to seize the fortress of Chliat (today Ahlat) on Lake Van, but the soldiers fled when fighting began.[21] Nevertheless, the emperor's troops acquitted themselves well, absorbing the Seljuk counterattack that followed the Turks' feigned retreat—an ancient tactic of the steppe nomads and one that destroyed many armies throughout history. The fight was bitter and prolonged and lasted into the second day, when Romanos was betrayed by the prominent nobleman Andronikos Doukas and captured by the enemy. Alp Arslan released Romanos, whose return to the empire triggered a civil war that allowed the Turks to continue their inroads.

The Seljuks and Turkmen nomads who ranged over the east posed an acute threat to the empire's stability. By the end of the eleventh century the Seljuks or independent Turkmen raiders had overrun most of Anatolia. Upland Asia Minor, with its vast lands, mineral resources, and pool of military recruits, was largely lost to the empire and the Seljuks had seized Nicaea, a mere 70 kilometers from Constantinople (Map 7). Even more serious than the Seljuk menace was the growing threat from the west. The appearance of the Normans in the

Mediterranean would forever change the delicate balance of power there and produce a new, bitter enemy whose capacities were unmatched. Norman adventurers had arrived in south Italy around the year 1000 where they found the fragmented, chaotic political situation to their liking. Norman soldiers in the pay of local Lombard princes fought against Byzantine troops during the Lombard revolt of 1009–22, and over the next decades Norman adventurers were frequently paid by both the Lombard princes and Byzantine commanders in south Italy. Norman troops—among them William "Iron Arm" of the Hauteville family—fought with distinction during the unsuccessful Sicilian campaign of the Byzantine general George Maniakes (1038–40). Following the failure of Maniakes's expedition, the Normans turned against their former Byzantine paymasters and ravaged most of south Italy. Iron Arm allied with Duke Guiamar IV, and under William and his successors the Normans steadily nibbled on Byzantium's south Italian possessions. Robert Guiscard, another of the Hauteville family, conquered Sicily (1061–91) and drove the Byzantines out of the Italian Peninsula with the capture of Bari in 1071. But the Normans had grander designs—the conquest of the empire itself.[22]

The emperor who found himself sorely tried by the Normans was Alexios I Komnenos (1081–1118), scion of a military family with connections to the powerful Doukas clan whose members had defected from the emperor at Mantzikert a decade earlier. Although just twenty-five years old, the emperor was an experienced commander, having fought in civil wars throughout the empire. He seized the throne as the emperor Nikephoros III (1078–81) prepared to meet the Norman onslaught. Alexios rushed to meet Robert Guiscard and his son Bohemund who had invaded in the spring of 1081 and laid siege to the important port of Dyrrachium (modern Durrës in Albania) on the Adriatic coast. In October the imperial forces lay within striking distance. Although advised by his local commander to avoid battle and to wear out the enemy, Alexios pressed for confrontation, probably because of his weak political footing. He screened the front of his force with the Varangian Guards (by now counting in their ranks many Anglo-Saxons who had fled the Norman conquest of England) supported by a unit of archers, and these units advanced against the Norman camp. The emperor commanded the Byzantine center, while the experienced general Gregory Pakourianos commanded the left and Nikephoros Melissenos, another battle-tried Anatolian commander led the right. Guiscard also divided his forces into three battles, commanding the center opposite Alexios while his son Bohemund commanded the left and a Norman count called Amiketas held the right. Much later Anna Komnene, Alexios's daughter, wrote an account of the battle and noted that a Varangian unit attacked the Norman camp through a salt marsh as the garrison of Dyrrachium made a sally.[23] Guiscard sent a detachment of Norman cavalry against the Byzantine center in a feigned retreat—a tactic which the Byzantines themselves knew well. When this failed, the two sides began a general skirmish. As the two armies closed, however, the Norman right under Amiketas clashed with the Varangians; the Normans fled to the shore where Guiscard's wife, Gaita, allegedly rallied them. Guiscard sent a strong detachment of infantry against the tired and isolated Varangians, who were surrounded and broke. Those who ran away took refuge in a church, which Anna accuses the Normans of burning down with the men trapped inside. In the general engagement that followed the Normans punched through the Byzantine lines and killed several prominent commanders. The empire's Turkish mercenaries fled and another ally, the King of Diokleia, refused to assist Alexios. The emperor bolted the field along with the rest of the army and made a dramatic escape by cutting down Guiscard's second-in-command and narrowly avoiding death several times. By winter the Normans had captured Dyrrachium and dug in, in preparation to push east toward the capital.[24]

Alexios maintained himself through the war by emergency confiscations of church plate and bought a costly alliance with the Venetians, who viewed the Normans as serious maritime rivals. The emperor also sent a huge shipment of gold to the Holy Roman emperor, Henry IV (1084–1105), who pressured the Norman homelands and Pope Gregory VII (1073–85), with whom Robert Guiscard had allied himself. Guiscard hurried back to Italy and campaigned against the Germans in the spring of 1082, and Alexios tested Bohemund, who inherited the strategic city of Dyrrachium and the Norman lands in Illyria. At Ioannina in western Greece, the emperor tried to break the ferocious Norman cavalry charge by using wagons, but Bohemund easily thwarted the effort and drove the Romans from the field. In a sub-

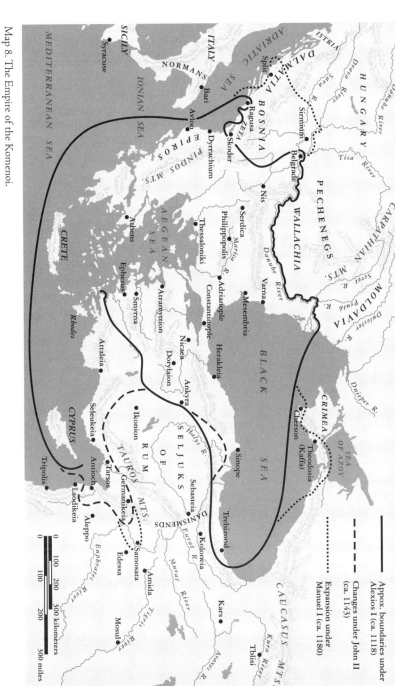

Map 8. The Empire of the Komenoi.

sequent engagement, Alexios laced the Byzantine front with caltrops (an iron ball with four sharpened spikes so that one side always pointed up, to pierce the feet of men and horses), but the Normans once more discovered the plan, outflanked the Roman army, and pressed both the right and left flanks. Bohemund laid siege to Larissa in Byzantine Thessaly, which held out for six months until the emperor led a relieving army against him. Alexios decided to employ the feigned retreat—given the Norman success against him a general retreat was certainly believable. As Bohemund pursued the fleeing Roman main force, the emperor sprang his ambush and overran the enemy camp while another force attacked the Norman rear. Bohemund withdrew, and although the following year Robert Guiscard renewed the war with an attack on the island of Corcyra, the old warlord died and his sons hurried to Italy to lay claim to their inheritance.

The first Norman war underscores how threatening new western powers could prove to Byzantine interests. Nor were the Normans the only rivals to be dealt with; in Anatolia the Seljuk Turks ranged unchecked. The penny-packets of Byzantine troops stood no chance, and fortresses and cities succumbed throughout the former hinterland of the empire, leaving Alexios with only scraps of territory along the coast. Pecheneg nomads from the south Eurasian steppe raided Thrace in force—a series of Byzantine victories and defeats drained the treasury and bogged down the empire when their precious resources were needed elsewhere. By the 1090s the emperor had managed to repair relations with the papacy. As is well known, it was Alexios's request to the pope for western mercenaries after the tribulations of his Pecheneg wars that yielded fruit of an entirely unexpected kind: the First Crusade.

When the crusaders arrived in Constantinople late in 1096, Alexios confronted the sour fact that the Norman prince Bohemund was among their leaders. The savvy emperor extracted oaths of allegiance from the westerners, then sent an army and offered logistical support as far as Antioch, where the Greek-Crusader alliance fell apart. The First Crusade did at least disrupt the Seljuks and regained Nicaea for the empire, but it nurtured western and Greek hostilities toward one another, and in the tangled relationship that followed, the Byzantines increasingly alienated western powers who were eager for a share of the eastern Mediterranean. While Byzantine military power remained formidable under the Komnenoi dynasty that Alexios founded, a major defeat at the hands of the Seljuks in 1176 at Myriokephalon in Phrygia spelled the end of Roman efforts to wrest control of Anatolia from the Turks. Ever after the Greeks were largely relegated to the coastlands and under pressure.

During the era of the Komnenoi the themes remained as administrative districts only while the army in the land was replaced by native professionals and foreign mercenaries, especially Frankish knights, Turks, and Pechenegs. Though these professionals were arguably of higher quality than their thematic predecessors, they were expensive and therefore never very numerous, and the Komnenoi apparently never had more than 20,000 soldiers on any campaign. The native element in the army was increasingly comprised of cavalrymen who held *pronoia* grants; these grants supported soldiers on revenues from the land tax in the locales where they were stationed. Initially such grants could not be inherited and, unlike the fiefs held in the medieval west, the state never relinquished its claims to the land from which the pronoiars were supported. While fiscally attractive, since it spared the state immediate cash outlays, the system fueled the regionalism and factionalism that plagued the later empire.

LATE PERIOD (THIRTEENTH TO FIFTEENTH CENTURIES)

The end for the empire as a major Mediterranean military power came in the spring of 1204 when Venice, the former imperial ally, diverted the army of the Fourth Crusade and trained it on Constantinople. In April 1204, after months of complicated political maneuvering and diplomatic failures, the western crusaders stormed the capital and for three days slaughtered inhabitants and burned and pillaged the greatest city in Christendom. The failure of Byzantine arms was total; inept command, a lack of funding, and the poor quality of the army that had degraded in the decades after the death of Manuel Komnenos in 1180 all contributed to the catastrophe. The military collapse led to a cultural tragedy rarely matched in history. In the ashes of the ruined Byzantine state the Franks and Venetians cobbled together a dysfunctional "empire" while rival Greek regional centers galvanized resistance in the provinces. The loss of power and prestige and the cultural winter of sixty years of foreign occupation rendered the Byzantine state that the emperor Michael VIII Palaiologos (1259–82) led a regional power.

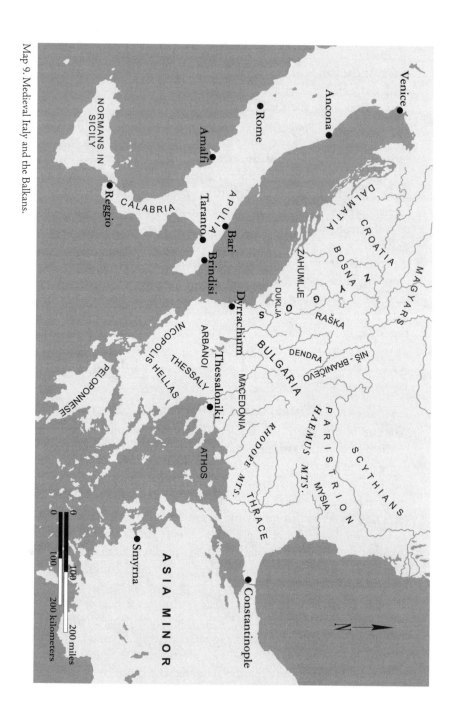

Map 9. Medieval Italy and the Balkans.

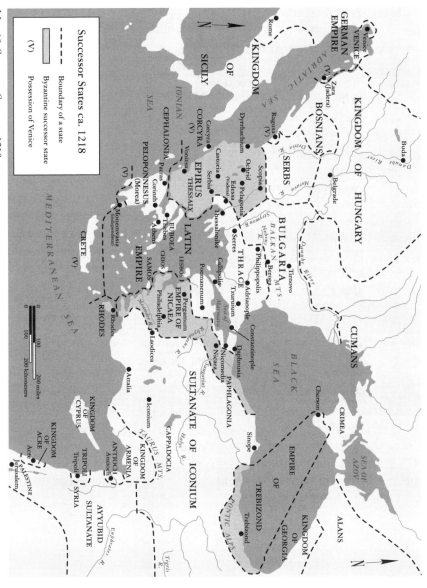

Map 10. Successor States ca. 1218.

Michael's dynasty, the Palaiologans, clung to power in Greece and portions of Asia Minor and the Balkans for nearly two centuries, wracked by factionalism and crippling self-interest. Their armies were pathetic compared with those of their predecessors and their enemies, and at no time after 1204 did a Byzantine campaign army ever total more than 5,000 soldiers, and it is doubtful that this number was ever fielded.[25] The broken reed of Byzantium fell into a familiar contradiction; without soldiers the empire could not capture more territory whose resources could support more troops for further security and recovery of lost territory. Although history presented opportunities for revival—the Mongol smashup of the Seljuks of Anatolia in the mid-thirteenth century for instance, or the heavy defeat of their Ottoman successors by the Timurids at the Battle of Ankara in 1402—the Byzantines could do nothing to reverse their political weakness. By the spring of 1453 when the Ottoman sultan Mehmed II (1444–46 and 1451–81) led his Turkish army to invest Constantinople, the defenders of the city that had once overawed the world numbered a paltry 7,000. They faced 80,000 determined Muslim opponents armed with gunpowder and cannons that bashed to rubble the Herculean walls of the city. On May 29, a mere thirty-nine years before Columbus landed in the New World, the Old World's longest-lived empire fell. Bereft of its resources and the arms that they sustained, Byzantium vanished into history, replaced by a Muslim empire that eventually grew to parallel its predecessor—stretching from Libya to the Danube and locked in an eerily similar struggle for survival on all fronts. Less remarkable than the slow march into twilight of the Byzantine army and its empire is the incredible fact of its thousand-year existence, one sustained in large measure by the resilience, adaptability, and professionalism of its fighting men.

TWO

LEADERSHIP

THROUGH MUCH OF THEIR HISTORY the Byzantines were exceptional not for the brilliance of the military commanders that they produced—after all, they suffered many defeats (see Chapter 1)—but for the general competence of their leadership that allowed them to defend their empire even after such setbacks. Though there does not appear to have been anything akin to West Point in Byzantium, a training campus where soldiers could learn military science and absorb the lessons of others, the Byzantines differed from most of their neighbors by writing down their thoughts on the science of warfare. There were numerous exceptions throughout the long history of the empire, but commanders tended to be professional soldiers with some degree of military competence. Given the value of the men and resources with which they were entrusted, they were held to a high standard.

One must be cautious in generalizing about a military institution and a culture of warfare that evolved tremendously over a millennium. In its most basic form, the ability to lead meant an understanding of strategy, tactics, and a combination of courage tempered by an acute sense of risk and reward. Neither the writings of Vegetius (fourth to fifth centuries) nor the *Strategikon* of the emperor Maurice (582–602) discussed the qualities of a general in detail, but the requisite knowledge and makeup that emerge from them show that an understanding of logistics was key, as was individual valor. A firm grasp of the morale and condition of one's forces were vital. In the *Taktika* of the emperor Leo VI (886–912) the traits of the general are enumerated and few will surprise the modern reader. A commander was to be self-controlled, serious, sober, and incorruptible. Further, he was to be intelligent and neither too young nor too old. Physical strength and endurance were prized. He had to have the ability to earn the respect of his men and to be a good public speaker. More surprising to a reader today were his spiritual qualities of exceptional piety and his parental status: Leo thought that men who had children were more motivated, and men of the aristocratic classes were preferred over those of obscure origin.[1]

These traits were thought essential to becoming *strategos* (Greek "general," pl. *strategoi*) and in holding other senior commands. Rarely do our sources tell us about the battlefield actions of lower officers and individuals in the rank-and-file, and even more rarely are the equivalent of today's NCOs or other lower ranks shown in pivotal leadership roles. The stress on professionalism and drill made soldiers who were tactically flexible and capable, but the lower ranks seem to have lacked initiative. There is no Byzantine *Anabasis* where an army bereft of its leaders pushed its way to safety, no Byzantine "soldiers' battles" where a group stripped of their high command fought to victory. The loss of a general or emperor in command of the host usually meant its defeat and dispersal. This picture is attributable partly to the nature of our sources, whose authors stress the deeds and heroics of men of their own elite class. The army remained professional at its core (although the standards of Dark Age thematic armies are debatable in this regard), so the inability of Byzantine armies to recover from the field losses of their high command cannot have been an attribute of army organization. The Byzantine army officer structure was of considerable depth and was quite advanced for the medieval era (see Chapter 3). And since junior officers seem to have gained their positions primarily through experience and merit, the apparent lack of ready response to battlefield crisis may be attributed to other factors.

Social influences clearly shaped soldiers' attitudes and responses. All men were not equal, and a poor recruit or even the best low-ranking fighter could not compare in worth to a well-born general. One's birth, wealth, and social standing endowed the elite not only with the connections to rise to high station, but also with an aura of superiority in all areas of life. One fulfilled one's role in the universe, and though not all well-born men accomplished great deeds, such expectations help explain why in the chaos of impending defeat it would not have occurred to the lowly soldier of the line to seize the standard and rally a crumbling army to victory even if such heroics were physically possible. While some common soldiers did rise to positions of authority, Byzantine society remained highly stratified. Many commanders of the early Byzantine era were elites, and most senior officers in the middle and late Byzantine periods were members of the aristocracy whose associates formed a hereditary military caste. This is in no way to say that such men were without merit. For example, Damian Dalassenos (d. 998) was one of many gifted leaders whose sons followed in their footsteps and, probably because they were known to imperial officialdom and high-ranking courtiers, found it easier to access high commands.[2] Status, however, had to be paired with success for one to keep imperial favor and maintain command, and while Byzantium had a number of incompetent commanders whose ineptness led to disaster, on balance the army was capably led throughout the empire's existence.

Although disciplined, drilled, and—as the handbooks and historical reality demonstrate—often capable of aggressive support of their comrades and complicated battefield tactics, there is no sense that the Byzantines prized individual initiative from below. The tactical realities of ancient and medieval warfare played a role in the apparent lack of junior officers rallying their troops or assuming command in place of fallen superiors. Throughout its history the empire faced aggressive and sophisticated enemies. With their range of movement, tactics, and weaponry, nomadic steppe warriors such as the Huns, Avars, and Cumans challenged the most skillful armies. Horse-mounted archery with its combination of striking power, range, and mobility combined with ages-old tactics of steppe warfare to create a dangerous tactical environment for imperial armies. Byzantine commanders were aware of the slender line between victory and defeat; an apparently beaten opponent could regroup quickly and inflict a reverse on troops disordered in pursuit or who stopped to strip the dead of valuables. The stress on discipline and the need to follow protocol made initiative among lower-ranking soldiers positively undesirable. The soldier who became an individual in either victory or defeat broke the cohesion of the unit and exposed his comrades to peril.

When we understand the expectations of a rank-and-file attuned to signs and symbols, the roles of leaders and those they led become clearer. The Byzantines, like most pre-industrial era peoples, were keen observers of omens. The final outcome of any endeavor belonged to God. The battle merely revealed God's plan: soldiers fought bravely because they were soldiers and thus such action was their calling, not necessarily because their bravery and individual skill would decisively affect the outcome. Of course this oversimplifies, but this distinctly fatalistic strand of Byzantine culture played a central role in military encounters. The perceived skill, piety, and well-being of the commander formed a major part of troop morale. Any sign of weakness, ill health, or other omens could panic the troops. Vegetius noted that the general who retreated from the line prior to battle fatally eroded the confidence of his troops.[3] In 917, when Leo Phokas's riderless horse bolted through the ranks and led the men to believe their general had been killed, the army panicked.[4] Just as the heroic encounters that often preceded battle were signs of God's favor or displeasure and hinted at the final outcome, the deeds of a heroic general were important spiritual markers. When in 623–24 Heraclius struck down the giant Persian soldier on the bridge over the Saros River it inspired his troops to victory, not because the emperor cleared the bridge, but rather because the deed's perceived spiritual significance vitally boosted his men's confidence.[5]

Thus, leadership flowed from the top; the general was perceived as both a superior person to his soldiers and a superior soldier, and had a spiritual aura about him. He was usually more experienced in strategy and tactics than most of his men. In essence the strategos and his staff council of high-ranking officers formed the nerve center of the army. Command resided with the general or generals who enforced iron discipline and tightly held authority; this was critical in the campaign environment throughout the empire's history, when soldiers were prone to disorder and when communications were cumbersome (signaling relied on messengers, flags, and musical instruments). The best army was unwieldy, and command and control almost nonexistent once battle was joined. If a general fell or disengaged, there was an abrupt loss of command and control and cohesion dissolved almost immediately as the elite fighters around the general perished or fled. Conversely, in engagements hard-fought over days, with the commanders in the fray,

Byzantine armies could demonstrate resilience, as in 971 at Dorostolon, though such encounters were rare.

There are exceptions to the lack of leadership apparent among lower ranks, especially in the early period. Perhaps the best example of a junior officer seizing control in a military crisis is that of Phokas, who was allegedly a lowly *kentarchos* (centurion, commander of eighty to one hundred men) in a tagma (a unit of about three hundred) under the command of the general Philippikos. Facing a mutiny over pay and conditions of service and unable to assuage his soldiers' wrath, Philippikos fled the encampment. The kentarchos Phokas, who was apparently of low birth, seized control of the situation and was raised on a shield by the troops, who proclaimed him emperor. Phokas led the mutineers to Constantinople where they eventually seized the city and killed the emperor Maurice. Such a usurpation of command by such lowly men during crisis was almost nonexistent outside the context of military unrest.

Combat leadership was most often learned by experience. The sixth-century historian Prokopios mentions many leaders who apparently rose through the ranks based on their abilities as soldiers. But in the early Byzantine period many leaders came from military families whose members followed in the footsteps of successful officers, such as John, nephew of the sometime rebel Vitalian (d. 520), or were barbarian elites drawn to imperial service, like Mundus, the son of a Gepid king who served Justinian loyally in both the Balkans and the eastern frontier.[6]

Early Period (Fourth to Seventh Centuries)

Until the disaster at Adrianople in 378, emperors often campaigned in person. Such soldier-emperors were often of low origin: Diocletian was from an obscure family and rose through the military ranks to the throne. Constantine I's father, Constantius Chlorus (ca. 250–306), was of humble origin, and men like him found opportunity, high honors, and power through military service. Constantine I, his son Constantius, and his nephew Julian were active soldiers who marched at the head of their forces. Into the sixth century, the rank-and-file continued to have the opportunity to achieve high positions. By the fifth and sixth centuries emperors no longer led their armies in person and commanders seemed to have been chosen more for their loyalty than their brilliance. Merit still played a key role in selecting leaders, however. Many of those whom the historian Prokopios mentions as leading men to battle apparently were of common birth and rose to authority via service. Once more the imperial palace provides the best story: the illiterate peasant Justin left his farm in Illyricum to join the army, whence he rose to service in the imperial guard and thence to the purple.

In the fourth century the *protectores* comprised an unknown number of corps under the magister officiorum. A *comes* (count) officered units of uncertain size and disposition. There were ordinary protectores as well as the domestici who, as their name implies, formed a corps in attendance on the emperor. Men normally selected for the protectores had distinguished themselves early in their careers as particularly promising and loyal. Promotion was based on seniority. Both the regular protectores and domestici provided staff officers—typically adjutants to the *magistri militum* marshals who seconded them on a variety of special duties, such as rounding up recruits, overseeing military depots, and inspecting fortresses. The emperor commissioned the protectores in person in a ritual of obedience, and thus such men were personally known to the ruler and his high command. Unsurprisingly, the combination of merit and loyalty often led to rapid advancement. Gratian, the father of the emperor Valentinian I, was an expert wrestler and was promoted to protector as a ranker.[7]

In the sixth century, both the emperor's bodyguard and the household men of senior commanders continued to be an important incubator for military commanders. The three-hundred-man palace guard of the Excubitors, a unit raised by the emperor Leo I (457–74), provided numerous officers as it drew to its ranks men of the greatest loyalty, ambition, and fighting abilities. *Boukellarioi* (named after the sort of bread they ate) comprised the private bodyguards of state officials and powerful private men. Unsurprisingly, men who served in the bodyguard of Justinian when he was magister militum (520–27) rose to high command once he became emperor in 527. Among them were Belisarios and Sittas. When Justinian ascended to the throne, he created a new army command in Armenia and named Sittas its chief officer. After a long career of loyal and distinguished service, Sittas fell in battle in Armenia in 539.[8]

Sittas's comrade Belisarios likewise rose to prominence when Justinian came to power. By 529 Belisarios was Master of Soldiers of the East (*Magister militum per Orientem*). His position allowed him to accumulate seven thousand boukellarioi; the illustrious general was responsible for their pay and maintenance. Some were common native soldiers who had proved themselves capable fighters. Boukellarioi were often given command of detachments of regular troops or sent on special missions, and leaders like Belisarios relied heavily on them. During his African campaign (533–34), Belisarios sent one of his bodyguard, Diogenes, with twenty-two other boukellarioi, to reconnoiter outside of the former Vandal capital of Carthage. The Vandals surprised the detachment and nearly destroyed it and Diogenes was wounded in the battle. In 549, when Belisarios prepared to depart Italy, he left Diogenes in charge of the three-thousand-man garrison of Rome.[9]

Though less common than in the early days of the empire, commands were sometimes given to high-born Romans. These seldom went to men lacking experience. When the Persian War of 502–6 caught the emperor Anastasios flat-footed, he dispatched four generals, among them his nephew Hypatios. The latter apparently had earned campaign experience during the wars against the Isaurian highland rebels in the 490s, but his lack of skill and daring let the emperor down and he was replaced and recalled in 503.

In addition to native sons, the Romans relied on officers of barbarian origin. A number of warlike neighbors surrounded the empire and provided fertile recruiting grounds for not only the rank-and-file but also their leaders. During the fourth to seventh centuries commanders of Germanic, Armenian, and Persian origin were common. The Gepid (a Germanic tribe living in Illyricum) Mundus was the son of a king and nephew of another. He entered Roman service in the late 520s and served as Master of Soldiers of Illyricum (*Magister militum per Illyricum*) and served with distinction. Mundus later replaced Belisarios as *Magister militum per Orientem* after the Romans were routed in the 531 debacle at Callinicum.[10]

DARK AGES, MIDDLE AND LATE PERIODS (EIGHTH TO FIFTEENTH CENTURIES)

The emperor Heraclius revived the practice of the emperor campaigning in person. Not all of his successors would lead their troops into battle, but many did. After the crisis of the Arab invasions, military men dominated the throne and emperors often campaigned in person. High officers were often drawn from the *spatharii* (sword men) who formed the emperor's bodyguard. The emperor Leo III (717–41) had once served as a spatharios under the emperor Justinian II. The state required leaders who understood military affairs and who could handle the army. When the last member of the Heraclian dynasty, Justinian II (685–95, 705–11), fell in 711, it was at the hands of a military coup led by an Armenian thematic commander named Philippikos Bardanes. Theophilos (828–42) was trapped with his army and barely escaped the battle of Anzen, while in 863, the emperor Michael III led an army into Anatolia to intercept the raid in force of the emir of Melitene.[11]

The high point of the soldier-emperors was the tenth century, when warriors like Nikephoros II Phokas and John Tzimiskes cultivated an image of imperial triumph and valor in arms as they personally led their men from victory to victory. By the reign of Basil II (976–1025), the grip of the military elite on the levers of power was such that the young emperor had not only to wrest it from their control through two painful and devastating civil wars but also to cast himself as the logical replacement, the vigorous, blessed soldier-emperor who led his troops to victory. Throughout his reign, Basil served in the army in person, often under the wing of more experienced generals.[12]

After Basil, emperors increasingly distanced themselves from the camps until the reign of Romanos IV Diogenes (1068–71), whose capture and humiliation at Mantzikert did not deter his later successors from campaigning at the head of their armies. Alexios I Komnenos (1081–1118), a usurper, personally led his troops, and though he experienced several reversals his successes on the battlefield were numerous and notable. By the time his grandson Manuel I Komnenos had followed his father's footsteps, the age of the great Byzantine soldier-emperors had come to an end. Though during the Palaiologan dynasty fewer emperors led troops in person and the armies progressively dwindled in size until the institution failed, in 1280–82 Michael VIII (1259–82) led troops into Asia Minor against the Turks when in his late fifties and thus very near the end of his life.[13]

Leaders in high commands in the middle and late eras of Byzantium were nearly always well-born men. The ninth to eleventh centuries were the era of the great Anatolian military aristocracy. Among the highest officers were several prominent foreigners, including the general and emperor John Tzimiskes whose family was of Armenian extraction and the Armenian-born Melias. Commanders from the family of the empress Theophano (wife of Theophilos) were also Armenians. The Persian (or Kurd) Theophobos served under Theophilos, Roussel de Bailleul (d. 1078) was a Norman, while during the First Crusade (1096–99) the Roman general Tatikios was a Turk. But during the heyday of the imperial resurgence of the ninth and tenth centuries, most of the senior commanders were native Romans (though many were descendants of immigrants). Families like the Argyroi, Phokades, Skleroi, Maleinoi, Melissenoi, Doukai, and Diogenai held estates in Anatolia and benefited directly from the recovery of vast territories seized by the Muslims over the prior three centuries. These Anatolian families produced some of the most skilled and capable commanders in imperial history, notably Bardas and Nikephoros Phokas, John Tzimiskes, and George Maniakes. Ultimately, their ambitions to seize and dominate the throne led to their downfall and the collapse of the eastern defenses in the face of the Turkish advance.

In the middle period, higher officers often took part in the fighting. After a banquet in which the emperor Romanos I roused his commanders to action, one of them named Saktikios led a dawn attack on the Bulgars encamped against Constantinople and was subsequently killed.[14] In 921 during the Bulgar siege of Adrianople, the city commander Leo was nicknamed Leo the Fool due to his rashness in personally exposing himself to battle.[15] Anatolian commanders frequently fought against the Muslims; in 953 Bardas Phokas (ca. 878–968) was surrounded and wounded by Sayf ad-Dawla's men in a defeat near Marash.[16] In pre-industrial war, before bullets caused generals to hunker behind the lines, the personal nature of war and the bravado of commanders were everywhere evident in Byzantium.

Following the fall of Constantinople in 1204 and the fracturing of the empire, leadership of the army remained with the emperor and elite-born commanders. Some, like Michael VIII (1259–82), campaigned in person at the head of what forces were left to them and even showed a talent for tactics and strategy. The career of the emperor John VI Kantakouzenos (1347–54) demonstrates that ideologically the emperor had to actively resist the Turks. John was himself a competent officer, but after his day the importance of the soldier-emperor faded as Byzantine decay deepened.[17]

BIOGRAPHIES

Byzantium produced its share of brilliant commanders, though few in the modern world have heard of them. Each of the men portrayed here shared the ability to act decisively in times of crisis, and they exhibited the key qualities esteemed among eastern Roman leaders: cool-headedness under duress, caution in the face of the enemy, and a thorough understanding of strategy, tactics, operations, and logistics. As compared with the more blunt tactics of leaders in neighboring societies, the Byzantine generals acted more like surgeons than butchers, with measured gains and a clear appreciation for the delicate instrument of the army in their hands.

Belisarios

The most famous Byzantine general and the one best known to western students of military history is Belisarios, who served the emperor Justinian faithfully over a long, distinguished career. He was born in Germania (today Sapareva Banya in modern southwest Bulgaria), a city in Thrace on the border of Illyria. The western regions of the empire were a rich recruiting ground and produced many late antique commanders and soldiers. Though we remain uncertain of his precise ancestry, Belisarios was apparently the scion of a local Thracian or Illyrian family probably of some means, as indicated by his ability to raise and pay a substantial cohort of personal household troops. Belisarios gained prominence as a commander after service in the bodyguard of Justinian when the latter was the right-hand man and magister militum of his uncle Justin I (518–27).

Despite his role as joint commander of a campaign that ended in defeat at the hands of the Persians in Persian Armenia, by 526 Belisarios had ascended to the office of dux of the province of Mesopotamia. The dux (Greek, *doux*) was the senior local commander of a mix of professional garrison troops and frontier guards (*limitanei*) of varying quality. He was thus headquartered at the city of Constantina (modern Viranşehir in southeastern Turkey) or Dara— both were key fortress-cities on the eastern frontier with the Persians. A document belonging to the late fourth or early fifth century, the *Notitia Dignitatum* provides some insight into what assets the dux had at his disposal; it lists four units (apparently cohorts of about five hundred men) of elite cavalry, all originally raised in Illyria, and six further units of local cavalry (probably cavalry *alae* of about a hundred men each, though these may have numbered up to five hundred each), along with two infantry legions of about 1,000 men.[18] The total number of troops under this frontier command then would have been at most 7,000, though units were not apparently uniform in number and they were commonly understrength.

In 528, Belisarios led elements of these units against the Persians in Upper Mesopotamia where they faced an invading Persian force. The Romans were attempting to construct a fortified city on the frontier and the Persians aimed to destroy the works. Belisarios was in overall command, but the young general (who was in his late twenties at the time) was joined by other duces of the east with their respective units and Arab allies. The combined forces joined battle with the Sasanians at Tannuris (Tel Thounenir) in the Khabur Valley of northern Syria. The Sasanians employed hidden trenches and pits, into which the rapidly advancing Roman lines fell headlong and a prominent leader, Coutzes, was killed. Belisarios fled back to Dara along with the Roman cavalry and left the infantry to be destroyed, but in the aftermath held onto his command as blame apparently fell on Coutzes. Three years later Justinian elevated Belisarios to the supreme command of the eastern army, the post in which he was to win fame and glory.

When Belisarios assumed command of the eastern forces, morale was low and Roman preparedness lacking. Since the era of Diocletian, the Romans had relied on strategic depth and linear defenses as a bulwark against the menace of their eastern neighbors. That the Byzantines had managed to hold the line was due more to good luck than to good management: within living memory the Persians had battered a large Roman army in the war of 502–6 that had few strategic implications but which served to expose deep fissures in the command structure and the feeble tactical punch of the Roman army.

In the wake of the debacle of 502–6, the government took decisive action. The emperor Anastasios built a massively fortified new city on the village of Dara (modern Oguz). Dara served as a forward staging post for imperial armies, a supply depot, and springboard against the Sasanian homeland. As dux of Mesopotamia, Belisarios made his headquarters there. Seated at the foot of the rough highlands of the Tur Abdin, Dara stared across the hot northern Mesopotamia plains toward the Persian stronghold of Nisibis, a mere 25 kilometers away.

Nisibis had been ceded to the Persians after the ruinous campaign of Julian in 363; its loss left a gap in Roman defenses and provided the enemy with a powerful salient. In 527 the Romans had suffered a defeat north of Nisibis at Mindouos while attempting to construct another fortified city to counter it.

When war resumed in 530, Belisarios and the general Hermogenes led a large Roman army of perhaps 25,000 toward Dara. The Persians under their general Firouz commanded a superior Persian force of around 30,000. The Romans decided not to endure a siege but instead arrayed their forces in a strong defensive position outside the walls of Dara. The fortifications shielded their rear, while to the front of the army they dug a lattice work of trenches with alleys that permitted the Romans to blunt the weight of enemy numbers while still permitting them to maneuver. These works shielded Belisarios's untried infantry (fig. 2.1). Belisarios and his bodyguard elite of boukellarioi stationed themselves behind the main body of Roman infantry in the center, while on the left flank were Herul (a Germanic people related to the Goths) cavalry under the command of Pharas and Roman units under Bouzes. The Roman right comprised Hun auxiliaries backed by a larger Roman cavalry force. Hun cavalry also provided a pivot force in the angles of the trenches that fronted the Roman lines. The historian Prokopios was an eyewitness and provides a description of the encounter that allows for a solid reconstruction. On the first day of the engagement, the Persians advanced in lines drawn up in standard fashion—two strong lines and flanking forces—and attacked the Roman left, which gave ground and exposed the Sasanians to a flanking attack by the Huns in the pivot point of the Roman force. The Sasanians withdrew with minor losses, and single combats followed in which the Roman hero Andreas prevailed over two Persian challengers. Given the role ascribed to fate in ancient warfare, these duels sharply raised Roman morale and proved to many of the untested that the Sasanians were not their betters after all.[19]

The next day the two sides parlayed and the Persians received reinforcements from Nisibis. The 10,000 additional Persians must have been the whole of the garrison in that city; their mobilization indicates that, based on his probes of the previous day, Firouz doubted the outcome. Battle recommenced (fig. 2.2), as the Sasanians attempted to soften the enemy lines with missile fire and the Romans returned their

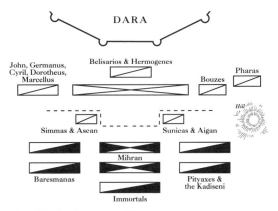

Fig. 2.1. The opening of the battle of Dara, 530.

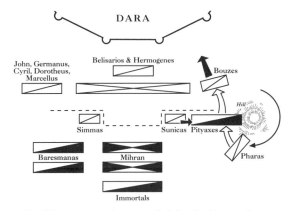

Fig. 2.2. Belisarios ordered Pharas to use the cover of a hill to lead his cavalry to an undetected attack behind the Persian line.

volleys which were more effective since the wind favored them. Firouz then ordered an assault across the line. Once more the Romans left under Bouzes gave ground, but as the Sasanians advanced, Belisarios sprung the trap—Pharas and 300 Heruls had hidden themselves behind the cover of a nearby hill and emerged on the Persian right as the Huns swept in from the Persian left. In the resulting crush the Sasanians absorbed heavy losses. Prokopios states that 3,000 Sasanians fell in the rout.

Firouz then ordered his reserve into action, the elite Immortals regiment (named after their illustrious Achaemenid Persian ancestors)

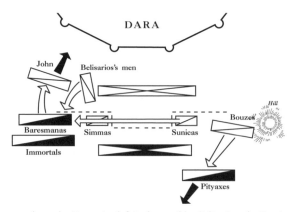

Fig. 2.3. Persian attack on the Byzantine left is thwarted by Belisarios; the Persian right flees the field.

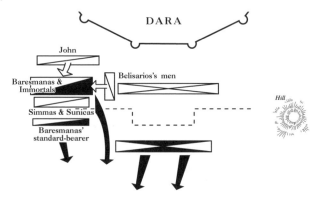

Fig. 2.4. Charge of the Persian reserve fails and Persian infantry flee; a general rout of the Persians ensues.

against John on the Roman right. Belisarios and Hermogenes sent 600 Massagetae (an Iranian nomadic group) to reinforce John. John's forces buckled under the onslaught of the Immortals and regulars, but once again the Romans in the angles of the trenches assaulted the Sasanian flanks in a vicious attack that split the Persians in two—the larger portion on the flanking forces' right and thus facing John's retreating cavalry, who saw their enemy falter and regrouped and counterattacked, surrounding a major portion of the Sasanian force. When Firouz comprehended the peril of his shock troops, he threw the remainder of his army into the fray along the whole Roman front. The

Romans absorbed the charge and held, while their officer Sunicas killed the one-eyed Sasanian general Baresmanas, who was second in command (fig. 2.3). The Persians panicked and broke but could not escape; the Romans surrounded the greater part of their army and killed 5,000 of the enemy. The wretched Sasanian infantry threw down their shields and bolted, only to be cut down in swaths by the pursuing Roman riders (fig. 2.4). For a Roman army that had not witnessed a major victory in the soldiers' lifetimes, and for the young magister Belisarios, the Battle of Dara heralded a critical shift. The Romans proved that they could take the field against a powerful opponent and defeat them, and Belisarios and his commanders exhibited outstanding tactics and leadership.

Though the Roman general went down in defeat at the Battle of Callinicum in 531, he regained Justinian's full confidence in his handling of the Nika Riot of 532, and was awarded the senior command of the emperor's grand expedition against the Vandal kingdom of North Africa. A century prior, this barbarian kingdom had rooted itself in the rich lands of former Roman Africa and battered the Romans in both the west and the east. In 468 the emperor Leo had launched an enormous force under his generalissimo Stilicho that went down in bloody defeat and alleged treachery. Belisarios landed his expeditionary force at Caput Vada on the eastern coast of what is today Tunisia. In two battles, Ad Decimum (September 13, 533) and Tricamarum (December 15, 533), Belisarios broke Vandal power (see Chapter 7). Belisarios displayed superb abilities in the Vandal War; he relied heavily on Hunnic and Roman horse archers against the Vandal lancers, who were helpless against the ranged weapons of their adversaries. He also maintained discipline among his forces and showed a keen understanding of the need to maintain good relations with the Romano-African locals on whose cooperation Byzantine success in Africa depended.

In 535, buoyed by his success in restoring Africa to the empire, Justinian dispatched Belisarios against the Ostrogothic kingdom in Italy, where the Byzantines quickly took Sicily, then Naples, and Rome. The Gothic counterattack led to the brutal siege of Rome in 537–38. Belisarios managed to break the siege of Rome by sending a flying column to the north that defeated an Ostrogoth force near their capital in Ravenna, which Belisarios besieged and seized in 540. By the time the first phase of the Gothic War ended, Belisarios held most of Italy for the empire. The outbreak of war with Persia required his presence in the East, for which he departed in June. In 541 he was once more at Dara on the frontier and the following year he repelled a major Persian invasion without a battle, his prior mastery of them having made the Sasanians wary of the Roman general's strategems. A plot against the emperor Justinian, who had fallen ill of the plague, implicated Belisarios, who lived in disgrace until 544 when he returned to Italy. In 549, once more under suspicion and starved of men and materiel, Belisarios fought in Italy with a force of only 4,000 men.

Belisarios was recalled to service in the twilight of his life when in 559 an invasion of Kutriger Huns threatened Constantinople which was largely bare of troops. Rallying rustics and town guardsmen to his side, he managed to end the threat. Enemies at court had apparently done their damage, however, as his ten-year hiatus in command demonstrates. He died in 565, the same year as his master, Justinian. In his career he had nearly doubled the size of the empire, handled his men with extraordinary skill, and exercised the cautious command that marked him as a brilliant general. Had he been given more with which to work, the war in Italy would have likely ended much sooner, and the imperial conquests strengthened and deepened.

John Tzimiskes

Probably the most vibrant commander in an age replete with fine leaders, John Tzimiskes oversaw the peak of the Byzantine revival in the eastern marches of Syria and Anatolia and personally commanded the decisive Byzantine victory over the Kievan Rus' at Dorostolon. A Byzantine historian described Tzimiskes as "enormously strong . . . possessed of a heroic soul, fearless and intrepid, displaying supernatural courage in so small a body."[20] In his portrait of John before his ascent to the throne, the Byzantine historian Leo the Deacon has one observer describe John as "ambitious, extremely aggressive, and good in warfare."[21] Tzimiskes was short but powerfully built and personally brave in battle to the point of recklessness. He was a vigorous soldier and leader, skilled with bow and javelin, and a good horseman. He was also a murderer and usurper who rose to power by killing his uncle, the great soldier and emperor Nikephoros II (963–69).

John Tzimiskes was born in northern Anatolia around 925, scion of the Kourkouas clan, a distinguished Armenian family who had settled in Byzantine territory and produced the general John Kourkouas whom his patron, the emperor Romanos I, named domestikos ton scholon (commander-in-chief) in 921. John Kourkouas achieved notable success on the eastern frontier of the empire, including the capture of the important cities of Melitene (934) and Edessa (944), but his star faded with the deposing of Romanos I in 948. John Tzimiskes's mother was the sister of Nikephoros Phokas, and his first wife Maria was the sister of the magistros Bardas Skleros. Tzimiskes was thus related by blood or marriage to the most powerful elite families of Anatolia who dominated the military establishment for the better part of the tenth century.

In 958 John Tzimiskes led a major invasion to the eastern frontier against the ruler of Aleppo, the Hamdanid emir Sayf ad-Dawla (945–67), who was a worthy and vigorous opponent of Byzantine power in Mesopotamia and Syria. Not far from Amid (ancient Amida, modern Diyarbakir), John encountered Hamdanid forces commanded by the Circassian general Naja at the head of an army of 10,000. Tzimiskes's forces utterly destroyed the Muslim army, killing 5,000 and taking 3,000 prisoners along with all the baggage. In autumn Tzimiskes captured Samosata, an important and wealthy Muslim city on the Euphrates.

When he seized power in a military coup, Nikephoros II elevated his talented nephew to the office of domestikos ton scholon. During the 964 offensive against the emirate of Tarsos, Tzimiskes led the Byzantine left in the engagement outside the city of Tarsos in which the Byzantines outflanked the emir's men who broke and ran to the safety of the walls. By 965, however, Tzimiskes was disgraced and cashiered for reasons unknown, and his forced retirement eventually led to his conspiring against his uncle, whom he murdered in December 969. Upon his accession John held the spear tip of the finest army in Europe and southwest Asia. He inherited from his uncle and forebears a veteran force hardened by frequent campaigning built on a core of professional, heavy cavalry (kataphraktoi—for more on these see Chapter 5). Unlike many of its ancestors, the Byzantine army of Tzimiskes was built for the attack.

Before he could return to the east, Tzimiskes had to deal with Prince Sviatoslav of the Kievan Rus' (945–72). After assisting Nikephoros II Phokas against Boris of Bulgaria (969–71), whom in

968 in a swift campaign Sviatoslav made a vassal, the Rus' ruler expanded his domain immensely—notably southwest to the Danube. The Byzantines watched with growing alarm as Sviatoslav ensconced himself there and transferred his power center to Pereyaslavets on the Danube some 600 kilometers south of his former seat at Kiev and far too close for Roman comfort. After failed negotiations in 970, a powerful force of Rus' and Pechenegs (a Turkic nomadic steppe people) invaded Thrace. Despite being heavily outnumbered, a Roman force under Bardas Skleros employed a feigned retreat and lured the enemy into an ambush in which the Romans killed thousands of the northerners. The following year the Romans helped to persuade the Pechenegs to withdraw their support from Sviatoslav, when the emperor himself led a massive force of up to 30,000 against the Bulgar capital of Preslav. After a brief assault, Tzimiskes took Preslav, slaughtering many of the 7,000 Rus' and Bulgars who held out in the royal palace.

Tzimiskes then advanced against Sviatoslav, who awaited him with a large Rus' army said to number 60,000. At Dorostolon (modern Silistra) on the Danube in northern Bulgaria the two sides clashed (fig. 2.5). Leo the Deacon, an eyewitness to the battle, described both sides as extremely motivated—the Rus' feared their loss of honor and reputation as invincible warriors and the Romans could not concede victory to a horde of barbarian infantry. The description Leo provides of the helter-skelter wild charge of the Rus', which was met with the cool discipline of the Romans, seems like an echo from an earlier era. Late in the day, after hours of fighting, Tzimiskes ordered his kataphraktoi heavy cavalry into the fray against the Rus' left. The kataphraktoi crashed into their infantry line, which Sviatoslav swiftly reinforced, only to be countered by Tzimiskes and his Immortals, whose repeated charges finally smashed the Rus'. The survivors fled behind the walls of Dorostolon.

The following day the Romans brought up their siege equipment and constructed a palisaded encampment, and the next day they assaulted the city walls but were repulsed. The Rus' attacked at daybreak in the early hours of the third morning. Over a number of days the Rus' repeatedly sallied against the Romans. In one encounter the Rus' slipped through the naval cordon and sailed upstream where they managed to slaughter many grooms as they tended the Byzantine mounts. The final climactic confrontation came on a hot summer day

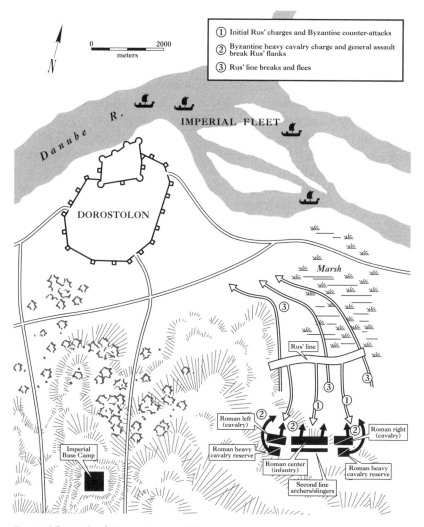

0 — 2000
meters

N

① Initial Rus' charges and Byzantine counter-attacks
② Byzantine heavy cavalry charge and general assault break Rus' flanks
③ Rus' line breaks and flees

IMPERIAL FLEET

Danube R.

DOROSTOLON

Marsh

Rus' line

Roman left (cavalry)

Roman right (cavalry)

Imperial Base Camp

Roman heavy cavalry reserve

Roman center (infantry)

Roman heavy cavalry reserve

Second line archers/slingers

Fig. 2.5. The Battle of Dorostolon, 971 (after Haldon, 2008).

in June or July when Sviatoslav again ordered a major assault against the Romans and led the charge in person. The Rus' forces made contact along a narrow front where the Byzantine cavalry could not maneuver—many horses and men were killed by the Kievan archers and throwing-spears. In the heat of the day, the Roman heavy infantry suffered from thirst and the emperor ordered wine mixed with water to be provided by rotation to the troops at the front. The deadlock was broken when the Romans executed a feigned retreat and lured the Rus' into open ground where the cavalry on the Roman wings shattered the Rus' shield wall and drove them back toward Dorostolon, but there the Rus' found their retreat cut off by Bardas Skleros and his eastern cavalry. The Rus' army dissolved in rout and the vast majority of them were butchered as they scattered across the plain. As many as 15,000 fell, according to Leo the Deacon. Sviatoslav sued for peace and abandoned his conquests.

In 972 Tzimiskes turned his soldiers' blades against the crumbling power of the Muslim princes of the eastern frontier. Roman incursions had battered and bruised Hamdanid power since the reign of Constantine VII, and Tzimiskes aimed to finish it. Tzimiskes apparently raided northward, since the emperor led his troops into the north of Mesopotamia, where he burned Nisibis. In 974 John again marched east and brought Amid to terms in return for heavy tribute. He then advanced 70 kilometers eastward to Mayyafarakin (ancient Martyropolis), another key Muslim stronghold in the Diyar Bakir region of eastern Anatolia: In Leo's account, "This is a famous and splendid town, superior in wealth and livestock of the other cities of the same region. And he brought it to terms and carried off numerous beautiful gifts in gold and silver and cloth woven with gold, which he demanded from the inhabitants; then he went to Nisibis."[22] John found Nisibis deserted and he apparently swung south to menace Baghdad, but the expedition stalled in the Syrian Desert—the fate of Roman armies since antiquity.

In 975 several of the Hamdanid towns rebelled against Byzantine authority, and the emperor again marched to Syria where he brought to heel the cities of the Syrian coast and marched on Damascus, which submitted. In a letter to the Armenian king Ashot III, John boasted that he would retake Jerusalem. Certainly the Muslim caliphate in Baghdad quaked—no Muslim force could stand before John and the Byzantine armies. On January 10, 976, at the age of perhaps fifty, John died—a victim of disease or the poisoner. With his death, the prospects of Byzantine expansion in the east vanished.

John II Komnenos

The son of Alexios I Komnenos, John has deservedly earned the reputation as one of the last outstanding leaders of the Byzantine army. The
multifront invasions and tenuous nature of his father's rule as a usurper limited his effectiveness, yet Alexios nonetheless passed on a stable
empire that had weathered the worst of its immediate storms. Despite
the threat of rebellion from within the ranks of the aristocracy, John
campaigned in Asia Minor in 1119 and captured Laodikeia-on-the-
Lykos in Phrygia (near modern Denizli, Turkey) and thereby set the
tone for the reign. John was a more measured commander than either
his father Alexios or son and successor, Manuel. John inherited a well-
disciplined and experienced army, as evidenced at the siege of
Sozopolis (modern Uluborlu, Turkey) in Phrygia. In 1120, John
marched into Asia Minor against the Seljuk Turks, who had increased
their territory steadily since the Battle of Mantzikert nearly fifty years
prior. Sozopolis was well fortified and could not be overcome using
siege artillery, so the emperor directed his commander Paktarios to
attack the walls with missiles (fig. 2.6). The Turks sallied to drive away
the Byzantine archers, who fled in a feigned retreat. Despite their own
persistent use of this steppe tactic, the Turks fell victim to the emepror's
trap. Some distance from the city the Byzantines sprang their ambush,
cut off the garrison from the city, and destroyed the enemy force. The
victory at Sozopolis is striking because of John's tactical judgment and
the discipline and coordination required for his men to execute his
strategy demonstrates that his forces were far from declining.[23]

Late in 1121 nomadic Pecheneg raiders bent on plunder swarmed
across the Danube. Once a major steppe power, these Turkic nomads
had been pushed from their homeland in southern Russia by the
Kipchak hordes. The Pechenegs nevertheless remained a formidable
power—in John's day the Byzantines still told stories of devastating
Pecheneg attacks on Thrace in the reign of his father and earlier. In the
winter of 1121–22, John marched north to meet the invasion and took
advantage of the seasonal lull in fighting to bribe contingents of the
enemy to his side. In the spring of 1122 John advanced to meet the
Pecheneg army which he found arrayed around a wagon-laager, their
families and animals inside the protective ring of oxhide-covered carts.
The emperor ordered a dawn attack and the two forces fought bitterly
to a draw; throughout the course of the fight the nomads retreated to

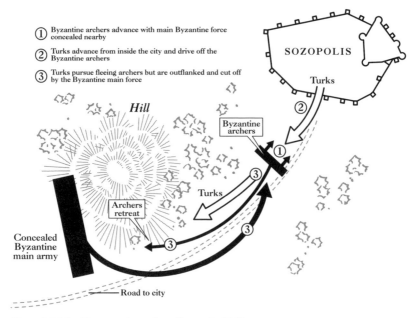

① Byzantine archers advance with main Byzantine force concealed nearby

② Turks advance from inside the city and drive off the Byzantine archers

③ Turks pursue fleeing archers but are outflanked and cut off by the Byzantine main force

SOZOPOLIS

Turks

Hill

Byzantine archers

Turks

Archers retreat

Concealed Byzantine main army

Road to city

Figure 2.6. John Komnenos's attack on Sozopolis, 1120.

the safe cover of their laager when they tired or the Romans successfully bloodied them. John himself suffered an arrow wound in the leg, but at the critical moment dismounted and led his Varangian Guard on foot against the laager, which his ax-men hacked through. The rout was complete and the emperor's men seized thousands of nomads captive and settled them in the Byzantine Balkans. Short, sharp engagements with Hungary and Serbia followed the defeat of the Pechenegs, but the emperor was able to raise a force to invade Hungary, with whom he established peace.[24]

In 1122 a Western crusading force spearheaded by Venice, the preeminent maritime power of the Mediterranean, laid siege to the Byzantine fortress on Corfu. The Venetians aimed to pressure John into renewing their lucrative trading privileges. John was forced to concede to the Venetians and restore their dominant position within the trade networks of the empire. The uneasy relations between the empire and Venice would simmer to a boil and lead to the disaster of the Fourth Crusade in 1204, a tragedy for which the Komnenoi bear some responsibility. The emperors of the dynasty were unwilling or unable to restore their fleet to a dominant position and seriously challenge the naval superiority of their ambitious western rivals.

Unlike both his predecessor and successors, John was most concerned with the Turkish threat from the east and, with the western front quiet, John turned his attention to Asia Minor. From 1130 to 1137 the emperor led campaigns against the Danishmends (a Turkoman dynasty) in northern and eastern Anatolia. Unlike their neighbors at Ikonion, the Danishmends took seriously the obligation of jihad and embraced its opportunities. In the power vacuum left in the wake of the Byzantine collapse on the high plains of Anatolia, the coalescence of another powerful raiding emirate thwarted the reunification of the coastal zones, much of which remained at least under nominal Byzantine control. John forced the surrender of Kastamon (Kastamonou), a Paphlagonian town where the Komnenoi family had previously owned land. In 1135 the emperor recovered the city of Gangra (today Çankırı about 140 kilometers north of Ankara). Elsewhere in Asia Minor, John sought to protect and expand his coastal positions in the southeast and to form a viable bridge to northern Syria, a relatively rich territory where a Latin principality exercised control and the Byzantines maintained some influence. In 1137, at Anazarbos on the Cilician plain (today Anavarza in southeastern Turkey), John employed a number of counterweight trebuchets, some of which the defenders burned by casting red-hot iron projectiles into the machinery. The Byzantines remedied this weakness by building brickworks around their artillery. A relatively new weapon to which some cities had not adapted their defenses, the trebuchets smashed the walls of the city, whose citizens promptly surrendered. Not much later, after a difficult siege, the Turks once more seized Anazarbos. This failure underscores the strain on imperial resources and the problems inherent in the emperor's strategy of piecing together a ribbon of fortified urban centers without securing the countryside from the Danishmends or the Seljuks based in Ikonion.

In 1137 the emperor again struck eastward and cowed his crusader neighbors. John's arrival at the head of a strong army intimidated the Franks and forced Raymond of Poitiers (1136–49) to pay him homage. By agreement, Antioch was to be ceded to the emperor if John could seize territory outside of Latin control, namely the capture of Aleppo

(Halab), Shaizar (Shayzar), and Homs (Hims). By seizing these strategic points, John hoped to undermine the growing power of Imad ad-Din Zengi (1127–46), ruler of Mosul and Aleppo who was tightening the noose around the exposed gullet of the Crusader States in the north—especially the County of Edessa ruled by Joscelin II (1131–59). In the spring of 1138, at Buz'ah (called Piza by the Latins), a town one day's march north of Aleppo, John's army encountered a strong Muslim garrison. The historian Choniates (d. 1216) stated that a sally of defenders drove back the Byzantine vanguard, but this was likely another feigned retreat, since John arrived on the scene with his elite Varangians and threw the Muslims back to the citadel. There the Muslims lay trapped as the Byzantine engines pounded the walls to rubble. The emperor seized immense plunder and committed it to a subordinate named Thomas. As John pressed on to Aleppo, Thomas marched back to Antioch but Zengi's men ambushed the Roman force and seized their spoils.[25]

John withdrew from Aleppo and turned south where he captured Kefar Tab and the city of Hama then wheeled northwest. Although he could not know it at the time, the decisive moment in Syria for John came in the spring of 1138 when he and his forces invested the important Muslim fortress of Shaizar. Raymond and Joscelin undermined the emperor by their delays and John had to withdraw in the face of a march-in-force by Zengi. The emperor did not wish to risk a major engagement with his powerful Arab rival; a loss would prove disastrous and unravel the strands of imperial policy in the east, while a victory would free the eastern Franks from the immediate Muslim threat that forced them so reluctantly into the arms of the empire. With Antioch brought to heel for the moment, John hoped to put one more stone in an arch of control from north to south that linked imperial territory along a defensible eastern line. Thus, in winter of 1139 the emperor again marched east, this time to Pontos in northern Anatolia, some 700 kilometers from Constantinople. There he threw a sizable army against the Turkish Danishmends and their stronghold of Neaocaesarea (Niksar) which commanded a fertile hinterland and access to the Black Sea coast, a region that had devolved from imperial control to that of the semi-independent Constantine Gabras. Determined Turkish defense and the bitter cold thwarted the emperor, who had to settle for seizing minor strongholds and captive-taking.[26]

When John learned that Raymond of Antioch rose in rebellion, he collected a large army—the sources for his reign rarely provide details—and in 1142 marched to Syria once more. The emperor's death the following year, aged fifty-six, was due to a hunting accident or murder. His son and successor Manuel paid less attention to Anatolia, and Byzantine hopes there waned.

John's record as a general is good but far from stellar, and his career underscores the problems facing the empire following the fall of the Anatolian plateau. Their route to the rich cities of Syria, which honor and economic interest demanded they possess, was effectively severed. The emperor was an indefatigable campaigner who understood geography, strategy, and tactics. It was a mistake, however, not to direct his full energies against the neighboring Seljuk Sultanate of Rum, which occupied the heart of the plateau. The loss of the recruiting grounds, resources, and strategic depth offered by central Asia Minor dampened the resources available for counterattack, and their continued possession by the Turks threatened the fertile coastal belt of the Aegean. Moreover, John misjudged his Latin crusader neighbors and consequently was checked by Raymond and his western allies. John embodied Byzantine caution. Unlike his father he suffered no heavy defeats but he likewise won no decisive victories because he sought no decisive battles; the dangers posed by defeat were too great. Instead he aimed to grind down his enemies and, by a combination of siege warfare and overwhelming shows of imperial force, to intimidate his opponents into cooperation or quiet. John is nonetheless accused of driving his men too hard; he led his forces on grueling campaigns year on year that netted plunder, but few permanent gains. The emperor's strategy of city-taking was a sound one to a degree—John wished to deprive the Turks of secure bases and gain permanent bridgeheads of his own. Thus his siege warfare maximized his forces and greatly reduced his risks. His aggressive campaigns in Anatolia disrupted the Danishmends and bullied the Seljuks, but did nothing to break the foundations of their power. In the final tally, John's leadership stabilized the Byzantine state; when he died he left a stronger empire than the one he inherited.

THREE

ORGANIZATION, RECRUITMENT, AND TRAINING

THE BYZANTINES MAINTAINED A professional standing army for most of their thousand-year history. During the early period, from the fourth into the early seventh centuries, there were large standing forces and elite units available for campaigning. The middle period army began its existence as a shattered remnant of this impressive late antique institution. While the precise nature of its forces in the turbulent era of the Dark Ages is unknown, over the course of the later seventh and eighth centuries the thematic system grew from the kernel of field forces that were consolidated and billeted in the provinces. Sustained offensive operations returned in the ninth century, by which time the state employed a mix of professional mercenaries and local thematic forces. The disposition of these troops, their recruitment, and supplement by thematic armies continued until the reign of Basil II. By the end of his reign in 1025 the thematic armies had run down, replaced by the tagmata, mobile armies stationed around the capital. The greater reliance on foreigners in imperial service and the corresponding decline of native troops is not a straightforward issue. The Byzantines always depended on foreign auxiliaries, and while there is little doubt that their role increased markedly from the eleventh century, we should not immediately disparage the loyalty or quality of such men. Native Roman soldiers served for pay in one form or another and were themselves mercenaries in the broadest sense—paid profession-als. In order to pay the soldiers and manage their deployment and to achieve their defensive aims, the state relied on a developed bureaucra-cy and military hierarchy.

ORGANIZATION

Like all armies, ancient and modern, the Byzantines arranged their mil-itary apparatus hierarchically. The handbooks portray deep organiza-tional structures, inherited from the Romans and persisting until the fall of the empire, with clearly delineated ranks to the level of five or four soldiers. The overall commander of the army was, of course, the emperor. In all cases emperors were expected to uphold the façade of military competence—even the most pacific possessed a smattering of training, could ride, wield weapons, and were literate in strategy and the structure of their forces. In many instances, the emperors were mil-itary men and possessed firsthand experience in the affairs of war. Since no head of state could manage security alone, even when he took the field himself, all relied heavily on practiced commanders.

Early Period

Constantine appears to have made radical structural changes in mili-tary organization; he removed the prefects from command and made theirs an administrative post. He further removed the troops stationed in garrison, the frontier guards (*limitanei* or *ripenses*), from the emper-or's guard units (*protectores*) and the field army (*comitatenses*), which he expanded in size. Units were uprooted and pulled from their old third-century bases. The Master of Infantry (*magister peditum*) and Master of Cavalry (*magister equitum*) commanded those branches of individual field armies. We would equate the various magistri with marshals in more modern military parlance, with control over armies in a given the-ater. After Constantine the empire was once more divided between emperors in east and west and some mobile units transferred to the frontiers where they formed the core of campaign armies and an effec-tive active defense supplemented by the limitanei. Such mobile region-al field forces were under the command of a Master of Cavalry who commanded both the infantry and horse.[1]

Prior to Constantine, Diocletian replaced the old Praetorian Guard—which had become infamous through fractiousness, rank insubordination, and regicide—with a new imperial bodyguard.

Constantine further increased the new regiments, the *Scholae* (Latin: schools, group), which totaled twelve units, each with 500 men divided evenly between eastern and western halves of the empire. The *magister officiorum* (Master of Offices) led them. These units formed an elite guard for the emperor on campaign through the time of Theodosius I (379–95), but most units gradually declined to a civilian honor guard by the later fifth century. By the sixth century a count (*comes domesticorum*) commanded units of the scholae.[2]

In the fifth century, the strategic disposal of forces and consequently the high command settled into the form it would resemble through the reign of Justinian (fig. 3.1). There were two imperial armies attached to the emperor's person led by the *magister militum praesentalis* (Master of Soldiers of the Emperor's Presence). These praesental armies comprised elite troops and mobile field forces that would form the core of any imperial expeditionary force. Five regional field armies (two praesental armies, Illyricum, Thrace, and the East) and their supporting frontier forces were under the command of the *magister utriusque militiae* (Master of Combined Forces [meaning of horse and foot]). His lieutenant, the *vicarius*, is known from the fifth century onward. There were frontier commands directed from the office of *comes rei militaris* (military counts) in Egypt and Isauria in mountainous and restive southern Asia Minor and thirteen dukes along the Danube, eastern frontier, and Libya. The magister commanded his field forces and also held authority over the armies under control of the *comites* and *duces*. The *legatus* (legate) or prefects held the reins of individual infantry legions. Infantry cohorts (regiments) of 500–600 still existed in the fourth century and their cavalry equivalent was formed of vexillations (*vexillatio*) or *alae* of up to 500 troopers. *Tribune* was the most common title for officers handling regiment-sized units, whether cavalry or infantry, but we also find the prefect in command of the cavalry vexilliations, *alae*, and among the limitanei.[3] Another *vicarius* (hence our word "vicar") was the lieutenant commander of the regiment whose duties and authority increased throughout this period. While much of the army underwent serious changes in organization and deployment, certain areas, such as Egypt, retained older structures and ranks.

Promotion within the ranks was a matter of service time or, not uncommonly, graft. St. Jerome (d. 420) provides a clear hierarchy of grades for enlisted men and noncommissioned officers in the early

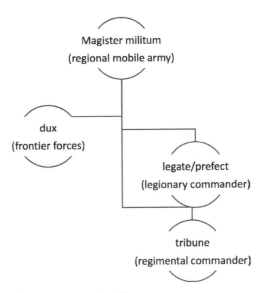

Fig. 3.1. Byzantine military structure in the fifth century.

Byzantine period. He lists from lowest to highest grade: *tiro*; *eques/pedes*; *circitor*; *biarchus*; *centenarius*; *ducenarius*; *senator*; and *primicerius*.

A recruit was a *tiro* (pl. *tirones*) until he was trained, and such men did not draw full pay or rations. The anonymous author of a late fourth-century document, the *De Rebus Bellicis* (*Military Affairs*), recommended that cohorts maintain fifty or a hundred tirones so that losses could be quickly and cheaply replaced.[4] Soldiers of the line were *pedes* (infantry) or *eques* (cavalryman). The *semissalis* seems to have been a senior ranker but below what we would consider noncommissioned officer status. At the base of the noncommissioned officer ladder of that time, the *circitor* at one time inspected sentries but little else is known of his authority or responsibilities. By the fourth century he may have been a junior *biarchus*,[5] (mess-leader; sometimes called *decanus* or *dekarch*, "leader of ten," even though he led eight soldiers, including himself) who commanded the *contubernium*, the squad or mess-group, which comprised eight to ten men who shared a tent and, as the name suggests, took meals together. By the fourth and fifth centuries the century numbered around eighty men, ten contubernia, commanded by the centurion with the rank of *centenarius*. The *ducenarius*, rather than commanding two centuries, was probably a higher-ranking centurion, since Vegetius stated that these men formerly commanded two hundred, an indicator that the title no longer reflected its old order. As historian Warren Treadgold argues, the *senator* likewise was probably a senior kind of noncommissioned officer with specialist duties, such as *adjutor* (clerk or scribal assistant), *campidoctor* (a centurion who drilled rankers and recruits), or *actuarius* (regimental quartermaster).[6] Each regiment also had an *optio* (quartermaster), a surgeon, two heralds, two standard bearers, *draconarii*—named for the dragon-headed pennons known in the fourth century, a cape bearer, a trumpeter, and a drummer.[7]

The lower command structure then looked something like fig. 3.2.

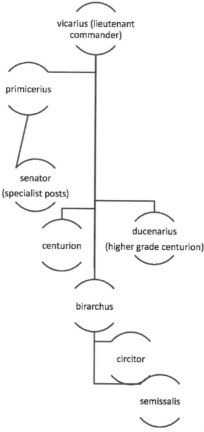

Fig. 3.2. Fifth century Byzantine army ranks.

The five regional field armies possessed an extensive administration that handled correspondence, pay, logistics, and judicial matters. These large staffs, numbering up to three hundred, mirrored their civilian counterparts in the provinces. Military tribunals were more or less the same throughout the staffs of the magister militum, the dux, or the comes. The army judiciary was staffed by a princeps assisted by a commentariensis and an adiutor and a libellis; the latter dealt with judicial petitions. Deputy assistants (*subadiuva*) and shorthand writers (*exceptores*) handled the judicial clerking. Another bureau headed by a *princeps* with his assistant, the *primiscrinius*, two *numerarii* (principal accountants), and their support staff of *scriniarii* (clerks) dealt with financial and supply matters.[8]

Scholars debate the tenor and role of the frontier forces (limitanei) who are sometimes characterized as "static" forces or even as "soldier-farmers" whose quality deteriorated in the fifth and sixth centuries. In a much-cited passage written no later than the year 550, Prokopios criticized Justinian for his elimination of their pay.[9] While the loss of payment in coin may be true, frontier garrisons staffed by local troops continued to exist in some areas of the empire. An Egyptian known as Flavius Patermuthis (the name "Flavius" was taken upon entry into imperial service from the reign of Constantine to show one's joining the imperial "family") served as a soldier in Elephantine (modern Aswan, Egypt) from at least 585–613. Patermuthis and his comrades were prominent locals, indicating that in some places the limitanei had come to resemble local self-help forces rather than disciplined professionals. Elsewhere, the picture is somewhat different. Isaac argues that the limitanei were not soldier-farmers but simply the troops under the command of the duces of the provinces and as such they were mobilized for police duties and patrols, manned the frontier posts, and joined the field army on campaign. From papyri recovered in Nessana (modern Nitzana in southern Israel) we know of a *numerus* of *dromedarii* (camel riders) who patroled the desert routes around Gaza; these men appear as landowners and prominent members of the community until around 590, when the unit was either disbanded or transferred.[10] Their duties were then probably assumed by allied Arab forces of the great confederation of Ghassan.

Federate soldiers (*foederati*) remained prominent in the Roman military structures of the fourth to seventh centuries. These troops served under a treaty (*foedus*) between the empire and tribes on the frontier. During the time of Diocletian and Constantine, federate troops served under their own commanders and were paid lump sums with which to provide for their soldiers' needs. They also received *annona*: payment in kind of foodstuffs and fodder. By the sixth century, some tribal groups served under their own leaders in this fashion, such as the Ghassanid Arabs who guarded the eastern frontier from the Euphrates to the Red Sea. Others federates were enrolled in regular military units that appear to have been mixed Roman-barbarian contingents under the command of Roman officers.[11] When not in the field these units were under the authority of the comes foederatorum, but for tactical purposes while on campaign they served under the magistri.

In 528, in light of new strategic realities in which the contest with Persia increasingly centered on Armenia and the Caucasus, Justinian divided the eastern command formerly under the *magister militum per Orientem*. He created a new command, the *magister militum per Armeniam*, headquartered at Theodosiopolis (modern Erzurum) whose army was drawn from both praesental units and the mobile forces of the old duces and comites of the frontier districts. Following their successful conquests, Africa, Italy, and Spain gained their own regional commands as well, which raised the number of army corps to nine, though there does not seem to have been a commensurate increase in troop numbers.

By the time of Maurice's *Strategikon* in the late sixth or early seventh century, the army had changed considerably. The old guard units, the Scholae, Domestici, Protectores, and Candidati (originally a picked unit of the Scholae) became mostly civilianized but remained intact. The limitanei degraded and Justinian seems to have drawn down some of these frontier forces.[12] The military returned to a purely decimal system of organization, with the main building blocks being the commands of ten and one hundred. A change in terminology reflects the decline of Latin in favor of Greek within the military, which was natural since the latter was the language spoken by most people in the eastern Mediterranean.

Book 1 of the *Strategikon* lays out the ideal officer structure of the Maurician army at the end of the sixth century. The general, now called by the Greek title *strategos*, held overall command of a given field army. A *hypostrategos* (lieutenant general) served as his second in command

and led the *meros* (division) in the center of the battle line; this indicates that tactically the *hypostrategos* was important, since his forces anchored the army. The handbook also says that armies of medium strength were 5,000–12,000, thus representing groups of one to three *meroi*. A *meros* (Greek "part," "portion") was a division comprised of around 5,000 men, officered by a *merarch*. The division meros was built from multiple units called *moira*. The moira numbered 2,000–3,000 under the command of a duke, *moirarch*, or *chiliarch*. The units that replaced the cohorts of the older army were variously called *tagma* (not to be confused with the imperial mobile army which had taken on the name *tagma* or *tagmata* after the Greek for "order" or "ranks"), *arithmos*, or *bandon*. The tagma and its equivalents numbered 200–400 led by a count or tribune, with his second in command, the *ilarch*, a higher grade *hekacontarch* who commanded a hundred men. The hekacontarch then was the successor to the old legionary centurion. The lowest levels of command were the *dekarch*, *pentarch*, and *tetrarch* who commanded ten, five, and four men, respectively (including themselves).

The *Strategikon* provides the order of march for a 310-man cavalry tagma, probably a common strength (for a number of reasons, unit sizes were not uniform). The commanding officer (tribune or count) held under his command two hekacontarchs (or ilarchs), 27 dekarchs, 29 pentarchs, 31 tetrarchs, a standard bearer, a cape bearer, and a trumpeter, with 217 troopers. Treadgold hypothesizes that the tactical units mentioned in the text, ranging from 200–400, represent deployments from standard, 500 men regiments (tagma or bandon) whose remaining 100–300 men remained in quarters.[13] This is a reasonable interpretation, given that unit sizes seem to have been based on decimal units grouped into thousand-man paper legions whose disposition varied according to the tactical situation.

The *Strategikon* names among mobile field meroi, the Optimates ("best men"), an elite cavalry regiment (bandon) unit of perhaps 1,000 men. In addition, elite cavalry units clearly owed their names to older Roman forces: the Vexillations, Illyriciani, and Federates, all mobile cavalry divisions that Treadgold estimates numbered around 5,000 each.[14] Haldon sees there being only three elite cavalry units: the Optimates, Boukellarii, and Federates, all formed sometime after 575.[15] These cavalry armies probably replaced the old praesental armies as the core of imperial campaign forces, since the author of the *Strategikon* envisions deployment of the three in the vanguard of an imperial campaign army.

The Persian War of Heraclius occupied more than a decade and drained the empire of men and resources. By the mid-620s the Romans had rebuilt their forces and attained victory, only to see them swept away by the armies of Islam. The Byzantines adapted to these exigencies by reconstituting their battered forces as best they could and billeting troops throughout the countryside of Asia Minor, the last large territory left in imperial possession. From the settlement of the military corps on the land evolved a new military and administrative apparatus called the *theme* system. *Thema (theme)* is a word of unknown origin, but may be derived from the army muster rolls or the tax rolls needed to support them. During the Persian campaigns of Heraclius the term simply meant headquarters of an army command.[16] The earliest attested themes seem to date to the mid- or late seventh century. "Theme" as a territorial and army designator probably derived from the association in the minds of administrators with the cataloging of military men and corresponding territory and material needed to sustain them.[17]

Dark Ages and Middle Period

The defeats suffered at the hands of Persians and Avars and the civil war led by Heraclius attrited the field armies considerably, and while it did not destroy them, it deprived many of them of their bases in Armenia and the eastern provinces. Heraclius gathered the mobile armies under his personal command; his immediate subordinate was the *comes Obsequii* (comes domesticorum), now a unified commander of the praesental armies and no longer simply the leader of the largely honorary Scholae and Excubitors.[18]

What we do know is that the names of the themes as they appear in the eighth century bear names derived from the old sixth-century army corps (see Map 4). The region around Constantinople comprising the Opsikion theme derived its name from Latin *obsequium*, the praesental army. The Thrakesion theme is attested in a letter of Pope Conon (686–87) and included elements from the old Army of Thrace, now garrisoned throughout western Asia Minor. The Anatolikon theme stretched from Cappadocia in the east to Lykia in the west with its northern and southern boundaries defined by the Halys River valley and the Taurus Mountains, respectively. Its name derived from the

Army of the East, that is, those forces under the old command of the *magister militum per Orientem*. The Anatolikon was reckoned as the premier theme in the military hierarchy, unsurprising given its location astride the violent frontier with the Muslims. The Armeniakon theme took its name from the Army of Armenia, formerly headquartered at Theodiosiopolis but in the seventh and eighth centuries headquartered at Amaseia (today Amasya). A short-lived naval theme, the Karabision, derived from *karabos* (Greek, "ship"), formed a permanent naval command possibly centered on the island of Keos (Chios); this theme was disbanded after repeated failures, their last being the siege of Constantinople in 716–17.[19]

Strategic passes were under *kleisourarches* (Greek, "guardians of defiles" = Greek *kleisoura*, pl. *kleisourai*). The kleisourai were hard points established by Heraclius and his successors to check the advances of Arab raiding forces in the dark days of the 630s and 640s. Nearly all of these commands lay in the east, among the mountain passes from Mesopotamia and Syria that the Arabs used to gain ingress into the Anatolian plateau. The institution is attested early; in 667–68 an unnamed kleisourarch apprehended an imperial rebel conspiring with the Arabs in his kleisoura of Arabissos (modern Afsin, Turkey).[20]

From the fourth to early seventh centuries, the economic strength and strategic realities of the empire favored the development of horsed units. These could respond to threats on multiple fronts with relative speed and counter the peril posed by nomadic tribes and Persian mailed cavalry; by the time of Maurice, the ratio of horse to foot may have been as high as two to one in elite forces. While nothing is known of the precise compositions of the army in the later seventh and eighth centuries, the loss of resources and impoverishment of the state must have reduced the cavalry arms substantially. Due to the Arab conquest of the east, by the 640s the state had effectively lost three-quarters of its revenue. Although the nature of the army, how it was supported, and its level of professionalism are highly debated, there can be little doubt that the troops suffered a decline in numbers and quality. Though cavalry remain prominent among the fragmentary notices we possess of the army of the Byzantine Dark Ages, the eighth-century army probably comprised a higher proportion of infantry than its predecessor. Treadgold suggests that the thematic cavalry represented one-fifth of the total, not an unreasonable number.[21]

The decimal system of organization of the sixth century seems to have mainly survived and been employed in the thematic structure; civilian sources of the late seventh and eighth centuries mention *chiliarchs* (also called *droungarios/droungar*, latinized as *drungar*), *komes* (count, who replaced the old tribune), *hekacontarchs* (also called *centarchs*), *pentecontarchs*, and *dekarchs*. The new officer here is the pentecontarch who, as the name suggests, commanded fifty men. Evidence is scant, but it seems that the old *merarch* became an officer called *tourmarch*, first attested in the eighth century.[22]

Theme Armies

The army regional commander, the theme commander, was after the seventh century called strategos (Greek "general") or *komes* (count). His office replaced the old magistri militum and strategoi of late antiquity. Apparently the komes vanished from the thematic landscape, meaning that there was no officer intervening between the general and the rank of kentarch, whose command was reduced at some point in the eighth century to command of forty men. In 840, the emperor Theophilos (829–42) created the thematic unit of the bandon to match the organization of the provinces to the tagma and abolished the office of pentecontarch, whose fifty-man units were obsolete due to the reduced command of the kentarchs to forty men. The staff of the strategos also reflected the army's Roman inheritance and its modification; the *komes tes kortes* ("count of the tent") probably took over the judicial and administrative role of the princeps. A *chartoularios* and staff domestikos handled the rolls, and financial and supply responsibilities, a *mandator* held specialist duties, perhaps comparable to the old senator title or provincial seconded protectores who served as regimental cadets or staffers.[23]

By the ninth century the empire had recovered somewhat from the shock of losses to the Muslims and began to salvage a portion of its wealth, power, and confidence. A contemporary account of Byzantine military matters compiled by al-Jarmi, based on his experience as a Byzantine captive in 837–45, provides some insight. Although al-Jarmi's original is lost, his report survives in reduced form in later writers such as Ibn Khurradadhbih, whose work dates from 846–70. According to the latter, the Byzantine command structure was as follows:

The *patrikios* [a court title given to top commanders, including strategoi] commands 10,000 men; he has two *tourmarchs* under his command, commanding 5,000 each; each tourmarch has under his orders 5 *droungars* in charge of 1,000 men each; under the command of each *droungar* are 5 *komites* in charge of 200 men each; each komes commands 5 *kentarchs* with 40 men each, and each *kentarch* has under his command 4 *dekarchs* with 10 men each.[24]

Thus, sometime between the sixth century and 845 the dekarch's command fell to forty but otherwise the organization largely mirrors that of the *Strategikon*. Throughout the eighth and ninth centuries the Byzantines never abandoned offensive warfare, but the return to the attack accelerated from the reign of Basil I (867–86). Purely Greek terms continued to replace the older Latin-based titles and professional mercenaries—both native and foreign—increased in importance. The thematic armies—built for defense, easily run down, and probably chronically understrength—gradually fell into a role not dissimilar to the old limitanei units of the sixth century, called upon seldom to campaign and mostly serving as a reserve and garrison force. This was especially true as the old central themes were broken up into smaller divisions.

Leo VI (886–912) again modified the command configuration. The emperor writes of a cavalry theme of 4,000 horsemen commanded by a strategos whose subordinates included two tourmarchs, each leading a tourma of 2,000 men. Below the tourmarch were two droungars (or chiliarchs) commanding a droungos or taxiarchia of 1,000 men, each comprised of five banda officered by a komites leading 200. Leo restored the 100-man units led by the kentarch, replacing their forty-soldier predecessor. This allowed for the restoration of the pentekontarch (tribune) over fifty men—a move which Treadgold links to an expansion of the cavalry.[25] Dekarchs and pentarchs round out the order of command. Tempting as it is to extrapolate that the increase of cavalry was general across all the themes, no evidence suggests an image of uniformity—indeed certain themes were cavalry themes, apparently with a preponderance of horsed units, and others were infantry dominant.

As the thematic commands and their armies shrank, the droungar became a tactical officer. In the themes his role as commander of thousand-man units faded, and the *douk* took on his provincial role as commander of smaller, more flexible, increasingly professional tagmatic units that formed a standing guard in the frontier regions. Thematic and tagmatic forces were brigaded to provide manpower to imperial expeditions, as seen in the attempt to recapture Crete in 949.[26]

The Tagma

Haldon has shown that the sixth-century praesental army evolved into the tagma (Greek "regiment") of the eighth century and that the foundations for the Byzantine army of the medieval period were laid by Constantine V.[27] The original field army of Heraclius was led by the *comes obsequium*. The Opsikion units descended from praesental armies and others attached to it over the course of the seventh century, including the units mentioned in the *Strategikon* such as the Boukellarioi and Optimatoi. As early as the 620s and no later than the 680s, the army of the Opsikion was established in western Asia Minor, with headquarters at Ankyra (modern Ankara). As Haldon notes, its composition and position in Asia Minor near the capital indicate that it was both the emperor's army and a strategic reserve to defend the capital.[28] The Opsikion proved fractious and unreliable; it was at the epicenter of five revolts and successfully elevated the usurper Theodosios III (715–17). In 741–43 under the emperor's brother-in-law, Artavasdos, the Opsikion waged a bloody uprising against Constantine V (741–75). Following the two-year conflict, Constantine broke the Opsikion into several themes. He also undertook the recruitment of new palatine troops to protect the capital and the emperor from the weight of the provincial armies.

Two new bodyguard units can be securely dated to his reign, the Scholai and the Exkoubitores. Both were commanded by an officer termed domestikos whose lieutenant commander was called *topoteretes*, an office that descended from an assistant to the old *doukes* in the provinces. We also find ranks continuing into the tenth century the command structure of the old cavalry vexillations of the sixth century: komites, kentarchs, doukinator, and specialists like drakonarioi (*draconarii*) are known.[29] The imperial tagmata were apparently a mix of new units and those drawn from older groups stationed in the new provinces around the capital. The empress Irene (780–802) added a new tagma, Vigla (Greek, "watch"), and her successor, Nikephoros I (802–11), raised the Hikanatoi (Greek, "able-ones"). Though Treadgold argues that each imperial tagma numbered 4,000, Haldon believes that in the late eighth and early-ninth centuries the guard divisions of the Scholai and Excubitors totaled around 1,300 while the Vigla and Hikanatoi had slightly double this number; 4,000 men in all is therefore a reasonable number.[30]

When Constantine V divided the Opsikion into three districts on a footing with regular themes, he turned the Optimates, who descended from the cavalry unit of that name during the sixth century, into a permanent supply regiment. The Optimates were responsible for marching with campaign armies and supplying and caring for mounts, weapons, and supplies.[31] Alongside these should be mentioned the infantry guard of the capital, the Numeroi, and the Walls regiments.

Throughout the ninth century emperors recruited new units into the imperial tagmata, such as Nikephoros I and his Hikanatoi and Federates, the latter a unit stationed originally in the Anatolikon theme whence the emperor hailed. Constantine V raised a new bodyguard unit called the Imperials. Leo V (813–20) apparently created a new corps of guardsmen, the Hetaireia (Greek: "companions" or "household cavalry"), which comprised three units and initially was recruited, like the old federates, from barbarian mercenaries. Michael II recruited Fortiers, men who were paid forty gold *nomismata* (the solid gold coin of the empire) annually for their service. The Hetaireia guarded the palace and accompanied the emperor on campaign and was commanded by hetairarches; one estimate puts these new eighth- to ninth-century guard units at 1,200 men total.[32]

Certainly tagmatic cavalry units seem to have expanded, but so did heavy infantry and other specialist troops. The recruitment of foreign soldiers paid in cash corresponded with the decline of the thematic armies—whether the expansion of the tagmatic forces was a cause or consequence or unrelated remains unknown. What seems likely is that the themes were rendered largely irrelevant by the new strategic situation; the 'Abbasid caliphate waned and the Byzantines aggressively sought to regain lost territory by first nibbling, then wolfing territorial emirates. The task of expansion was more easily conducted by professionals centrally directed from a focused high command.

The domestikos commanded the tagma. His lieutenant generals each commanded 2,000-man brigades, each in turn further divided into ten banda of 200 men officered by a komes (count). Each bandon comprised two kentarchiai under a kentarch leading 100 men.

Officer	Officers Numbers and Unit Numbers	Troops per Officer
domestikos	1 tagma	4,000
topoteretes	1 or 2	2,000
komes	20 bandon	200
kentarch	40 kentarchia	100

The emperor Leo VI reformed the kentarchies to comprise 100 men. He also created the 50-man cavalry bandon and the ten-bandon, 500-man cavalry *parataxis* and the introduction into the *tagma* of the 1,000-man command under the droungar who had prior to this been a thematic officer.[33] This officer structure among mobile troops prevailed for most of the height of imperial power in the late ninth and tenth centuries. Described here is the administrative organization; these were "paper structures" and had to be adapted in the garrison and the field, where units were drawn from across theaters for action. Tagmatic units were increasingly stationed on the frontiers where the eastward expansion brought new territories to garrison and new scope for offensive operations against the crumbling 'Abbasid state.

The need for tactically capable offensive units meant that tagmatic forces and thematic soldiers were combined under new battlefield commands. The taxiarchia, a unit of 1,000 infantry, appears in the tenth-century military treatises. The taxiarch took over the role of the old infantry legion and is parallel in the themes to the chiliarchs. As Haldon has noted, the struggle for new terminology to describe campaign forces hints that the thematic structures and officers were themselves eroding. By the late ninth century, the domestikos ton scholon, divided into two commands of east and west, was commander-in-chief of the army. Operational officers, such as the eastern and western field marshal called the *stratopedarches*, served as a proxy for the domestikos ton scholon. Nikephoros II Phokas bestowed the rank on his brother Peter, a eunuch who was therefore ineligible to be domestikos ton scholon.

The themes were apparently not up to scratch in their ability to provide campaign-capable forces, and their overall numbers probably declined throughout the tenth century. The replacement of the droungos of 1,000 with the smaller bandon as the major building block in the themes continued apace throughout the later tenth century; Nikephoros II Phokas noted that a normal cavalry banda numbered

50; but another source notes some banda of 400 strong. The bandon structure provided a more flexible command with units more easily integrated into field armies; it probably also reflected the inability of some themes to provide tactically useful, full-strength droungoi. While the reliance (from Theophilos around 840 onward) on the 50-man bandon as the building block allowed for the creation of smaller themes with garrisons of under 1,000, it also reflects a general weakness in thematic arms and the rise of tagmatic forces. The text attributed to the emperor Nikephoros II Phokas, *On Skirmishing*, noted that a *large* army in the common eastern lightning campaigns numbered only 3,000 (though very large forces to counter major *ghazi* or holy warrior expeditions are encountered elsewhere in the text) and continues:

> If you are present with only your own theme, General and the force under your command is a small one, then you should follow the enemy cautiously and at a good distance to avoid being detected by them. You should launch your attacks only against those charging into the villages and spreading out.[34]

The army available for counterraiding of an individual tenth century theme must have been well below 3,000, a situation that reflects both smaller themes and reduced thematic forces.

As the empire took the offensive against the Bulgars in the north and the Arabs in the east, the rise of tagmatic forces is partly reflected in the division of the army into western and eastern commands under the domestikos ton scholon, whose role shifted from being commander of an elite palatine unit to the head of imperial forces. This change occurred by the end of the ninth century at the latest, when we find the Cappadocian Phokas family holding the position over multiple generations. While on the whole successful, the Phokas clan proved too rebellious and the domestikos ton scholon fell out of the hands of the military aristocracy after the rebellions of the Anatolian military magnates in the first half of the eleventh century. Alongside the domestikos were the stratopedarchai and the *ethnarches* who, like the lapsed comites foederatorum of the fifth and sixth centuries, headed foreign troops; the ethnarches were sometimes themselves foreigners who led their troops in battle.[35]

The establishment of new tagma corps continued. John Tzimiskes raised the Athanatoi (Immortals), a heavy cavalry unit whose gilded armor impressed contemporaries.[36] The Immortals formed an imperial vanguard for the emperor while on campaign. They fought in the victories over the Rus' in Bulgaria and probably also in the Syrian expeditions of John, but their existence was short-lived—they were apparently disbanded when the emperor died in 976 and only revived under Michael VII (1071–81) by his chief minister Nikephoritzes.[37] The Immortals were probably among those units destroyed in the first decade of Alexios I Komnenos's reign in his wars against the Normans or Pechenegs.[38] Other units, such the Satrapai and the Megathymoi, make rare appearances in the literature. The rise of these new mercenary units supports the view that professional, mobile units increasingly replaced the theme forces as the wars of conquest proceeded through the tenth and early eleventh centuries.

The army of the tenth and eleventh centuries was structured for expeditionary action and the organization proved capable of supporting extensive conquests in the Balkans and in the east. As the Turks overthrew the established order in the 1060s, the condition of the thematic forces was deplorable; in his eastern campaigns, Romanos IV Diogenes (1068–71) tried to rally the remnants of these regiments to his banner, but by then the system was impossibly broken. The tagmatic forces did survive both these campaigns and the defeat at Mantzikert in 1071. When he seized power in 1081, Alexios I Komnenos inherited this structure and maintained it, though the field armies suffered severe attrition during the wars of the first decade of his reign and the ranks were increasingly filled with foreign mercenaries. The structure of the eastern and western domestikos commanding mobile armies survived until the fall of the capital to the forces of the Fourth Crusade in 1204. In the provinces, the arrival of the Turks destroyed the old thematic organization. The thematic strategoi, the mountain passes held by their kleisourarch, the dukes in charge of small "bandon" themes, and katepans as governor-dukes mostly eroded, though the Komnenoi used the latter for keeping the scraps of Byzantine eastern holdings around Antioch.[39] Foreign mercenaries often served under their own commanders and were seldom integrated into the structure of the Byzantine army; sometimes conquered foreign elements were absorbed, as were the Pechenegs under Alexios I, but this was rare.

Late Period

After 1204 and, more particularly after the restoration of the capital and Thrace to the rule of the Byzantine Palaiologan dynasty, there was an attempt to re-create some centralized fiscal and military administration in the European provinces. The late imperial army seems to have been a checkerboard of structures. The state reconstituted a theme system whose territorial units were often quite small; these territories were called *katepanikion*, governed from a *kastron* (fortress). The kastron was typically a stronghold governing a small district, but may have included villages, a group of islands, or even large towns or cities. The *kephale* ("head") governed the *kastron*. The *allagion* (squadron) commanded by an archon formed a core unit like the old bandon; Constantine, the brother of emperor Michael VIII (1259–82), commanded eighteen allagia totaling 6,000 men, but we cannot be certain about how many men commonly comprised this division.[40] The kephale and his subordinates were responsible for the maintenance of his troops, the repair of the walls, and ultimately the security of the kastron. His lieutenant was the *kastrophylax* ("castle guard"), a position that was often granted in concession to prominent aristocrats who fortified their settlements and received in return lifetime privileges from the emperor. The kastrophylax managed the maintenance, watch, and security of the kastron. Some frontier posts and forts were manned by soldiers enrolled in the *megala allagia*, the "great allagia" (or "big squadron"), and took their names from their administrative capitals or the theme in which they served. An officer called *tzaousios* (from Turkish *çavuş*) usually commanded the megala allagia.[41] But by the end of the thirteenth century the army was devoid of offensive capability and was outpaced by its neighbors who threatened the absorption of the tattered empire. In the Palaiologan era (1259–1453) the mercenary element, both natives and foreigners, remained prominent. Paid troops frequently served in companies (*syntrophiai*) organized and serving under their own leaders rather than imperial officers. Sometimes such companies were absorbed into the empire's permanent forces via grants of cash, *pronoia* (proceeds in cash and kind from tax allotments or farms), or land.[42]

RECRUITMENT

Early Period

From the fourth through seventh centuries the Roman state ingested soldiers primarily in four ways: through native volunteers, through enforced hereditary service, by conscription, or by hire of foreign mercenaries. Native volunteers were the mainstay of the army and were generally sufficient to fill the requirements of the state. The hereditary obligation for sons to succeed their father in military service, introduced by Diocletian, was soon after abandoned for recruits to the comitatenses, but maintained among the limitanei. The era of Diocletian and Constantine witnessed annual conscription in the provinces in which state agents levied recruits based on regional resources as assessed in the minute reckoning imperial officials had made; villages and estates had either to furnish a set number of men based on their population and expected agricultural surplus or to buy out of their obligation. Slaves were not accepted. In the troubled years of the fifth century when the eastern army suffered from the aftermath of Adrianople and civil war, supplemental conscriptions fell upon elites who had to provide able-bodied men to serve or a cash payment of 30 solidi (the gold coin struck from 309 on at 72 to the pound)—a steep price, since a worker would have received around 12 solidi maximum annually.[43] Unsurprisingly the draft was unpopular and seems to have been employed only in times of significant stress.

With the exception of the ranks of the limitanei, in which service was hereditary, the practice of conscription was generally abandoned. Justinian allowed slaves to join the army rather than resort to general forced levies, which were unpopular among elites and rustics alike.[44] Limitanei did enroll in the regiments in which their fathers served until the end of their existence; there were incentives on both sides for the frontier guard to be maintained. For the state the provincial soldiery still served a useful role as garrisons and as logistics and police forces, even if those outside Syria and Mesopotamia rarely took part in campaigns. Soldiers still received payment, supplies, and certain tax and status privileges that somewhat offset the risks posed by service, which in places like Egypt was infrequent.

Although Justinian did eventually allow for slaves to be enrolled in the army (and these must have been provided as substitutions during episodic ad hoc conscriptions) volunteers usually staffed the mobile armies and imperial guards units. Justinian and his general Belisarios are good examples of this—both sought service as an escape from provincial obscurity. Volunteers continued to provide the manpower for the army through the reign of Phokas, though Maurice provided that sons of fallen soldiers would succeed their fathers in the comitatenses. This was a privilege rather than a burden that the soldiers welcomed—it assured their families salaries and support. When Heraclius found himself chronically short of manpower in the midst of the Persian War, he restored the old hereditary recruitment of all soldiers, something he managed to accomplish in a time of crisis.

Native recruits generally came from the rural, rough-and-ready regions of the empire. Illyricum (the modern eastern Adriatic coasts and mountains) provided an ample pool of military manpower. Countless troops and officers came from this and other regions south of the Danube from Diocletian's time through the sixth century. Isauria, in the mountain lands of southeastern Anatolia, furnished large numbers of military men from the fifth century onwards, when the emperors were especially active in recruiting them to offset Germanic influence in the army. The rugged upland areas of Paphlagonia, Cappadocia, and Pontos also produced surplus men with martial prowess who helped to fill the legions.

Foreign recruits formed a major component of the army. Armenians provided excellent quality cavalrymen and infantry to both Rome and Sasanian Persia. Armenians dominated the imperial scholae after the fifth century.[45] Hunnic horse archers provided a major tactical advantage for Byzantine armies of the sixth century—they were recruited in groups following a native leader and placed under Roman command. Iranian nomadic elements, such as Massagetae, also called "Huns," and Alans in the sources formed another source of mercenary manpower. They fought as both cavalry and infantry. Three hundred "Hun" or Massagetae horse from Belisarios's boukellarios proved decisive in the opening engagements of the battle of Ad Decimum (September 15, 533) when under the command of the Armenian adjutant John, they slaughtered the 2,000-man Vandal lancer vanguard and killed the king's brother, Ammatas.[46] Captured Sasanian Persian soldiers were brigaded into units that served among Byzantine forces, and some Persians or Armenian-Persians rose to high positions in the military command.

Germanic-speaking peoples also provided excellent warriors for the Roman army up through the sixth century. Among these groups we find the east-Germanic Goths, who dominated the ranks of the eastern field army after Adrianople and were still found in Roman service in the sixth century. The east-Germanic Heruls feature prominently in Prokopios's description of Belisarios's campaigns; they are often seen undertaking special missions and were brave to the point of reckless.

Their east-Germanic neighbors, the Gepids, formed another tribal confederation that emerged from the shadow of Attila's Hunnic Empire in the fifth century and also provided troops until their defeat and destruction by the Lombards. The west-Germanic Lombards provided significant manpower in Italy—5,500 of them served the Romans during the 551–54 campaigns of Narses.[47]

The loss of most of the Balkans in the seventh century to Slavs and Avars deprived the Romans of some of their finest soldiery. This recruiting ground was replaced mainly with Anatolian Greek-speakers from the rugged interior. Armenians became especially important; at the beginning of the seventh century, the emperor attempted to transfer 30,000 Armenian troops with their families to Thrace.[48] The army that Heraclius reformed in 621–22 was largely from native Roman troops—since the emperor was in the midst of an empire-wide collection of loaned church plate to melt down to coin money, there was little cash to pay foreigners. It was at this moment when Haldon proposes that the emperor made military service once more hereditary, as it certainly was by the end of the century.[49]

Middle and Late Periods

Anatolia formed the heart of the medieval empire and consequently its most vital recruiting ground. As noted above, the soldiers who survived the defeats of the early and mid-seventh century formed the core of the theme armies. To these we can only guess were added local Anatolians drawn from places like Galatia, Phrygia, Cappadocia, Isauria, Lykaonia, and Pontos—the uplands that produced an abundance of durable men knowledgeable of local terrain and capable of the kind of skulking warfare the authorities would soon adopt to slow down Arab raids. Added to their numbers were Arab defectors—the rump of the Christian Ghassanid Arabs and other tribal elements who had fought in the Syrian campaigns. A few Persians adopted into the ranks during the chaos at the end of the Persian Wars and Armenian elements mitigated Roman losses somewhat.

In the Dark Ages the state relied mostly on native troops and Armenian groups that migrated into the empire or were recruited into service, but the use of barbarian mercenaries never really ceased. In 664–65 Constans settled thousands of Slav prisoners in Anatolia—five thousand of these deserted to the Arab army of 'Abd al-Rahman.[50]

Fig. 3.3. Thomas the Slav and his army assault Constantinople in 822. (*Madrid Skylitzes Fol32v*)

Justinian II (685–905 and again 705–11) introduced Slavs into the army in large numbers, most notoriously through a program of capture of thousands of Balkan Slavs and their transferal as soldiers to the eastern front, where as many as 30,000 were shifted. In a spectacular failure of imperial policy most of these troops deserted to the Arabs at the battle of Sebastopolis (Sebaste in Cilicia) that led to a Byzantine rout.[51]

During the reign of Michael II (820–29) the tourmarch of the Foederati of the Anatolikon theme revolted, led by Thomas the Slav whose army is said to have included nearly a dozen different ethnic groups (fig. 3.3). Thomas himself had served under the domestikos ton scholon Bardanes Tourkos ("the Turk," probably a Khazar). Theophilos increased foreign elements into the tagma and palatine units; after 840 a unit of the Hetaireia was at least partly staffed by Turkic Khazar mercenaries from the empire of the south Russian steppes and another of Pharganoi (Iranian or Turkic inhabitants of the Fargana Valley in Central Asia).[52] Occasional immigrations of outsiders who fled the caliphate, as in the Persians who defected to Theophilos and the Arab Banu Habib in the tenth century, added temporarily to the manpower available in the themes and on campaign. But the most plentiful recruiting ground for the Dark Ages and Middle Byzantine period of Byzantine history was Armenia. Armenians were an important element in the rank-and-file of the Anatolian armies and many of their commanders rose to prominence within the military hierarchy.[53]

Together with native Romans they formed the bulk of the armies from the seventh to early eleventh centuries.

In the eleventh century, the foreign element increased steadily. The formation of the Varangian Guard, a palatine regiment, during the reign of Basil II was precipitated by the arrival in 988 of 6,000 Rus' mercenaries from Kiev to help the emperor quell the fiery rebellions of the Anatolian military magnate Phokas. By 1034 the Varangians formed the regular palace and imperial bodyguard, replacing the older units noted above. The Varangian Guard was known for its steadfast loyalty to the emperor and their devotion was handsomely rewarded; so lucrative was service in the Byzantine army that one Varangian, Harald Hardrada, bought the throne of Norway largely with loot gained in the east. Though the Varangians were mainly recruited from the Kievan Rus', many Scandinavians served. After 1066 and especially after 1080 there was a strong Anglo-Saxon presence in the guard.[54]

At the end of the eleventh century, with the Turks possessing much of the Anatolian plateau, Alexios I Komnenos and his successors faced the loss of the central recruiting grounds of the empire. The Komnenoi therefore turned to the European core of the empire—Thrace, Macedonia, and Epiros in western Greece. But the reliance on foreign men became especially pronounced; Alexios enrolled many Normans in his service—it was these heavily armed and excellent cavalry that the emperor desired when he asked for aid from Pope Gregory VII, a request that helped spark the First Crusade (1095–99) when Norman adventurers spearheaded the western expedition into the Levant. Turkish horsemen feature prominently in Alexios's campaigns against the Normans and Pechenegs. Alexios's general Tatikios was a Turkopole (Gr. *Tourkopouli*—"sons of Turks"), a Turkish former mercenary who had converted to Christianity and became part of the emperor's inner circle. In 1081 Tatikios commanded a unit of Vardariotai against the Normans in Greece. The Vardariotai, probably Hungarians, were established in the valley of the Vardar River (in modern western Macedonia near the Serbian border) and continued to provide troops until the Serbs conquered the region in the thirteenth century—after this the Vardariotai continued to exist as a palatine regiment, probably staffed by other foreigners. They were horse archers or light lancers who wore distinctive red dress and carried whips.

After his defeat of the Turkic Pechenegs in 1091, Alexios settled them inside the empire and raised troops from among them. The

Cuman (Kipchak) confederacy that replaced the Pechenegs on the south Russian steppes and in Bulgaria posed the same challenges as enemies and opportunities as allies; they were superb horsemen and archers and would later form one of the major sources of Mamluk recruitment for the Egyptian state. In 1241 the emperor of Nicaea (one of the successor states that arose following the crusader sack of Constantinople in 1204) John VIII Vatatzes (1221–54) settled 10,000 Cumans in Thrace; they proved useful but fickle allies.

By the Palaiologan era, one-third of the soldiers in the imperial allagia were ethnically Byzantine recruited from Thrace and Macedonia.[55] Emperors supplemented these native soldiers with mercenaries of opportunity—for example, Andronikos II settled 10,000 Alans in Thrace. The enlistment of the Catalan Grand Company perhaps best underscores the lack of native Byzantine manpower and military competence. In 1304 the Byzantines hired the Catalan Company with its 6,000 mercenaries under its mercenary captain Roger de Flor to fight the Turks in Asia Minor. The Catalan Company affair ended in disaster. The empire had neither the money to pay these unruly professional freebooters nor the military force to contain them; the sad affair ended with the capture of Athens and Catalan dominion there until 1388.

Pay

During the era of the Tetrarchy, soldiers' pay was rendered largely in-kind. This was a result of the rampant inflation that plagued the empire in the third century. Since the time of Septimius Severus (193–211) the empire had levied a tax in-kind to support the troops, the *anonna militaris* and accompanying *capitus* to supply animal fodder. The state issued clothing, arms, and horses to soldiers. Pay was measured in annona, rations paid annually to rankers. Prior to Anastasios (491–518) each annona was reckoned at 4 solidi. Officers received multiple annona; the primicerius of the fourth-fifth century legions typically earned five annonae. During the reign of Diocletian annual pay in coin continued but was modest to say the least—perhaps 7,500 denarii a year plus donatives and special payments made on accession dates of the emperor and other imperial holidays. Fourth-century pay has been calculated as equivalent to about 12 solidi plus arms and equipment, but by the mid-fifth century had fallen to the equivalent of 9 solidi.[56]

To provide some frame of reference, a stone cutter in contemporary Egypt might earn something less than 12 solidi per year.[57] Upon their accession and in anniversaries of their reign, emperors paid substantial bonuses called donatives; Julian paid 5 solidi and a pound of silver, a standard sum offered through the sixth century.[58] Donatives paid every five years from the emperor's accession were about five solidi for soldiers of the line. But over time, by reckoning arms issuances and equipment in annona, the state deeply cut soldiers' pay while theoretically maintaining their ability to fight. One wonders how such issues worked, since a soldier could have hardly worn out a spear or sword in a normal year; possibly these allowances were convertible to food or fodder.

In the fifth century the cumbersome and easily abused in-kind system was replaced by payments in coin; the stability brought by the fourth-century creation of the gold solidus and economic recovery of the empire permitted a remonetization of military pay. Anastasios seems to have spread the five-year donatives out as annual payments and offered cash instead of supplying arms and equipment; prior to his reign soldiers in the field army received something like 9 solidi plus equipment. Under Anastasios field troops earned 20 solidi annually, an increase of as much as two-thirds; the raise was probably a response to a lack of recruits and the general poor condition of the soldiery. By the beginning of the reign of Justinian, soldiers in the comitatenses were then well paid when compared with the average worker.[59]

Limitanei received far less, perhaps 5 solidi and an equipment allowance. Justinian's pay scale for the African limitanei survives. The *dux* earned 1,582 solidi, the cavalry *primicerius* 33 solidi, infantry centurions 20 solidi, and their cavalry counterparts 16.5 solidi while infantry rankers earned 5 solidi and cavalry 9.[60] It is probable that even this modest wage was eventually cut by Justinian and that the state paid frontier troops only annona payments in-kind in equipment and capitus issuance for their mounts.[61] Allied units on the frontier, like the Ghassanid confederacy, received annona in cash and kind. But like their comrades in the mobile armies, limitanei received tax exemptions for certain family members and were exempt from corvée labor, among other burdens.

In response to the fiscal and military crisis sparked by the Persian War, in 616 Heraclius seems to have ended the cash allowances for uniforms and equipment, which amounted to reducing pay by one-half. The state returned to issuing clothing and equipment to the soldiery. Constans II (641–68) apparently cut this salary in half again and probably replaced the lost salary with grants in land from which soldiers could support themselves. Annual base pay for the rank and file was thus around 5 solidi during the Dark Ages.[62] To put into perspective this abysmal remuneration, we should note that a carpenter in eighth-century Egypt might earn 16 solidi per year.[63]

By the tenth century, the situation had improved and cash payments in gold had expanded. Officers in the tagma were well paid by contemporary standards. In the mid-ninth century average pay had doubled to about 10 *nomismata* (singular *nomisma*, the Greek term for solidus). A tagmatic commander earned 144 nomismata, a topoteretes 72 nomismata, a pentekontarchos 24 nomismata, and a ranker in the tagma 9 nomismata.

The health of state finances and the fineness of the nomisma declined sharply in the middle of the tenth century. Alexios I replaced the nomisma with the *hyperpon* (pl. *hyperpyra*) a coin inferior in fineness to the solidus/nomisma of the past. As most soldiers were by this time native and foreign mercenary professionals, they earned cash payments and donatives. The limited data suggest that soldiers in service in the late Byzantine period were well paid. In 1272 a soldier in Asia Minor earned 24–36 hyperpyra, well above the salaries of common workers, such as cooks or domestic servants (10 hyperpyra each) or doctors (16 hyperpyra). Even though the currency was further inflated by the fourteenth century, the 288 hyperpyra paid to a Catalan mercenary cavalryman even though he had to equip himself, was exorbitant.[64]

Many of the soldiers of the Palaiologan allagia served on the basis of pronoia grants. The origin of these grants is obscure but, like the settlement of troops in the themes centuries earlier, they served to shift the burden of maintaining troops from the central government to the provinces. Pronoia grants included tax revenues or rents from dependent peasants—a system often likened to the "feudal" customs that supported the landed aristocracy of the West. Unlike the medieval western arrangements, however, the pronoia were at first held for the lifetime of the grantee; they became hereditary under Michael VIII. In contrast to the medieval west, the state remained the owner of the land and in control of the fiscal mechanisms by which the pronoia were administered.

Over the centuries the Byzantines showed a continuous tradition of army organization that evolved from the Roman imperial system but was adapted to the strategic and tactical realities with which the empire was confronted. Until the twelfth century, the organizational structure of the army was relatively conservative—were he to view the army of the eleventh century, the emperor Maurice from some five centuries prior would have recognized many units and their officer structure. There was, however, adaptation and reorganization in response to the defeats at the hands of the Arabs, but the seventh-century wars did not expose the system as completely broken and thus most structures continued, albeit in modified form. There was a generally deep command structure present in the organization, with officers down to the level of four or five soldiers which undoubtedly preserved discipline and offered considerable tactical flexibility.

On the whole the state managed the well-being of the soldiers reasonably well—service was often dreary, unpleasant, and dangerous. Only during times of severe crisis, such as the inflationary era arrested by Diocletian and Constantine, and the seventh-century military collapse faced by Heraclius, did the empire economize at the expense of its troops. Even during the worst of the crisis, cash payments were never halted, though they were apparently sometimes paid in copper and in arrears. Since the military was by far the largest governmental expense, it was frequently the only place that such economies could be enacted. However, once the crisis of the Dark Ages ended, pay rates climbed to an average well above those of most workers.

FOUR

EQUIPMENT AND LOGISTICS

"The harsh necessity of war has invented the guild of *fabricenses*, which guards the decrees of the emperors with a kind of immortality . . . for the guild arms, the guild equips our army.

1. Hence provision has been made that such persons shall be subservient to their own skills, and when they have been exhausted by their labors, they, together with their offspring, shall die in the profession into which they were born."[1]

These words, preserved in the law code compiled under Theodosios II (408–50), intrigue for many reasons. Noteworthy is the attribution to war of causal force, a creative energy that produced a guild of skilled craftsmen. Also striking is the mental image the decree conjures of men wearing down in toil and age, and for the draconian harnessing of the children to their fathers' profession.

The Roman state traditionally equipped its warriors and developed an extensive network with which to supply the soldiery. As with all other ancient inheritances, these institutions evolved over the centuries, yet even at the nadir of Byzantine power in the seventh and eighth centuries, the supply system functioned (albeit at a lower level than previously) and was adapted to the new norms of defensive, skirmishing warfare and the rural disposition of the soldiery. By the ninth and tenth centuries the Byzantines sought more offensive capabilities and developed both these and the supply capacity required to push the borders of the empire to the north and east.

PRODUCTION AND ISSUANCE OF MATERIEL

During the era of the Tetrarchs the department of the *sacrae largitiones* distributed the shirt, tunic, and cloak that formed the basic uniform of the troops. Boots were requisitioned from the local community as tax-in-kind. By the fifth century soldiers were generally paid cash with which to purchase their uniforms, in part because the imperial linen works could never produce enough clothing to keep up with demand; six solidi for gear seems to have been standard. Soldiers might also opt to spend their uniform money elsewhere, as probably the case with the fourth-century Egyptian ranker Apion, who was glad to be supplied a cloak from his loved one Artemis.[2]

A system of imperial arms factories (*fabricae*) owned and managed by the state was spread throughout the east, where in the fifth century fifteen are attested. The fabricae lay on major routes, close to sources of raw materials, such as wood and iron, and often close to the frontier. The Danubian sector possessed six works: in Thrace there were shield and arms production centers at Adrianople (modern Edirne in Turkey) and Marcianople (Devnya in eastern Bulgaria). In the jurisdiction of the diocese of Illyricum, there were four: armories producing unspecified weaponry were established at Naissus (today Niš in southwest Serbia), Ratiaria (the village of Archar on the Danube in northwest Bulgaria), and Thessaloniki, and a shield works at Horreum Margi (Cuprija in central Serbia). By the year 539 Constantinople had a fabrica as well. In the diocese of Asia, in western Asia Minor, there was an armor and shield maker at Sardis in Lydia, while the Pontic diocese had a general arms works at Nicomedia as well as a *clibanaria*, which manufactured gear for the heavy cavalry, probably including the tack and scale barding for the mounts.[3] There was an additional *clibanaria* at Caesarea in Cappadocia, which probably also possessed a general arms factory. In the eastern frontier districts, there was a spear factory (*hastaria*) at Irenopolis in Isauria (in modern southeast Turkey), and general armor-works at Antioch, Edessa, and Damascus. Antioch also possessed a *clibanaria*. From this pattern it can be seen that the empire benefited from a planned network of arms-makers. The absence of imperial factories in Egypt in the earliest period is striking, but with no close enemy it made sense for Egyptian troops to be supplied by sea from Antioch or Irenopolis. By the sixth century there was certainly an arms trade in Alexandria, which was mentioned in Justinian's legal code as being a place where the illicit trade was to be curbed. The state had a monopoly on weapons manufacture and it was illegal to produce or traffic in arms without imperial permission.

The Master of Offices (*magister officiorum*) oversaw the fabricae workshops. Although the workers were civilians, they were organized along military lines. Each group of workers served under a tribune or praepositus with a subordinate primicerius. Workers received annona as soldiers and tended to come from the middle classes. They were bound to continue their service, probably for the twenty years that was standard for army recruits. Advancement was based on years of service, with men who had worked for two years attaining the rank of *protector*. Each worker was responsible for a monthly quota of objects in which they specialized. At Antioch, regulations dated to 374 ordered workers there to produce six bronze helmets and gild eight others every thirty days.[4]

Although settlements like Ratiaria, Naissus, and Horreum Margi suffered sack or were lost to the empire by the mid-seventh century, other major centers, such as Constantinople, Nicomedia, and Thessaloniki, remained unconquered. While these cities witnessed attacks throughout the seventh and eighth centuries there is no reason to suppose that arms-making ended there. In the capital region, the state supplied arms and equipment to the troops of the tagma from its stores.[5]

In the themes the situation is murky. When in 616 Heraclius halved military pay, part of the cut involved withdrawing the annona reckoned to cover arms and equipment; these had to be made up by the state if the army was to function, and all the more so when in the 660s Constans II again halved pay.[6] Prior to this, during the sixth century, there were imperial arms depots as well as urban warehouses for the storage of weaponry which would be distributed to limitanei and citizens in the event of a siege or used to resupply the losses of campaign armies. Given the lack of evidence, scholars are deeply divided about the question of central supply of weaponry and uniforms in the Dark Ages. On the one hand, Hendy and Treadgold have argued that a modified form of issue existed probably based on a system of the *apotheke* warehouses spread throughout the themes and known from lead seals to have been overseen by officials called *kommerkiarioi*, who were previously associated with the imperial silk monopoly. Soldiers were issued arms or exchanged copper coins or, after the mid-seventh century, agricultural produce from lands assigned to them. They transacted this exchange either at the imperial warehouses, with private weavers and smiths, or with whatever remained of the imperial arms factories. Haldon, on the other hand, believes that state reverted to the old Diocletianic method of requisition among the provincials and collected arms and clothing as tax which was then distributed at the *apotheke* warehouses.[7]

In the middle Byzantine period the main arsenal was at Constantinople, and an official called an *archon* probably oversaw the works where arms and "Greek ire" were made, but nothing is known about the size, capacity, or organization of these works. Maurice built an imperial *armamenta* (arms workshop, storehouse, or factory) in Constantinople adjacent to the Magnaura palace. The emperor Constantine V is accused of turning a church into an arms depot or factory. The central fisc maintained control over the office of the *archon* into the period of the Komnenoi, and arms-making, like production of other "forbidden" products, remained a state monopoly; the state maintained a certain level of control over the fabrication and distribution of weaponry.[8]

What of the *fabricae?* In the provinces it is likely, though not certain, that some kind of state supply continued. We have no clear indication of the continuation of major arms-making cities, such as Caesarea in Cappadocia. After the reforms of the seventh century, Cappadocia lay mostly in the Anatolikon theme and was in part garrisoned by elements of the old elite cavalry Federates regiment of Maurice's day. These men would have had at least some regimental smiths who kept their horses shod and their gear in repair. The region of the Anatolikon was rich in iron working, and even throughout the lowest ebb of its power the state worked hard to hold onto these precious assets. The needs of the garrison, the availability of raw materials, and the past history of manufacture in Cappadocia lend weight to the idea of continuity. A tenth-century mention of armorers in Caesarea may indicate that the armory there functioned through the troubled times of the seventh and eighth centuries.[9]

By the 840s, when cash payments to the soldiery resembled sixth-century levels, the troops probably once again purchased their equipment, from either the market or the state. In areas where the tagma was based, western Asia Minor, Thrace, and Macedonia, access to urban markets and specialized production was not problematic. However, requisition remained a part of the supply system, especially for major campaigns. Thessaloniki may have supplied its stores from a still functional state armory there or via purchase from private suppliers, although Haldon prefers to see the system of supply in the themes as based on state requisitions. In certain instances, though, private purchase was used, as the *strategos* of Samos raised cash to pay for nails to support an expedition.[10]

In the tenth and eleventh centuries, in addition to their salaries, soldiers received a cash allowance for food and personal equipment as well as provender for their mounts. This should remind us once again of the old Diocletianic *annona* system, and just like its ancient relative, it was equally open to abuse. The thirteenth-century Byzantine historian Niketas Choniates—who wrote with the hindsight afforded by the debacle of the Fourth Crusade—groused that Manuel I Komnenos allowed soldiers to profiteer among the provincials:

> He was not aware that he was enfeebling the troops by pouring countless sums of money into idle bellies and mismanaging the Roman provinces. The brave soldiers lost interest in distinguishing themselves in the face of danger, as no one any longer spurred them on to perform glorious exploits, and now the concern of all was to become wealthy. The inhabitants of the provinces, who in the past had to pay the imperial tax-collector, now suffered the greatest horrors as the result of military greed, being robbed not only of silver and obols but also stripped of their last tunic, and sometimes they were dragged away from their loved ones.[11]

On campaigns there were large-scale levies imposed, and imperial officials scoured the countryside to drum up recruits, ox wagons, and provender. In 1153 Manuel I ordered his troops preparing to campaign against Hungary to provide wagons and food to the imperial encampment so that supplies would be on hand when reinforcements arrived; such victuals were no doubt procured by draconian round-ups.[12] In the era of the Second Crusade when the armies of Conrad of Germany bore down on the capital with dubious intent, Manuel ordered imperial cavalrymen to Constantinople where they received issues of mail, horses, and cash.[13] Thus we should consider that the origin and supply of weapons varied across time, but even during periods of prosperity and strong centralization, there was not a single way in which the emperor equipped his soldiers but rather a mix of private purchase and state requisition and supply.

TRANSPORT AND SUPPLY

The supply challenges for the empire were, stated mildly, significant. The frontiers were far from the center—in the east the Arab frontier was 600–800 kilometers and had nearly doubled by the end of the expansion begun under the Macedonian emperors, while to the west the upper reaches of the Danubian frontier stretched for 600 kilometers.[14] The Roman logistical apparatus, overseen up through the sixth century by the *Praetorian prefect*, managed to maintain large standing forces and garrisons scattered over a vast crescent of the eastern Mediterranean world from the rugged Balkans to the snowy lands of Armenia to the desert wastes of Arabia and Sinai. It was no mean feat to equip, provision, and maintain an army of over a half million men. By the Dark Ages the resources available and the strategic realities of the empire rendered supply more localized, with mounts and weapons procured in the neighborhood of the troops from private or state sources. According to the emperor Leo VI, soldiers were to be supplied during the winter, which must have been impossible for units stationed in Armenia and the mountain passes of Anatolia where snows blocked the routes for months. Units in such places must have taken in large stores of provisions in the warmer months and waited, often in isolation, for contact with their superiors.[15]

Throughout its history the empire sustained a network of roads that bound the capital with its provinces. In the west, the main artery of communication was the Via Egnatia (Map 1). This route crossed the Balkan Peninsula from the second European city of the empire, Thessaloniki, via Pella in Macedonia, Edessa, Herakleia Lynkestis, and Ohrid, reaching the Adriatic Sea at two termini—Dyrrachium and Apollonia. The route continued to be used and thus repaired until the end of the medieval period. A northern trunk, the Via Militaris, built in the first century, linked Constantinople to the western Danubian

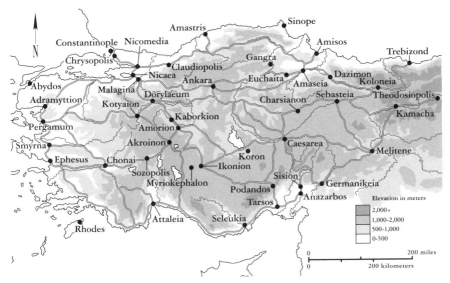

Map 11. The road network in Anatolia.

regions via Adrianople, Philippopolis, Serdica, Naissus (Naissos), and thence on to Viminacium on the Danube in what is today eastern Serbia. Recent archaeological work shows that sections of the Via Militaris were built of large, well-dressed blocks; the road was 8 meters (26 feet) wide. Another route hugged the coast, departing Constantinople and going along the Black Sea via Anchialos, Mesembria (Nesebar, Bulgaria), and Odessos (Varna, Bulgaria), finally reaching the Danube at Noviodunum (Isaccea in Romania).

Eastern links (see Maps 5 and 10) were maintained by a series of routes originating from opposite the capital. Abydos was a critical transportation node and customs waypoint where goods flowing to the capital were controlled and assessed and a staging post where east-moving armies gathered. A route from Abydos skirted the western edge of Asia Minor and linked the rich cities of the coastal plain such as Pergamum and Ephesus. From Chrysopolis also ran the great trunk road that crossed the plains and mountains of western Asia Minor and climbed to the plateau via Nicomedia and then on to Ankara. At Ankara the road bifurcated—the northern route led across the highland hills across Galatia and Cappadocia to Sebasteia (Sivas) and then on to Theodosiopolis, where a north-south route linked the city of

Melitene on the Euphrates with other garrison cities on the frontier and then Antioch in Syria. The southern trunk road in Anatolia from Ankara crossed the high plateau to Caesarea in Cappadocia and then forked southward, where it crossed the Taurus Mountains via the ancient pass of the Cilician Gates, onto the Cilician Plain and thence to Antioch. In the early period, and once Byzantine control returned to Syria in the tenth century, Antioch was a connecting hub of two major north-south military routes; the Via Maris and the desert route to the Red Sea. The first of these, the Via Maris, followed the course of the old Philistine road along the coast of the Mediterranean, linking the prosperous and important seaports of Phoenicia with Gaza and ultimately, after crossing Sinai and the Nile Delta, Alexandria. The more easterly route ran from Antioch, south via Raphanea to the desert steppe city of Bostra on the Arabian frontier, across the deep rift valley, to Aila on the Red Sea. An outer military road from Bostra to the Euphrates, the Strata Diocletiana (Map 5), ran along the desert margins of Syria via Damascus and then to Palmyra. Alongside these major roads were a host of other major and minor routes, the latter generally not suitable for conveyance of an army and its supplies. By law minor public roads had to be 8 feet wide in open country or 16 feet wide in difficult ground, and such widths, even if observed, would have been of limited use for a large force on the march.

A glimpse of the range of installations along major routes used by the military may be drawn from the example of the legionary base at el-Lejjun, dating to the period of the Tetrarchy and located near the Via Nova Traiana, the military highway later subsumed within the network of the Strata Diocletiana. Lejjun is a fortress measuring 242 by 190 meters and covering 4 hectares. Probably built during the reign of Diocletian, the fortress is a massive structure and symbolized an unmistakable statement of imperial power and might in the desert, but it also fulfilled a practical role of outpost, support base, and logistical node.[16] Despite the effort put into these large strongholds at Lejjun and nearby Udruh, neither was occupied for long—they were abandoned by the late fourth century, probably in the aftermath of a devastating earthquake. Justinian's reign saw a great deal of building activity in Syria, including the construction and refurbishment of forts and fortresses in the *limes*, such as the fortress (*kastron*) at Androna (modern al-Andarin in Syria), which preserves an urban citadel dated by inscription to 558 A.D. The Andron kastron is about 80 meters on a side and built of large blocks of dressed basalt. It protected a large village and agricultural region on the desert fringe. Watch towers, like that found at Kerratin near the imperial estate and supply depot of Taroutia Emperon, measured less than 10 meters on a side, but were constructed of fine basalt ashlars with a strong sloping talus that shows this is not simply an ordinary, private watch tower.[17]

The imperial post system supported communications across the empire, both in the fast movement of orders and in the slow movement of men and materiel. After Constantine, the post system (*dromos*) was divided into the fast post for officials and urgent business and the regular post for heavy goods mainly drawn by oxcarts, which moved the bulk goods of taxes in-kind, bullion, and raw and finished products requisitioned by the state. Regular rest stations (Lat. *mansiones*, Gr. *stathmoi*) and relays of mounts for the fast post, and draft animals and oxcarts for the slow post, were maintained along major routes of travel. Though the fate of the regular post following the Muslim raids and repositioning of the army is uncertain, the dromos as an institution certainly continued, and corvée labor to maintain roads as well as the burden of supply provender and sometimes animals to the post persisted. By the end of the eleventh century, since most of the lands that supported the *mitata* (imperial lodgings) and stud farms and imperial holdings on the plateau were in the hands of the Turks, the dromos suffered greatly. However the Komnenoi must have relied on elements of the dromos that survived, or at least the practice of levy that had long been practiced to support it, in order to move their large siege trains around Asia Minor. The Byzantines depended especially on heavy weaponry during the reigns of John II and Manuel I, when large, cumbersome counterweight trebuchets formed an important part of the Byzantine arsenal and siege warfare a cornerstone of imperial strategy and tactics.

The postal system *stathmoi* were at regular intervals, often a halfday's or full day's journey on foot. Egeria, a fourth-century pilgrim to the Holy Land, left an account of her journey in which she describes Roman troops accompanying pilgrim caravans from station to station along the route from Clysma on the Red Sea to the interior of the Sinai. In addition to forts, such routes possessed *mitata* (sing. *mitaton*) which served as a kind of merchant khan in certain areas but as a military installation in others. Installations at the imperial stud of

Malagina are referred to as *mitaton* and in the middle and late Byzantine era the term is also applied to the burden of billeting soldiers, indicating clear links with military and logistical functions. Though we do not know what the *mitata* typically looked like, if there was a typical design, we can imagine a complex of stables, barracks, and warehouses. In pre-Arab conquest Syria several *mitata* are known from inscriptions, at Deir Soleib outside of the important city of Apamea and another at Raphanea, south of Epiphaneia (Hama), where units of the Third Gallic Legion (*Legio III Gallica*) were stationed in the fourth century and probably later.[18]

By the Dark Ages, the state warehouses or *apotheke*, functioned to receive goods collected as tax, some of which supported the army. Most likely these occupied roadside centers where the *mitata* or *dromos* already possessed appropriate infrastructure or on imperial estates where produce and labor were available. As early as the fifth century the term *apotheke* may have been used in Asia Minor to designate such regional military warehouses; an early inscription is known of an *apothekarios* (warden of a warehouse) in Phrygia.[19] The apotheke was an accounting system and in-kind warehouse network and which dealt military stores, among other goods. Additionally, there were "marching camps" called *aplekton* (pl. *aplekta*) spread along major routes on which armies traveled and where they could be resupplied. Most famous of these was the imperial stud and warehouse at Malagina in the fertile Sangarios River valley. Malagina was the center of an imperial estate whence came many of the emperor's horses, military remounts, and equids for the imperial post. From at least the eighth century, Malagina served as a mustering point for the themes of the *Anatolikon*, *Thrakesion*, and the *Opsikion*.[20]

We have details of only one purely logistical unit, the tagma of the *Optimatoi*, which was charged with supporting imperial campaigns and fighting units dispatched to frontier wars. In the sixth century this unit had been an elite cavalry division comprised of Goths or their descendants, but it fell victim to Constantine V's breaking of the Opsikion and became infantry escorts and support troops. This logistical regiment was headquartered in Asia Minor, opposite the capital, with its headquarters at Nicomedia. Its 4,000 men were charged with obtaining mules and other pack animals and for moving military supplies where they were required. Some notion of the transport arrangements and capacity of the *Optimatoi* can be gleaned from Constantine VII's writings on expeditions, where he states that 1,086 pack mules were required for the imperial baggage alone, along with thirty saddled riding horses as tribute or from among beasts raised in the imperial studs.[21] In addition the *Optimatoi* would have carried the baggage of the certain elements of the tagma while on campaign. By the tenth century, heavy infantry regiments were provided one mule per pair of soldiers on which to carry their shields, spears, and victuals.[22] Even with these provisions, the baggage train and the large numbers of men involved in expeditionary forces, as well as the need to locate a suitable site and fortify a camp each day, made marches ponderously slow. A maximal distance for a fast-moving tenth-century army was 16 miles (25.7 kilometers) per day; something like 12 miles was probably more typical, although forces stripped of their baggage trains or their infantry forces or those making forced marches could obviously as much as double this.[23]

When an emperor's army prepared to campaign, the emperor and his inner circle decided on the target and the scale and route of march, then issued orders to provincials in advance of the army's muster. This allowed officials to purchase foodstuffs and equipment needed by the army and to be deposited at the way stations along the proposed route, or to collect it from the provincials by levy. Often the needs of the army were simply drawn out of the provincial treasury's storehouses where they had deposited taxes received in kind. In tenth-century inventories that survive we can see that planning for imperial expeditions involved numerous state departments and not only drew on large reserves of gold and silver, but also required inland thematic lands to provide food and fodder as well as basic stuffs for things like sail-making and cloth for uniforms.[24] Haldon has shown how immense the needs of a tenth-century expeditionary army could be: he estimates that for a two-week (or at most three-week) march, a 15,000-man force needed about 634,500 pounds (about 288,400 kilograms) of grain for soldiers' rations alone, a figure that excludes drinking water/wine and other foods like cooking fats and provender for horses.[25] Once in enemy territory these needs could be met at least partly by foraging or by purchase from merchants, whom we know often supplied military forces, but nonetheless the burden of any major military undertaking to the state and its citizens was immense.

Equipment

Clothing

The basic clothing of soldiers was a long-sleeved tunic made from goat hair, rough wool, or linen. Such tunics were frequently colorfully embroidered with medallions on the chest and shoulders and are known from mosaics and other pictorial evidence such as the hunting scenes from the late Roman villa at Piazza Armerina in Sicily. By the late sixth century Goth-type tunics were part of normal Roman military dress; these were longer than traditional Roman versions and fell to the knees. By the late Roman period, breeches seem to have been common. Wool leggings, often bound with laces, were normally worn. Soldiers' shoes, *kampagia* (from Latin *campagus*), were high open toed, heavy-strapped sandals. High black leather boots (*krepides/hyopdemata*) were increasingly common throughout the empire's history, and high-ranking officials preferred tall, white leather boots.[26] Woolen or linen leggings, often decorated in imitation of Sasanian silk versions, afforded some protection for the lower legs, and in the most heavily armed men these were covered with greaves, scale, or chainmail leggings. For inclement weather conditions, soldiers were required to have a heavy cloak, a *sagum* or *gouna* that fell to the knees and was spacious enough to cover the fully armed and armored trooper, including his bow.[27] These heavy cloaks served to camouflage soldiers—they were often gray in color and, according to the *Strategikon*, provided extra protection against arrows. The same text indicates that many infantrymen went to battle without the armor protection available to elite troops, even though they fought in a close-order, heavy infantry phalanx.

By the middle Byzantine era, the *kremasmata*, a quilted, padded skirt worn beneath one's armor, became a common article of clothing. This garment came to below the waist to protect the rider's legs while mounted. A similar item, the *kabadion*, owes its origin to Iranian garments which were long and buttoned down the front. Attached at the waist, the kabadion had a skirt with front and rear panels that could protect the legs of the rider, as well as the horse's back.[28]

The *Strategikon* notes that cavalry had saddles and thick saddle cloths and saddle bags large enough for four days' rations. The saddle probably had a high front, with prominent cantles (rear supports) to provide stability. Cavalry troops carried a lasso, an adoption from the steppe peoples who increasingly influenced Roman arms from the fourth century onward.[29]

The baggage train that formed part of the army is also discussed in the handbooks. Light ox-drawn wagons, each of which the author of the *Strategikon* instructed should carry a hand mill, axes, hatchets, an adz, two picks, a hammer, shovels, baskets, a scythe, and caltrops. Separate wagons carried the arms of each arithmos.[30] Packhorses were also part of the standard army baggage train, and these could be separated from the main supply train to accompany fast-moving battalions and carry enough rations for eight to ten days, probably for each contubernium. The handbooks stress that the supply train carried spare equipment, such as extra bowstrings and arrows for each campaign; Nikephoros Ouranos stipulated that a supply of 15,000 arrows for each division be carried on pack mules and horses, 100,000–200,000 total for each campaign.[31]

Armor

The equipment used by Roman units varied depending on their function. Since no contemporary surviving examples survive in the archaeological record, it is unknown if use of the muscled cuirass depicted on artwork up through the seventh century continued. There is considerable debate about how heavily armored and equipped and how uniformly outfitted were the legionnaires of the fourth century and after. Unlike the legions of the Republic and Principate, the forces of the fourth to sixth centuries certainly witnessed a downgrade in their panoply. Haldon argues that only the men in the front ranks of the army would have worn the entire defensive battle gear.[32] The fifth-century author Vegetius noted that one of the reasons for Roman failure against the barbarians was that they were no longer heavily armored:

> For despite progress in cavalry arms thanks to the examples of the Goths, and the Alans and Huns, the infantry as is well known go unprotected. ... Thus with their heads and chests unprotected our soldiers have often been destroyed in engagements against the Goths through the multitude of their archers. Even after so many defeats, which led to the sacking of so many cities, no one has troubled to restore either cataphracts [cuirasses] or helmets to the infantry.[33]

This is only partly true. While the days of each legionnaire being protected by *lorica segmentata* (the segmented plate-armor cuirasses famous from Hollywood movies) were over by the third century, it seems that the mobile field forces of the comitatenses would have been more heavily armed and armored than many of their adversaries.[34] But there was a decline in infantry protection, especially after the disaster at Adrianople, where massive losses of equipment were difficult to make up. Most costly and problematic to replace were the chain mail tunics of the elite infantry and praetorian units, since such coats required skilled smithies and many man hours to produce. Much equipment was lost simply due to age and retirement rather than battlefield losses, and an emphasis on cavalry tactics was also to the detriment of infantry arms.

The *Strategikon* offers a view into the kit of officers and elite infantry and cavalry of the late sixth and early seventh centuries:

> They should have hooded coats of mail reaching to their ankles, which can be caught up by thongs and rings, along with carrying cases; helmets with small plumes on top, bows suited to the strength of each man … spare bow strings in their saddle bags; quivers holding about thirty or forty arrows; in their baldrics small files and awls; cavalry lances of the Avar type with leather thongs in the middle of the shaft and with pennons; swords, round neck pieces of the Avar type made with linen fringes outside and wool inside.[35]

Most of the rank-and-file infantrymen seem to have worn a heavy wool felt gambeson (padded jacket) called a *thoracomachus*.[36] The author of the *De Rebus Bellicis*, a fourth-century work advising the emperor on military affairs, stated that the felt *thoracomachus* should have well-sewn covers of African leather to wear in the rain so that soldiers were not burdened by sodden garments.[37] Since the weight of mail fell mostly on the shoulders, the thoracomachus would have protected the wearer from chafing and injury caused by mail and from impact and penetrative blows from swords and arrows as well as blunt force from maces and clubs against which mail offered inadequate protection.

Quilted coats, *kabadion*, were adopted from Persian kaftans. These were split at the groin and fell to the knees and were the most common form of basic protection in the middle period. The kabadion was a tightly quilted garment with sleeves slit at the armpit; when not needed the sleeves were buttoned to the back. The strong, heavy kabadion served as the undergarment for armored troops or as the only form of defensive clothing for light-armed soldiers. When made of coarse silk, they would have offered some protection, especially against arrows.

Chain Mail

The *Strategikon* depicts infantry forces less well equipped than the cavalry arms and indicates only the first two ranks of the infantry were normally equipped as heavy infantrymen with full armor. Heavy infantry in the fourth to sixth centuries wore mail cuirasses (*cataphracta*; Greek *zaba*) of mail, developed from an evolution of the older *lorica hamata*, a chain mail shirt made from a combination of drawn wire and riveted rings, or from rings punched from sheets of iron. Mail was used alone or in conjunction or in composite body coverings with plate, scale, or other protections, and was the better choice for leggings and long sleeves because of its flexibility. Coifs offering protection to the neck or full face coverings like those used by the Sasanians were also adopted by the best-equipped Byzantine troops (fig. 4.1). In the sixth century, the historian Agathias (d. ca. 594) described men in the front ranks as armored in mail down to their feet, and ankle-length mail is depicted in contemporary art.[38] By the end of the sixth century, the *Strategikon* refers to the *zaba*, usually a long chain-mail ankle-length coat. Chain mail was best against slashing weapons such as swords, though it could absorb some punishment from piercing thrusts of spears or arrow casts. Modern experiments have shown that mail could sustain multiple arrow strikes without failing—penetration and torn rings did not always result in any harm to the wearer and although limited, such experiments show that some felt-backed mail provided adequate protection against the bodkin-piercing arrows of the medieval era.[39]

Experimental archaeology has also shown that chain-mail production required skills that placed its manufacture closer to the realm of a jeweler than a smith, since ring diameter was normally about 12 millimeters with the smallest rings having a diameter of 3 millimeters. Extant examples demonstrate a high degree of accuracy and standardization. Good quality mail required hammering of the rings to slightly flatten them which increased their hardness, then riveting of these rings together at intervals to form fabric. At a minimum, a mail cuirass comprised 12,000 riveted rings and may have required about 4,800

man hours (1.3 work years) to produce
a coat of first quality. Twenty of
Maurice's tagmas forming an army of
about 6,000 may have had approxi-
mately 1,240 such heavily armored
men, and while probably not all of
them would have worn chain cuirasses,
if they had done so, 1,240 coats would
be needed for the two front ranks. As
much as 1,600 man-years of labor
could have been required for making
this armor. Even if this figure is cut in
half, the production of mail cuirasses
was both time consuming and costly.
While chain mail seems to have been
less costly to produce than the best
lamellar (discussed below) it was not

Fig. 4.1. Seventh century Byzantine
infantryman wearing a chain mail
cuirass. (*Metropolitan Museum of Art*)

cheap; the resources required to produce first-quality body protection
for the troops were intensive and consequently armor availability
declined as the resources of the state diminished.

The infrastructure, skilled labor pool, and materials required to
equip and maintain heavy cavalry and infantry were vulnerable to economic and military disruption. Military losses, wear and tear, and the
loss of skilled manufacturers in times of stress meant an immediate and
widely felt decline in armor availability, especially during the Dark Ages
(seventh to ninth centuries). Nevertheless, chain mail seems to have
remained in common use throughout the history of the empire. The
advantage of mail's adaptability to hot weather, relatively simple (if
time consuming) construction, and adequate protection against the
missiles and lighter weapons common among Byzantium's foes made it
a logical defense.

Scale and Lamellar

Scale armor had a long history of use in the east prior to the advent of
Roman power and provided an alternative to the lorica segmentata
plate armor of the early empire. Scale armor was constructed from
small scales of bronze, leather, or iron overlapping one another and
attached to a fabric backing (fig 4.2). A clear depiction of this type

Fig. 4.2. A detail from the manuscript *Alexander Romance* depicting Middle Byzantine troops wearing scale (front row, far left) and lamellar (front row, second from left) armor. (*Istituto Ellenico, Venice*)

appears on coins of the emperor Aurelian (270–75). Fragments of scale armor have been found, mainly in the Roman West, indicating widespread use. Ammianus Marcellinus left a vivid account of an encounter in 363 with Persian heavy cavalry wearing such equipment:

> Moreover, all the companies were clad in iron, and all parts of their bodies were covered with thick plates, so fitted that the stiff joins conformed with those of their limbs; and the forms of human faces were so skillfully fitted to their heads that, since their entire bodies were plated with metals, arrows that fell upon them could lodge only where they could see a little through tiny openings fitted to the circle of the eye.[40]

The fearsome impression left by these formidable foes is obvious, and it seems also from the description that Ammianus was not used to seeing such men among the Roman ranks. Throughout the following centuries, though, especially through their contact with the steppe peoples of the north such as the Sarmatians, the Romans recruited and developed more such horsemen. These heavily armed horsemen appear already on Trajan's Column (AD 113) where they are depicted wearing full-scale armor and riding horses with scale barding (fig. 4.3). A tomb painting of the second century from Kerch, Crimea, is taken to portray Sarmatians, and two of the infantrymen depicted there wore

Fig. 4.3. A manuscript detail depicting cavalry wearing ankle-length scale armor. (*Istituto Ellenico, Venice*)

scale cuirasses. The Alan-Sarmatian cavalry noted in the fifth-century *Life of St. Germanus* calls these men "iron cavalry" indicating their full armor that influenced Roman equipment and tactics.[41] Scale mail coats are also depicted on soldiers in fifth- and sixth-century Egyptian tapestries and wood carvings, signifying that these coverings were in wide use and were stereotypes in the minds of contemporary artists. Like chain mail and lamellar, scale mail seems to have continued in use thoughout the empire's history.

By the seventh century, under the influence of the steppe peoples with whom the Romans had frequent and often violent contacts, the latter adopted lamellar armor, that is, crafted from leather, bone, or metal *lamellae* (sing. *lamella*) sewn together (fig. 4.4). The materials and techniques of construction were very similar in lamellar and scale armor. Lamellar tends to be made of larger metal plates—predominantly iron, as opposed to bronze often used in scale armor—and while some consider that the plates were sewn to one another, Dawson has

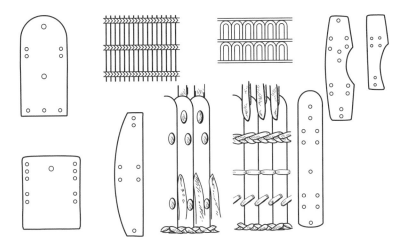

Fig. 4.4. Lamellar armor components and construction.

argued that this form of construction is impractical and that lamellae were instead first sewn onto a backing so as not to shear their bindings when one flexed the torso. Following their attachment to the backing, rows of lamellae with rounded tops and square bottoms were bound to one another. This technique, of affixing rather large plates (those found in excavation at Birka belonging to a long Turkic or Byzantine coat comprised lamellae measuring 27 by 100 millimeters or 1 by 4 inches) onto a thick leather backing rendered a heavy, protective garment. The overlapping lamellae effectively doubled the depth of defense and the leather added additional protection. The defensive quality of such pieces is exemplified by the encounter of the emperor Alexios I with the Normans at Dyrrachium in October 1081 when Norman knights assaulted the the emperor from two sides. The knights' spears lifted the emperor from his saddle but did not pierce his coat; Alexios was able to cut away the spear points that had lodged in his armor and make his escape. From this it is apparent that the best lamellar was impervious to arrows and other light projectiles.[42]

Lamellar cuirasses (fig. 4.5) were heavy, often weighing 5–6 kilograms (11–13 pounds) and offered superb protection. The Byzantines developed a technique of inverting the lamellae so that shoulder pieces had the rounded ends of the plates on segments protecting the limbs at the bottom of the rows. This is clearly depicted in an eleventh-century steatite icon of St. George of Mount Athos.[43] Fashioned this way, lamellar offered improved defense to horsemen against blows from below, which typically came from infantry spears and swords thrusting upward at acute angles. Unlike solid plate, the composite nature of lamellar armor meant that energy from strikes were distributed more evenly across the face of the cuirass, helping to reduce damage to the coat and its wearer. Likewise, the failure of an individual lamella could be contained; even if the plates became dislodged from one another they remained anchored to their backing, or vice versa. This heightened protection and reduced the need for frequent repair. Lamellar coifs and limb protection were probably adopted widely around the period of the sixth-century Maurician reforms when Avar influence on the Byzantine army was strong.

Fig. 4.5. An end of the tenth or early eleventh century painting from Hosios Loukas (Greece) depicting a soldier with a lamellar cuirass and upper arm splints.

From the tenth century onward, lamellar armor seems to have been the most frequently used type in Byzantine armies. It is the common form depicted in contemporary art. But while Dawson sees in its absence in Prokopios and Maurice a telling omission indicating it was not used in Roman armies from the sixth to tenth centuries, Haldon views it as utilized throughout the empire's history from the sixth century onward.[44] But by the later imperial period, after the sack of Constantinople in 1204, the soldiers' armor came under increasing western influence and lamellar probably declined. The common coat of the late period was apparently the shorter chainmail hauberk (*hauberjon*) that generally fell just below the waist and had short or long sleeves. A mail gorget (*gorgeré*) protected the neck and head. This mail

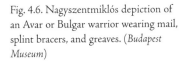

Fig. 4.6. Nagyszentmiklós depiction of
an Avar or Bulgar warrior wearing mail,
splint bracers, and greaves. (*Budapest
Museum*)

shirt was sometimes worn underneath a mail or lamellar cuirass of
Turko-Mongol form.[45]

Splint armor was used in protecting limbs, as depicted in the tenth-
or eleventh-century fresco in Hosios Loukas monastery, Greece, where
a soldier wears upper arm guards of horizontal strips (fig. 5.4), probably of hardened leather, riveted together. The *Strategikon* notes that
heavily armed cavalry wore arm guards (*cheiromanika*), probably of
splint type made of wood, bone, or metal. This equipment probably
reflected modifications to classical Greek and Roman patterns based
on experiences gained from contacts with the Persians and steppe
nomads, especially the Avars. The sixth to tenth centuries Treasure of
Nagyszentmiklós, a hoard of gold vessels with a range of Byzantine,
Iranian, and steppe influences, depicts a warrior of Avar or Bulgar type
with splint forearm bracers, splinted greaves, and a chain-mail coat
falling below the knees (fig. 4.6). Leg armor, perhaps lamellar or scale,
is also portrayed in the illustrations of the twelfth-century manuscript
of the history of John Skylitzes. This panoply probably closely parallels
Byzantine cavalry protection from the sixth and seventh centuries,
which developed under Avar influence.

The author of the *Strategikon* stipulated that greaves were to be worn
over fabric leggings and were to be as smooth as possible in order to
effectively deflect missiles and attacks to the legs. They were not to be

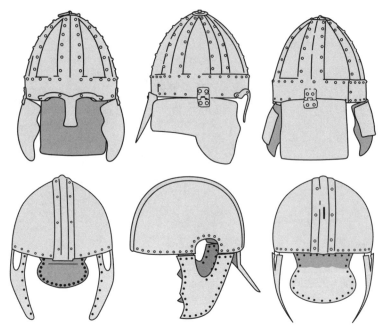

Fig. 4.7 (top). Spangenhelm helmet type; after James (1965). Fig. 4.8 (bottom). Ridge helmet type; after James (1965).

so heavy as to impede movement or wear down the soldier, but had to be sturdy enough to sustain punishment on the battlefield. Wooden greaves are also mentioned.[46] The recommendation for the creation of smoothed surfaces does not eliminate the likelihood of splint greaves, but it may indicate that molded metal leg protection common in the Classical period and depicted in the Dura Europos fresco of the crossing of the Red Sea of ca. 250 may have continued in use through to the early seventh century. There are no archaeological finds of splinted greaves from within the eastern Roman provinces, but those found in the sixth-century Vendel period in the Valsgärde 8 burial near Gamla, Uppsala, Sweden, are believed to have been derived from Roman models.[47] By the tenth century, most soldiers wore *toubia*, padded leggings made of wool, felt, or coarse silk.[48] Chausses (leg guards) generally of chain mail, were worn during the Palaiologan period, sometimes underneath greaves and thigh and knee armor (*cuisses*). The Frankish influence is again here evident.

Helmet design evolved considerably during late antiquity and in the medieval period. Unlike the Gallic-type helmets with sloping neck guard, the whole skull covering beaten from a single sheet of iron or brass, late Roman types show manufacturing shortcuts. Typically the design of these helmets (Greek *kassis*) was influenced by the eastern and northern neighbors of the empire, especially the Sarmatians and Sasanians. There were several designs in use, including the ridge helmet and *spangenhelm*.[49] Small, skull-cap kassis-type helmets are known from an excavated example from the Dead Sea region. The spangenhelm (fig. 4.7) consisted of four to six pieces curved into the center of the helmet where

Fig. 4.9. Kettle helmet type similar to that depicted at Khirbet al-Mafjar.

a band of metal joined the plates together, often carrying prominent cheek pieces and intricately decorated. The ridge helmet consisted of two metal halves joined at the centerline by a metal ridge that often carried a crest (fig. 4.8). Such helms were often high-peaked. These changes reflect adaptations based on encounters with well-armed neighbors whose technology matched or exceeded the Romans' own, as well as manufacturing increases required by the expansion of the army under the Tetrarchy. The multipieced helmets required less skill and time to turn out but still offered adequate protection. An intriguing example of helmet development comes from the eighth-century Arab estate of Khirbat al-Mafjar in the Jordan valley, where a Byzantine archer is shown wearing a kettle-type helm with a conical peak and a wide, arched brow piece or brim (fig. 4.9).[50] By the twelfth century, the kettle helmet was widely employed over a mail hood. Kettle helms had a flat or angled brim, and usually an aventail (a curtain of leather or mail suspended from the rear of the helmet for neck protection).

The shield (*skouta*) was the soldier's most important body protection. Along with the helmet it formed the basic defense of light-armed troops. Shields were convex and constructed of wood planking and covered with colorful painted insignia (fig. 4.10). Affixed to the back were rope handles and a shoulder strap through which one's arm could

Fig. 4.10. Soldiers with ovoid
shields depicted in a fourth century
mosaic in Piazza Armerina, Sicily.

be threaded. Shields typically measured 0.75–0.9 meters (2.5–3 feet) wide and 0.9–1.1 meters (37–43 inches) long, while smaller shields akin to later bucklers were used by mounted archers.[51] The Byzantines developed the familiar drop-shaped shield with a rounded top and pointed bottom which was easier to use on horseback, since for the mounted warrior the tapered end rested more easily to the left side than a round or ovoid.[52] In later centuries, perhaps under Frankish influence, they adopted the flat-topped kite-shaped shield, though the drop-shaped variety remained the most common.

Arms

Close Combat Weapons

Throughout the empire's history the two main arms of the military, infantry and cavalry, were similarly outfitted with a variety of arms. Personal equipment depended partly on one's role as heavy or light infantry or heavy or light cavalry but there was considerable overlap in basic gear, with the spear and sword forming the standard weapons of the line. These were supplemented by a number of secondary and tertiary weapons. To see late antique infantry in the eastern empire as purely swordsmen is probably wrong. The primary weapon of the late Roman legionnaire instead was the spear (*hasta*; Greek *kontarion*), about 2.5 meters long (just over 8 feet) and consisting of an iron tip, wooden shaft, and butt spike. Shafts of spears and lances were usually lathe-turned from saplings of cornelian cherry (the choice for the ancient Macedonian *sarissa* pike famous in the battles of Alexander the Great), myrtle, ash, hazel, willow, poplar, or other durable woods with good strength. A spear found at Qasr Ibrim in Nubia was made of tamarisk, a local wood that indicates that soldiers had to adapt to conditions of local supply and could not count on arms from imperial distributions.[53] Spear heads were socketed and usually triangular and rather broad-headed with a narrow cross-section. Spearheads found at Corinth from the early medieval period were of several types, typically 11–14 centimeters long, and usually square in cross section tapering to a narrow piercing point. Others were broad and triangular, gradually tapered (leaf shaped) or barbed.[54] The cavalry *kentron* was a longer version of the spear, with a length of about 3–4 meters (11.5–13 feet). By the tenth century, this length was usual for infantry spears, which accords well with the generally heavier weaponry of the Macedonian era foot soldier.

The Middle Period treatises describe troops (*menaulatoi*) who carried the heavy spear, *menaulion*. This weapon measured about 3.5 meters long and carried a socketed metal tip 35–45 centimeters (about 12–18 inches) long, probably resembling in make the ancient Macedonian *sarissa*. Like the sarissa, the menaulion was built from a single sapling trunk, honed down and fitted with its blade tip. The menaulion probably also had a butt spike that served as a backup fighting point should the main tip break off, but which more importantly allowed the weapon to be anchored into the ground to help the user sustain the weight of a cavalry charge. Anastasiadis, however, offers an alternative interpretation of the weapon, which he views as a shorter, heavy thrusting spear whose users served as a tactical support against cavalry, especially if the primary heavy infantry wall was penetrated by enemy horse.[55] Even in the last years of the empire, the Byzantines seem to have eschewed the use of pole arms, though this question has not been adequately investigated.

In certain instances infantry used long lances as well, since the *Strategikon* ordered that in wooded environments foot were to discard such weapons and substitute the standard infantry spear instead. These shorter spears seem to have been based on Slavic examples. By the time of the *Strategikon*, unskilled soldiers armed themselves with "Slavic" spears, a shorter weapon closer to a javelin than the kontarion

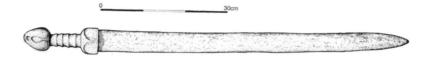

Fig. 4.11. Spatha. (*T. C. Jacobsen*)

but useful in close combat, especially in woods where fighting space was limited.[56]

The fourth- to fifth-century *spatha* (*spathion*), the single-handed straight sword of the later Roman Empire, is well known and was used by both infantry and cavalry. The tanged blade was pattern welded, a method that involved forging different metal wires together to form a distinctive design, a longstanding and simple smithing technique with many uses, including providing a softer iron core to an edged weapon. Suppleness and hardness were required in balance, the former to keep the blade from breaking, the latter to keep the blade from bending in action and to hold an edge. The spatha was typically 65–80 centimeters (25–31 inches) long, depending on the type, and about 4.5–7.5 centimeters (1.7–3 inches) wide, with a tapered point and double edge (fig. 4.11). The guard of these weapons was slightly concave and quite narrow, only slightly protruding beyond the width of the blade. Pommels were usually parallel to the guard and flattened. A good example of swords of this general type comes from beyond Roman borders in the north, from the Nydam Mose burials in southern Jutland (250–550), where a cache of blades exhibits these traits and was possibly even made by Roman smiths.[57] By the later sixth century, this spatha type had been replaced by the so-called Herul sword (*spatha Heruliska*), named for the Germanic barbarian mercenary allies of the Justinianic era. Although the exact form of this weapon is uncertain, it likely fit into the broader family of Germanic swords found in burials throughout central and southeastern Europe that seem unremarkable. Rather than a morphological difference, the novelty in the Herul sword perhaps lay in the quality of its metal. There is the possibility that the Herul blades were forged using the Germanic techniques that yielded high-carbon, fine steel blades such as attested archaeologically in northern Germany at Heeten (a region close to the presumed homeland of the Heruls) rather than via Mediterranean traditional iron processing.[58]

The find of a sword from Anatolia indicates probable Avar or Sasanian influence on some Byzantine swords of the later sixth and early seventh centuries. The weapon unearthed at Aphrodisias in central Asia Minor has a long (1.8 meters, ca. 6 feet) narrow, double-edged blade that tapers to a steep point. The utility of this long sword for cavalry is apparent, as are its piercing characteristics designed to defeat heavier armor.[59]

Fig. 4.12. St. Bakchos with spathion, eleventh century.

By the tenth century, the curved saber was common. In one famous illustration, the emperor Nikephoros II Phokas is shown with a *paramerion*, a thin, long blade that curves slightly upward to the tapered point. This paramerion saber had a wider guard than the late antique examples discussed above and is well-suited to the slashing and downward cuts of cavalry warfare conducted by the heavily armed horsemen (*kataphraktoi*) that by Nikephoros's time formed the main offensive arm of the military. Straight, double-edged swords continued in use and Nikephoros ordered his kataphrakts to carry them, as the paramerion was prone to breaking in the thick of battle.[60] The eleventh-century depiction (fig. 4.12) of the military martyr St. Bakchos in the Daphne Monastery in Greece shows the saint holding a straight blade *spathion* with a wide guard and decorated scabbard similar to types used throughout the Mediterranean.[61] By the later days of the empire, Theodore Palaiologos (1355–1407) described soldiers equipped with the *glaive*, possibly a Frankish long sword (rather than a pole arm of the later western medieval era) because he mentions it might replace the sword (*espee*). Alternatively, this may be a scribal error for *clava*, the mace, which was a common soldier's weapon from at least the tenth century onward.[62]

The mace was long used in the ancient Mediterranean—it is mentioned in the *Iliad*—and such a simple weapon was probably widely distributed, since the mace is simply an improved war club fitted with a symmetrical metal head. The latter is frequently studded to make easier the smashing of armor, bone, and soft tissue. The Romans of the early imperial centuries do not seem to have used it, probably because they only rarely encountered heavily armored enemies. The Sasanians particularly favored the mace, especially for their heavy cavalry, who wielded it with great effect; the Romans probably adopted it amid their confrontations with the Persians. A seventh-century source mentions the maces carried by the bodyguard of the emperor Maurice. In the ninth century, the emperor Basil I was proficient in the use of the mace; he is said to have shattered the legs of a bounding deer with a well-placed throw, a feat he repeated against a wolf. The war club (*rabdion*) was the favorite weapon of the mythic hero, Digenis Akrites, the "two-blooded border lord" of Byzantine medieval epic; with this weapon Digenis overcame the Arab emir who opposed him. The late ninth-early eleventh-century military handbooks of Leo VI, Nikephoros II, and Nikephoros Ouranos demonstrate that the mace made entirely of iron had become part of the regular weaponry of both infantry and cavalry, carried sometimes as a primary battle weapon and sometimes in addition to the sword and spear. Numerous examples of knobbed mace heads from the Balkans confirm that by the middle and later periods of the empire its use was ubiquitous.

Another weapon that gained in popularity was the battle axe. The weapon also was known to the Greeks from Homeric times, although it was not used by the Romans of the Republic or early empire. The Germanic peoples whom the Romans contacted used war axes, primarily single-bit types for close combat or throwing, such as the Frankish *francisca*, an elegant S-curved blade that tumbled when it struck the ground and skipped at the legs and lower body of its targets. Prokopios described the *francisca* as able to shatter shields and kill the soldier taking cover behind it.[63] The *Praecepta militaria* of Nikephoros II attests to infantry carrying the axe (*tzikourion*) as a primary weapon. The Byzantine battle axe was a one-handed, single-bladed infantry weapon with the blade backed by a hammer or spike. These were wielded as primary weapons on the line; the manuals show that tactically armies were a mix of "best weapon" men, who used the tool most suited to their training, experience, and physique.[64] The presence of axe-men among the armies of the tenth and eleventh centuries may also indicate a high number of Scandinavian mercenaries in imperial service. The

Vikings and their Rus' descendants, who favored axes, were prominent in the Varangians Guards. These men were famous for their use of the *pelekys*, the two-handed, double-headed axe that they wielded with great effect in battles around the Mediterranean world.

Missile Weapons

Javelins were a main weapon of light infantry throughout the history of the empire. Vegetius describes two types, a heavy version called the *speculum*, the replacement of the old *pilum*, measured 1.7 meters (about 5.5 feet) and carried a 22 centimeter (9 inch) tip. A lighter version was just over 1 meter (3.5 feet) with a 12.7 centimeter (5 inch) head; this weapon was called alternatively *vericulum*, *verutum*, or *beretta*.[65] In the sixth and seventh centuries, there were apparently multiple javelin types carried including short Moorish varieties. These were throwing weapons carried by light troops and sometimes by forces unskilled with the bow. By the tenth century, javelins had evolved somewhat into longer, lighter weapons of more than 2 meters, with socketed heads. The Rus' were apparently especially proficient with the javelin, which seems to have been their primary missile weapon.

Darts (*martzobarboula*), with a cast-lead weight on a fletched shaft, were another secondary weapon. Vegetius described palatine legions under Diocletian as especially proficient in the use of the dart; they carried five apiece in slots on their shields. "If soldiers throw them at the right moment, it seems as if shield-bearing infantry were almost to imitate the role of archers"; the range, he states, was similar to that of a javelin.[66] In the *Strategikon*, darts were to be used by both front-line heavy infantry phalangites and lighter skirmishing troops.

One prominent but overlooked weapon, mentioned frequently from Vegetius's day to the end of the empire, is the sling. The sling is cheap to produce, as it consists of a simple leather thong with central pouch in which is placed a smooth stone or lead projectile weighing 50–75 grams (1.8–2.6 oz). The sling is a humble weapon, its use commonly a skill acquired by shepherds and other rustics, and thus a weapon of the poor. The slinger's range was quite good—modern slingers have a cast of over 400 meters, a distance that rivals or surpasses that of archers. It is therefore interesting that the author of the *Strategikon* recommended both heavy infantry and light infantry carry slings, which shows something of a combined-arms approach gaining prevalence in the Maurician "new model army" of the later sixth and early seventh centuries. This perhaps also represents an effort to continue or revive older legionary training practices mentioned in Vegetius, who recommended that recruits be trained to use the sling. The tenth-century military handbook *Sylloge Tacticorum* mentions the use of staff-slings (*sphendone/sphendobola*) 1.4 meters in length (about 4.5 feet).[67] This weapon, which had a pouch affixed to the end of a staff from which rocks and other missiles could be hurled, is attested by Vegetius with the Latin name *fustibalus*.[68] It had a length of about 1.25 meters (ca. 4 feet).[69] Staff slings allowed one to cast heavier bullets or grenades and needed little space to operate, which made them useful on board ships or in sieges.

In numerous instances the tactics of the Justinianic era reflect the prominent place of archery in the warfare of the day. Belisarios relied heavily on native Roman and foreign allied horse archers. Since the arrival of the Huns in the fifth century, the Romans had clearly developed an appreciation for the utility of mounted missile troops and recruited as well as trained their own. It was not the Huns who introduced the composite bow to the Mediterranean and Near East, nor was it simply the Huns' proficiency with that weapon that caused such headaches for opponents. What posed such tactical and strategic challenges for the sedentary empires of Byzantium and Sasanian Persia was the Hunnic proficiency as horse archer swarms; the mobility of the horse and the striking power and speed of delivery of arrow fire from their composite bows were nightmares for Mediterranean and Near Eastern armies.

The bow used by the Romans in the sixth century was a composite, Hun-type bow with projecting ears and built up of wood pieces backed by sinew and horn glued together (fig. 4.13). The draw weights of such bows obviously varied from one piece to another—though this could be controlled reasonably well due to the precision making of these pieces—but 80 lb (36 kg) draws for a composite horse bow is a good estimate. While maximum flight distance may have been 300 meters, effective range against an armored target was within 100 meters.[70] The Byzantines seem to have favored the Mongolian release, which used the thumb with a thumb ring and index and middle fingers to draw the bow. In the sixth century, the Byzantines drew their bowstring to

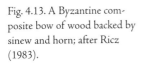

Fig. 4.13. A Byzantine composite bow of wood backed by sinew and horn; after Ricz (1983).

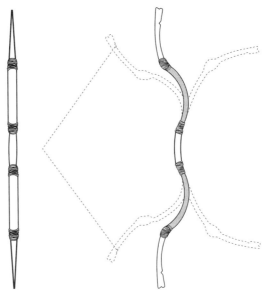

the ear and thus packed considerable force and outranged Persian weaponry. This bow remained relatively unchanged until the end of the empire. A good example is the eighth-century depiction of a Byzantine archer at Khirbat al-Mafjar.[71] The Byzantines relied heavily on archers in the expansion of the middle period—light-armed horse archers as well as kataphraktoi wielded them, and one quarter of the infantry were typically bowmen. The bow and arrow was thus the most important projectile weapon and, along with the sword and spear, of critical importance to the success of imperial forces.

While the crossbow was known to the Romans, its use seems to have been limited and faded away in the east; only after the Fourth Crusade, and the heavy Frankish influence on Byzantine arms, do crossbowmen appear in Byzantine service.[72] Although the Greek word *solenarion* may have meant a crossbow, it more probably implied an arrow-tube used for shooting short, heavy darts over distances greater than those achieved by conventional archery.[73] The solenarion seems to have been a Byzantine invention from around the time of Maurice—it is mentioned in the *Strategikon* and in the manuals through the tenth century.

Artillery

The Romans used a variety of artillery in both attack and defense, and their medieval successors continued to employ a number of different missile projecting machinery. A passage from a law of Justinian indicates that the Romans regularly defended cities with war machines:

> We also desire that those who are called ballistarii, and whom We have stationed in different cities, and authorized to manufacture weapons, shall only repair and place in good condition those belonging to the government, which are deposited in the public arsenals of each town. Where any workmen have manufactured arms they must surrender them to the ballistarii, to be placed with those belonging to the public, but they must by no means sell them to anyone else.[74]

Ballistarii were, of course, men who operated the *ballista*, which here probably implies artillery generally. The text shows the emperor's concern not only with the manufacturing of artillery, but informs us that cities typically had such heavy weapons stored in public arsenals and trained crews to operate them. The ballista (fig. 4.14) is a torsion-powered bolt and stone thrower that resembled a heavy framed crossbow with vertical springs at each end consisting of twisted fibers; the operators drew the bow arms with a winch and ratchet. There were several varieties and sizes, built to cast bolts 77 centimeters (2.5 feet) long with 200 gram (7 oz.) heads or stones weighing from 2.5 to 40 kilograms (5.5 to 88 lb.) with an optimal range of 100–170 meters, though they could cast projectiles as much as 450 meters.[75] Late Roman examples of iron-framed ballistae are known from the early second century onward and Belisarios's men used iron-framed ballistae during the Gothic campaigns.[76] The small *cheiroballistra* was apparently a hand-held torsion-powered bolt and stone thrower used by the Romans, but it is doubtful that it continued in use beyond the Arab conquests. The Romans did not seem to make use of torsion weapons beyond the sixth century.

In the fourth century, Ammianus Marcellinus described the torsion-powered *onager*, a catapult (fig. 4.15) with a vertical arm drawn back using a windlass. It was a difficult weapon to manufacture, maintain, and use on the battlefield, although when working properly and with a skilled crew it could launch projectiles on average weighing around 32 kilograms (70 lbs).[77] The onager was replaced in the

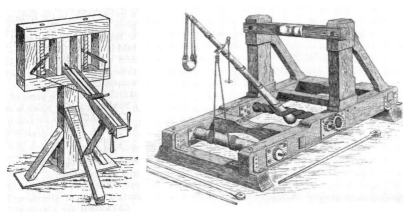

Fig. 4.14 (left). Ballista. Fig. 4.15 (right). Torsion powered onager.

Byzantine military arsenal with the traction trebuchet (fig. 4.16), a machine built on an upside down Λ-shaped timber frame with a cross beam at the top; a horizontal axle also at the top of the frame received the end of a pole whose unanchored end had a sling fitted to it. Using straps attached to the center axle, a crew of men hove on the lines and once the arm snapped forward, the sling released and launched the projectile. These traction trebuchets were simple and easy to construct and maintain. They were equal or superior in effectiveness to ancient torsion powered examples. The seventh-century *Miracles of St. Demetrios* records details of the Avar siege of the city in 597 in which they assembled fifty trebuchets:

> These trebuchets had quadrilateral [trusses] that were wider at the base and became progressively narrower toward the top. Attached to these machines were thick axles plated with iron at the ends, and there were nailed to them pieces of timber like the beams of a large house. Hanging from the back side of these pieces of timber were slings and from the front strong ropes, by which, pulling down and releasing the sling, they propel the stones up high and with a loud noise. And on being discharged they sent up many great stones so that neither earth nor human constructions could withstand the impacts.[78]

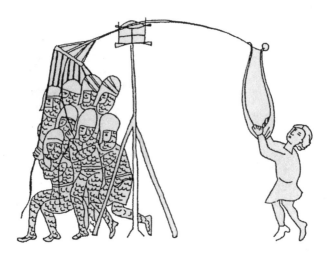

Fig. 4.16. Medieval illustration of a traction trebuchet.

The Byzantines also developed the counterweight trebuchet, which we shall discuss further in Chapter 7.

The above thumbnail sketch of Byzantine logistics shows that military officials faced considerable challenges in supplying and maintaining both static and campaign forces but in their mobilization, fielding, and sustaining defensive and offensive campaigns over centuries of near-continuous warfare, Roman logistics personnel achieved a remarkable record. Massive supply failures do not really appear in the sources, and given a culture that seemed to embrace the lessons taught by failure, we should expect to see these had they been a common occurrence. The provisioning and equipping of troops was always a state and private endeavor, with one featuring more prominently than the other depending on the era and the soldier's status and location. The equipment that the state issued or the soldier bought was nothing like a modern uniform—in its appearance the Byzantine armies of any age would have presented a far more colorful and varied aspect to an observer who would have seen many different forms of dress, armor, helmets, and weaponry represented in the ranks. Partly this was due to expediency—the state certainly would have struggled to maintain the depth of supply and uniformity of stocks required at all times, and it was partly due to simple adaptability to the realities that soldiers could be drilled without one standard-issue weapon.

More interesting is that during the time of Maurice, but especially in the ninth and tenth centuries period of reconquest, while one's unit affiliation of heavy cavalry, lancer, or light or heavy infantry was clear, one's tactical role was extremely flexible. Cavalry might be called to dismount and fight like infantry, and infantry forces served both offensive and defensive roles. This flexibility and training that clearly backed it is one prime reason for the success of Byzantine arms.

FIVE

STRATEGY
AND TACTICS

STRATEGY

The *Oxford English Dictionary* defines "strategy" thus: a. The art of a commander-in-chief; the art of projecting and directing the larger military movements and operations of a campaign; b. An instance or species of this.[1]

Said the emperor Leo VI: Tactics is the science of movement in warfare . . . Tactics is the military skill [that is concerned with] battle formations, armament, and troop movements. . . . Strategy is how good commanders put their military training in practice, their drilling with strategems, and putting together ways of defeating [the enemy].[2]

For Leo, strategy is the application of theory and practice in adapting to the exigencies of warfare. The Greek word *strategia*, from *strategos*, the general, implies the military art, military wisdom—the art of war. It is in this all-encompassing sense, covering what modern thinkers conceive of as strategy, operations, tactics, logistics, and geography that Byzantine military planners understood the term. We cannot therefore see clear dividing lines between strategy and tactics, nor to expect the Byzantines to understand geography and the organization of war as each forming separate disciplines. Such compartmentalization, to use the present expression, belongs to the era of modern total war as practiced from the nineteenth century onward.

As Haldon has noted, two pillars of Byzantine military doctrine—even if never expressed in explicit fashion—are known from both statements of imperial ideology and the actual waging of warfare throughout the centuries.[3] Emperors were protectors of the Christian people first and foremost, and while they claimed to rule the universe (Greek *oikumene*, roughly, the inhabited world) these ideological statements were limited by the belief that the "universe" meant the Roman world of the high empire, or in its most ambitious embrace, the Christian world. When Constantine claimed to be protector of the Christians of Persia, he was making fundamental claims to the dominance of the new religion and the extension of imperial beneficence to those who followed the imperial faith. Such grandiose claims were not pursued in lands traditionally outside of direct Roman political control—the Romans did not wage wars of conquest in Persia, for example, to yoke all Christians under their authority. But the emperors did vigorously pursue the maintenance and recovery of territory in the Christian west and Islamic east that had formerly been ruled by the Roman state, and emperors still considered themselves the only divinely selected universal rulers. All wars were defensive. Even offensive campaigns were considered defensive, in that they aimed to recover land that had been seized from the empire and rightfully belonged to it, and this notion of the "forward defense" or "active defense" was something that the Romans probably imparted to Muslim *jihad* theorists. Even after Charlemagne was crowned "emperor" on Christmas Day 800, the Byzantines operated under the belief that the real Roman emperor resided in Constantinople; the Franks and all other comers were interlopers, inferior culturally and politically. All of this imperial panache was tempered, however, by a generally clear understanding of the actual military capabilities of the empire. Rarely did Byzantine strategists overreach in their attempts to regain territory or in the defense of their core areas of the Balkans and Anatolia.

One notable example that illustrates the practice inspired by the ideological pillars of aggressive action to recover lost territory and the emperor's role as a Christian was the eastern offensive of Justinian II of the 680s and 690s. Justinian's thrust east was partly buoyed by his success over the Balkan Slavs, tens of thousands of whom he pressed into the army. But the emperor was more than a little inspired by an apocalyptic mood that had seized a considerable portion of the Christian population of the empire and beyond, a mood inspired by the new taxation and Arabization efforts of the caliphate that particularly ruffled the Arabs' Christian subjects. Justinian seized the moment, issuing coins with the inflammatory image of Christ on the obverse as tribute that were expected to circulate in the Muslim empire and in the process incensing the caliph 'Abd al-Malik (685–705). The emperor may even have believed he was a divinely anointed figure, as his ancestor Heraclius had proved against the Sasanians. Whatever the specifics, there were compelling psychological, material, and strategic reasons to pursue what was, in hindsight, a series of debacles that ultimately cost Justinian his throne.

The Byzantines often went to great lengths to avoid armed confrontation. While many empires relied heavily on nonmilitary dealings as a primary tool in advancing self-interest, Byzantine diplomacy was perhaps the deftest in history. This was at least partly due to the fact that through most of its existence, the Byzantines did not have the vast resources at their disposal, a fact which made diplomatic action a logical first response and stands in sharp contrast with Roman ideological expressions of eternal victory and overwhelming force that was rarely achieved.

Byzantine diplomacy encompassed many aims; through exchanges of embassies the emperor forged alliances, gathered intelligence, managed clients, or attempted to negotiate peace. In the embassy of the Byzantine courtier Priskos to the Huns in 449, members of the embassy had a more sinister purpose: to assassinate Attila.[4] Usually, though, Byzantine diplomacy used enticements; rich silks, silver services, plate, embroidered cloths, gifts of imperial rank along with the insignia and cash salaries. These tangible inducements demonstrated the wealth of the emperor and enticed many foreigners to imperial service and kept others neutral. The age-old adage "the enemy of my enemy is my friend" was keenly followed and exemplified by an endless scouring for potential alliances which could threaten the flanks and rear of existing enemies. Heraclius's alliance with the Western Turks brought the Sasanians to heel during the war of the 620s, and Byzantine payments to the Rus' and Pechenegs were used in the ninth and tenth centuries against the Magyars and Bulgars who menaced the empire.

Embassies also gathered information and bribed men to the emperor's side. In the ninth century the Arab Samonas, the right-hand man of the emperor Leo VI, used contacts inside the caliphate to ruin the pretender to the throne, Andronikos Doukas. On another occasion, during the regency period of the child Constantine VII's reign, a Byzantine agent in the exchequer of the caliphate, a Greek "deserter" Nicholas, informed Constantinople that Andronikos Doukas's son, Constantine, planned a revolt which would fail because the Arab authorities would not support it.[5]

The sophisticated diplomacy and defensive posture of the empire contrasts with the marked military expansion of the Macedonian era (867–1056). But to view Macedonian actions in isolation from earlier and later efforts is misguided; even in the dim twilight of the seventh century the emperors waged numerous campaigns to recapture lost territory or, barring this, destroy enemy capabilities along the frontier. Likewise, though they are often criticized by modern scholars for their failures to hold onto or reclaim lands in Asia Minor from the Turks, the Komnenoi expended considerable resources in the region and campaigned frequently there. Clearly by the eleventh century, the Byzantine doctrine of "protect and survive" as Haldon has described it, was anchored on the desire to preserve the richest provinces now forming the imperial center—Constantinople and the Balkan hinterland— from enemy ravage and conquest.[6] Imperial intentions never changed but what did alter was the empire's ability to make and sustain territorial gains.

While there were certainly permanent bureaucracies and institutions in the empire that imparted a mandarin flavor to administration and politics, we know of no standing central command responsible for long-term strategic planning. Rather, individual emperors and their commanders and bureaucrats responsible for supply dealt with military situations as they arose. Any discussion of overall strategy of the empire must be recognized to be our own imposition; the Romans themselves never articulated (or if they did it is lost to us) a comprehensive form of long-term war planning envisioning specific scenarios and reactions intended to preserve their borders for the existence of the empire. It can be argued that such actions were more organic and reflexive, though, and it is certain that a body of practices emerged from the fourth century onward whose general application could be termed strategy. The Romans operated under several fundamental doctrines which can be gleaned from the military handbooks, histories, and writings of emperors over the centuries. As in all historical studies that attempt to sketch more than a millennium of history, we are bound to flatten distinctions and differences that may alter the picture in its particulars at any one moment in time. But, as Luttwak has recently argued, in aggregate these fundamental tenets can be taken to comprise something we may call today a "Grand Strategy"; these were deeply embedded doctrines and practices that were passed from one generation of leader to another and subject to minor modification.

Just what, then, were the fundamentals of Byzantine war preparedness and practice? From the historical documents we can discern values and actions stressed by Byzantine authors throughout the centuries.

If You Desire Peace, Prepare for War

This maxim of Vegetius in the fifth century was followed throughout the empire's history. The *Strategikon* urged leaders to always expect conflict, a sentiment repeated centuries later by the emperor Leo VI:

> Always be vigilant and alert against confrontation with the enemy. Do not let a period when hostilities have ceased lull you into a period of carelessness. Do not become negligent before the conclusion of firm peace. Always be on guard against the machinations of the enemy. Be careful and watch out for their unfaithfulness. After you have been injured, regret is not of much help.[7]

The handbooks stress constant training, not allowing the soldiers to be idle, enforcing discipline, looking after supply stores, and paying meticulous attention to the mood and equipment of the troops on which success depended. Both the author of the *Strategikon* and Leo VI advised that households should possess a bow and at least forty arrows and that men should practice archery throughout the year in preparation for conflict, though we do not know how widely these desires reflected reality.

From the fourth century onward, foreigners attacked the empire with astonishing frequency. The military costs borne by the state were immense; by far the bulk of the budget was spent on maintaining, training, and equipping the troops and fleet. It is thus no exaggeration to view Byzantine society as one geared first and foremost to the defense of its territory. Experience taught the emperors that any period of peace was fleeting; never did this come into such sharp clarity more than in the events of the late 620s and 630s, when Heraclius found himself at the top of the wheel of fortune with his victories over the Persians, symbolized by his triumphant entry into Jerusalem in a spirit of millennial jubilation. The wheel turned, however, and within a decade Arab forces seized the whole of the Levant. Such episodes, and countless others, reinforced among the Byzantine elite that there was no shortage of enemies and that one defeated foe would soon be replaced with another. Therefore the state not only maintained standing, permanent forces, but also attempted to maintain and control production and stocks of arms and materiel. The imperial bureaucracy drew on centuries of experience in the needs of the soldiery in material resources and logistical support on campaign. Although we take written knowledge for granted, the vast collection of state archives in the capital provided the Byzantines an immense advantage over most of their neighbors. Detailed intelligence briefs, battlefield reports, and accounts accumulated over centuries of imperial expeditions provided information on most military challenges that confronted the authorities.

The collecting of ancient military writers, much of whose work was adopted in the military treatises of the seventh to eleventh centuries, demonstrates the importance of literacy in maintaining imperial defense. Moreover, beyond the assumption of the army as an institution implicit in their production, these handbooks show a concern for standardization and replication in military experience. They also demonstrate a keen self-awareness in terms of the cost of warfare and the limits of Byzantine material resources. Thus, as the handbooks suggest, the Byzantine army was trained, drilled, and perpetually prepared for conflicts that always arose.

War Was not Merely Material but also Spiritual and Psychological

The Byzantines regarded themselves as inheritors of a Christian empire, guarded by God and the saints, and their state destined to survive until the end of days. Since the reign of Constantine I, the Romans had understood that the universe was ordered according to the principles of Christianity and the world was a reflection of the unseen cosmos: one God, one faith, one emperor, one empire. Christianity was a vital ingredient in the understanding of the place of the empire in the world, and of the individual in action. War was a sinful space in which activities normally considered impious, such as deceit, were acceptable. Such actions as aggression and duplicity were not exculpated by war,

though, and soldiers were enjoined to remain always pious and prayer-
ful so that God would favor the Roman cause. Commanders were
urged to purify themselves before campaigns and battles, and to always
maintain their piety, as in this directive from the *Taktika*:

> It is necessary to worship the Divinity at all times. Especially, O
> general, should you offer worship when you plan to enter upon
> the dangers of war. If at that time, you genuinely worship God,
> then, when the time is full of terror, you will be confident that you
> can offer your prayers to him as to a friend and you can seek your
> salvation with utter confidence.[8]

Especially in conflicts with the Persians and Arabs, when Heraclius
cast himself as the biblical David—the weak shepherd boy following
the moral right, against the physically superior but heathen Goliath—
the psychology of conflict was tinged with Christian notions of just
war and its moral virtues. Priests accompanied armies, holy icons
served as battle standards, and the *kyrie eleison* (Lord have mercy) was a
battle cry for the army in the seventh century and later.[9]

The Byzantines clearly understood the psychological nature of warfare and the use of psychological means to manage one's forces and to
undermine the enemy and there are numerous examples in the handbooks: "The bodies of soldiers who have been killed in battle are sacred,
especially those who have been most valiant in the fight on behalf of
Christians. By all means, it is necessary to honor them reverently and
to dignify them with burial and eternal memory."[10]

To those who observe them, the practice of commemorating the
fallen is a powerful reminder of communal bonds, a key ingredient of
identity, and a strong inducement to collective action. Just as the early
saints of the empire were killed by infidels, the soldiers who perished
against the barbarians bore a heroic example to the Christians of the
empire. The morale of men was to be safeguarded through provision of
adequate provender, equipment, and especially by the careful scrutiny
of their needs by commanders. Leo stated, "When you do not provide
your army with necessity of supplies and food, even without the enemy
attacking, you have been defeated."[11] The dead were to be buried cere-
moniously, but at night, so that soldiers could be assured of respect for
their sacrifice but to conceal the numbers of dead from the enemy. The
wounded were cared for and their comfort and morale overseen by

commanders who were instructed to visit them. Families and friends were to be placed in units together in camp and on the battle line, so that the emotional bonds that tied them checked their fear and sparked the desire to protect.[12] Signs of fear were to be observed by careful commanders, and bad omens shrugged off or spun as good signs in order to maintain and elevate morale. These remarkable measures show a clear understanding of the mental and emotional toll of warfare and the dangers of low morale.

Subterfuge, bribery, and disinformation were prized bloodless means to undermine or dissolve enemies and were always preferred to open battle. The military manuals instruct, whenever possible, to bribe enemy commanders. Before campaigns on the frontiers, the general Nikephoros Ouranos (ca. 950–1011) ordered that gifts be sent to the emirs along the border in order for the bearers to collect intelligence and possibly induce the enemy to the Byzantine side or at least inaction in the coming conflict. Sowing dissent within populations under siege was a standard tactic:

> You must make this announcement to the fortress, that "all the *Magaritai* (probably Arabic muhajirun = refugees), Armenians [Christians], and Syrians [Jacobite Christians] in this fortress who do not cross over to us before the fortress is taken will be beheaded." These are the things you will proclaim first to those within the fortress, for it causes disagreement and dissension among them.[13]

Even though imperial officials took war for granted as part of the sinful condition of fallen man, they usually went to great lengths to avoid it. In addition there were strenuous diplomatic efforts, like the payments of thousands of pounds of gold to the Persians and Avars throughout the sixth century, that the Romans made to ensure neighbors did not attack. Though often a fruitless exercise, given the wealth of Byzantine society relative to many of their neighbors and the militant nature of most societies on their borders, emperors paid bribes and subsidies to foreigners to keep them from waging war. Gifts were critical to imperial prestige, to demonstrate the superiority of the empire, and to forge ties with outsiders.

As Maurice's *Strategikon* observed, the cause of war must be just.[14] Just war was by definition defensive. On those occasions where the

Byzantines pursued what modern observers would call offensive war-fare, their view was that these were conducted to recover lost territory that legally belonged to the empire, or to punish enemies and thereby discourage them from further attack. Examples of the former are Justinian's western campaigns in Africa and Italy and the expansion of imperial boundaries in Bulgaria, Syria-Mesopotamia, and Armenia in the ninth and tenth centuries. A good, though failed, example of the latter case is Manuel I Komnenos's 1155–58 campaigns in Italy which, while they restored suzerainty over a sliver of former Byzantine lands, their main purpose was to punish the Sicilians for their 1147 attack on the Balkans.[15] In the series of conflicts that pitted the empire against Persia during the early period, war aims were always limited to attaining a favorable negotiated settlement. For instance, in 578, in response to Persian invasions in Mesopotamia, Maurice, then magister militum, led a Byzantine raid in force that was retaliatory but aimed to bolster Roman positions in the peace talks to follow. Later, the Macedonian emperors accepted the submission of Arab and Caucasian princes along the eastern marches rather than attack them, and the Komnenoi, especially the emperor John II, took seriously their treaty obligations as overlords of the Latin crusader state of Antioch, despite the duplicity the latter often exhibited. Throughout the history of the empire, when an enemy wished to negotiate, the Byzantines were quick to oblige them: "When the enemy, after God has granted you victory, should seek terms of peace, do not be rigid, but listen graciously to them and make peace. Keep in mind the uncertainties of war and of fortune."[16]

Seek Allies in Conflict and Turn Enemies into Allies

Time and again the Byzantines turned to neighbors who were neutral or well-disposed at the start of conflict to oppose invading forces. In addition to the recruitment of steppe archers and barbarian cavalry and infantry for the campaigns of the Justinianic era, the Byzantines creat-ed a network of dependents among frontier peoples who offered addi-tional manpower and specialist troops in wartime. The Ghassanid Arabs were among the most important and effective clients in the east-ern regions, and in the west the Muslim conquest of Africa shows that the Roman-Berber alliances forged there from Justinian's day onward continued to function; imperial titles, gold, and weapons flowed to the Berber confederations who provided manpower for the defense of the North African provinces. The arrangements that Heraclius made with the Western Turk Empire against the Sasanians tipped the scales of power in favor of the empire and confronted the Persians with the possibility of war on multiple fronts that their crumbling political structure could not sustain. In facing the Arabs, the intervention of the Bulgars on behalf of the empire during the siege of 717 was decisive; Bulgarian arms constantly harassed the Muslim encampment and added to the misery of the long winter of the siege. The Byzantines also turned to the Khazar khanate on the southern Russian steppes to pressure the Muslims from the north, and this buffer yielded considerable advantages in the seventh and eighth centuries when Justinian II and Constantine V married Khazar princesses and forged personal bonds with the khagan.

The litany of northern peoples who invaded the empire and were defeated in turn and settled on imperial lands is extensive. The Goths in the fourth century were among those who crossed the Danube and were provided with land; some of them maintained distinctive communities from which soldiers were drawn centuries later. Throughout the Dark Ages, Slavic groups were defeated in the Balkans and drafted into the army or settled in Anatolia. The Pechenegs defeated by Alexios I were settled in Thrace and likewise provided recruits, as did the Cumans after them. In the wake of the First Crusade Alexios also tried, unsuccessfully, through lavish gifts of goods and gold to turn the fractious Norman lord of Edessa, Tancred, into a vassal.[17] The settlement of refugees, such as the Alans from the steppes of the north or refugees from lands formerly belonging to the territory, and recruiting their capable men continued into the Palaiologan era.[18]

The quest for alliances to blunt the asymmetry of forces ranged against them remained a constant until the crumbling of the empire; in 1282 in the last great coup of Byzantine diplomacy, Michael VIII, persuaded the Aragonese King Pedro III (1276–85) to intervene in Sicily against the French, who like their Norman predecessors threatened invasion of the empire. Michael VIII also married his daughter to the Nogai khan of the Golden Horde, who in 1282 provided the emperor with 4,000 Mongols for the invasion of Serbia.[19]

Fight Attritive Wars

In the sixth century, no political group bordering the empire possessed a professional standing army. Apart from Persia, no neighbor could even claim to be a state with a developed bureaucracy and other machinery of government. With rare exception, the lack of standing armies in kingdoms and political groupings remained true until the fall of Byzantium. Unfortunately, this made adjacent powers only slightly less dangerous, as Byzantine forces were not in a position to pursue the use of aggressive, blunt force. Only for a brief moment of its history during the fifty years or so from the accession of Nikephoros II Phokas to the death of Basil II did the empire possess the combination of wealth, skilled commanders, and veteran forces to engage in frontal attacks against strong enemies—the direct assault of Nikephoros Phokas and his immediate successors in Syria broke with some of the cautious and patient strategies of the past. The presence of professional, standing forces in and around the capital and in the themes by the ninth century made it possible for the Byzantines to respond fairly rapidly to threats from without and to wear down an enemy by harassment and clever use of geography. In the histories and military handbooks the conduct of war was consistently described and practices repeated; these habits were germane to the Byzantine art of war, even if they were not seen by contemporaries as part of a grand strategy.

By the later sixth century, strategic realities thrust the empire into a defensive posture. Twenty years after the death of Justinian, his far-flung conquests were under attack on multiple fronts—Germanic groups menaced their scattered holdings in Spain and Italy, while the Avars pressed the Balkan frontier and the Persians waged war against the Armenian and Syrian borders. Despite the considerable wealth and men at their disposal, the Romans lacked the resources to contain every threat and their losses mounted. The collapse of the eastern *limes* (frontier zone) under Persian assault in the 610s destroyed the defensive integrity of the eastern marches and lay open the route across Asia Minor and the capital. After the seventh century, maintaining hard frontiers was not possible and the Byzantines understood that warfare, fluid by its nature, required a set of flexible responses. Among these was knowledge of the paucity of forces, which could only rarely be tested in full-scale engagements; said the author of the *Strategikon:* "Well aware of our weakness, we have been motivated solely by devotion to the nation."[20] It was this recognition of the structural limitations of the military that prompted one commentator, obviously weary of the manifold warnings of an anonymous Byzantine writer, to observe: "He has a distinctively defensive mind, and sees clearly what the enemy may do to him more than he has time to think of what he may do to the enemy."[21] Unlike most peoples, the Byzantines prepared for the eventuality of battlefield defeat; these were both inevitable and the fault of the commanding officer who had been prepared in the methodical, cautious, and proper way to conduct war. The cautious, defensive tone changes only during the tenth century, when the work *On Skirmishing*, attributed to Nikephoros II Phokas, expresses great confidence in confronting and overwhelming the enemy. This was the work of an experienced commander who in his lifetime had witnessed Byzantine military resurgence in the east.

On Skirmishing is not only one of the most interesting works of Byzantine history, it ranks as one of the most interesting works on guerrilla tactics ever written. In it the adaptation to the small war, the raid, skirmish, and running battle, is complete. *On Skirmishing* depicts a method of warfare generations in the making, in which Arab raiders penetrated the highlands of Asia Minor in annual forays to enslave the inhabitants and rustle cattle. The Byzantine theme strategoi called up their troops, watched the passes, evacuated the inhabitants, and shadowed enemy forces. Night attacks, ambushes, assaults on encampments, and surprise movements are described in detail. In many instances, the thematic soldiers strike raiding columns that have already plundered their targets and were plodding back to Syria loaded with booty. The fatigue and slow pace of the encumbered columns made the *ghazis* vulnerable to the hit-and-run tactics of the thematic light cavalry. Such a defense was born of failure; their employment is an admission that the empire was not strong enough to stop enemy columns from entering their lands. But the methods that *On Skirmishing* shows were honed to perfection. Ultimately, as the caliphate fractured into disparate political entities, the raiders of the themes turned to the offensive and from the small war to a full onslaught against the border emirates. Envisioning a confrontation with a strong enemy force in Syria, the author of *On Skirmishing* describes how the vanguard of a divided column would attack the Muslim lines near sunset,

> then charge against them, and by the favor of Christ you will be able to defeat them. But if the enemy commanders present there have a large force, they may be able to hold their ground and will struggle to come back from defeat, which is impossible, for with

night already falling nothing untoward will happen to you. If, therefore, you do things in this manner, the enemy will be amazed and terrified of you, and they will not dare to ride from their army without food. Finally, the lack of food will force them to return to their own country.[22]

Defense in Depth

From the period of the reorganization of forces under Diocletian and Constantine, the empire's strategic footing indicates that imperial authorities understood not only their own defensive and logistical challenges, but the obstacles that invasion of their territory posed to enemies. Although we need not see an integrated and centrally planned and managed static line of defense on the order of massive modern linear fortifications, from the fourth to sixth centuries the frontier zones were studded with fortresses and fortress cities with substantial garrisons; strategic routes were guarded, and storehouses supplied armies near the frontier. Certainly the Romans grasped strategic geography; following the conquest of Africa, Justinian's surveyors and military architects conceived of a series of strong points and fortified cities that stretched along the rich corn lands at the foot of the untamed Aures Mountains, home to unvanquished and warlike Berbers; the result was a fortified military road that could serve commerce and be patrolled and defended. Heraclius made his headquarters at the well-placed city of Caesarea of Cappadocia, which controlled routes to the east and south of the Anatolian plateau as well as providing many of the raw materials vital to his war effort against the Persians. The Balkan and Anatolian landscapes of the Dark Ages were studded with watchtowers, fortresses with at least modest garrisons, and refuges where threatened civilian populations took refuge from attackers. Much later John II Komnenos pursued the strategy of gradual recovery of lands in Asia Minor by steady advancement of one fortified post to another, a strategy which, though it failed, showed a clear awareness of strategic geography and the role of fortified cities in Byzantine military planning. Until 1204 the sheer size of the empire exposed the enemy to risk; in the north the Danube was used to land troops to the rear of enemy columns, and the Anatolian passes provided natural barriers and ambush points from which to attack eastern enemies.

Fight Small Wars

Large pitched engagements rarely favored the empire, and even when imperial forces were superior in numbers and arms, chance had too much of a factor in the outcome. Decisive battle in which the field forces were put at risk in one stroke were increasingly avoided after the collapse of resistance to the Muslims during the first decades of the seventh century. Instead, small-scale regional warfare, containment, and raiding were favored in order to punish the enemy and keep them off balance. Managing the theater of action was a vital component; the Byzantines repeatedly had to stall invaders on one front in holding actions while making peace with or dispatching other invaders in order to free up resources required for effective action. In their understanding of their own material weakness and the relative strengths of their opponents, the Byzantines show great pragmatism in the prosecution of warfare and patience exhibited by few states in history. Partly this was because of their perpetually threatened position and the limits of imperial resources and partly because of heavy defeats absorbed over the course of the fourth and fifth centuries. The Battle of Adrianople in 378, the 443 defeat of Roman forces at the hands of Attila, the 468 catastrophe dealt by the Vandals—all at great cost of blood and treasure—served to convince the authorities that payments of even heavy indemnities, such as those doled out to the Huns by the eunuch chamberlain Chrysaphius's government under Theodosius II, might be unpopular, but were often a better option than war. The policy of Heraclius to avoid massive confrontation in decisive battle persisted— the Battle of Yarmuk in 636 demonstrated a tactical failure in the local command, not a flaw in the strategy. Such losses merely reinforced the belief that warfare was best limited; the empire simply could not put its field armies at risk except on occasions when the potential damage to their population allowed no other option. Aided by successful defense of the capital in the 670s and 717, the Byzantines frequently negotiated long truces with the caliphate, despite the empire's relative weakness. Although imperial raids were launched to punish the Arabs for incursions into Byzantine territory in the border region under Constans II, and his successors did no lasting harm to the caliphate, nevertheless they showed the local populations that the empire intended to resist and could do so.

After the glaring failures of the mid- and late seventh century, Byzantine strategy continued earlier philosophies of general avoidance of decisive battle. With the vast bulk of their tax base sundered from imperial control and their army increasingly depleted through battle-field losses and lack of funds, the Byzantines were forced on the defensive. The creation of an Arab fleet under the Muslim governor of Syria, Mu'awiya (governor of Syria 640–61, caliph 661–80), posed an existential threat to Byzantine rule in Cyprus and the Aegean, already under Muslim attack, and threatened Constantinople itself. Constans was forced to engage in direct, massive naval action that ended in defeat of the Byzantine navy at the Battle of Phoenix (655). When civil war broke out in the caliphate, the Byzantines were spared further advances for a time and Constans probably was able to address the fiscal and military crisis that confronted him by settling his troops on the land in the provinces, thereby creating the rudiments of the thematic structure.[23] Constans's departure to the west, where he arrived in 663 or 664, was an attempt to shore up the situation in Africa and Sicily. His relocation may indicate that the themes of Anatolia were already established sometime in the 650s, perhaps during the period of truce that existed between 655 and 661 when the Muslims were embroiled in civil war.

The creation of the first major themes and settlement of the army of the land blunted offensive capabilities and reinforced Byzantine reliance on the small war. Containment, harassment, and raiding governed warfare in the seventh to ninth centuries. *On Skirmishing* portrays a world of constant raid and counterraid, of flying columns and stealth tactics all honed in more than two centuries of border conflict with the Muslims. Preservation of force and the ability to reply to enemy attack, if only in a symbolic way, were paramount. On those occasions when the Byzantines were forced to mass armies to defend targets whose loss was too heavy to contemplate—Constantinople or the thematic capital and major military base of Amorium in Phrygia—their record was mixed. The successful defense of the capital during the series of attacks of Mu'awiya's forces from 674–78 and those of 'Umar II in 717 high-lighted Byzantine strengths: the powerful defenses of their capital city that was virtually impregnable, the adroit use of allies in 717, and the defensive depth that the sheer size of their empire, although much reduced, afforded them. In the disastrous invasion by the Arabs in 838, the Byzantine army collapsed in defeat and the key city of Amorium fell to the Muslims. On numerous other occasions, though, when forced to large-scale confrontation against the Arabs, Rus', Normans, Pechenegs, Cumans, and Magyars (Hungarians), imperial forces successfully held the line or scored victories that established long-lasting peace.

The admonition of the emperor Nikephoros II Phokas, although offered in a tactical context, was applied as strategic practices as well:

> If the enemy force far outnumbers our own both in cavalry and infantry, avoid a general engagement or close combats and strive to injure the enemy with stratagems and ambushes. The time to seek general engagements with the enemy is when, with the help of God, the enemy has fled once, twice, or three times and are crippled and fearful. . . . Avoid not only an enemy force of superior strength, but also equal strength.[24]

Divide and Conquer

Sowing division and attempting to dislodge elements of the enemy from opposing ranks was a standard Byzantine strategy. In war or peace, Byzantine diplomatic efforts sought allies from among potential enemy populations and recruited them either as imperial agents or into the military forces. Lulls in hostility were used to open negotiations with those prone to enticement, usually through material rewards. At the heat of the bitter conflict between Heraclius and the Sasanians, the emperor retained back-door communications with senior officers within the Persian hierarchy that eventually yielded the coup that overthrew Kosrow II. After the upheavals of the war, many prominent Sasanian commanders and their households joined Roman service. The emperor Theophilos negotiated for the services of the Khurramite Persian rebels against the 'Abbasids that for a time provided a boost to the emperor's military capabilities.[25] His tampering in 'Abbasid internal affairs temporarily strengthened the emperor's hand and weakened his most dangerous enemy. In later eras, the Komnenoi used bribes of money, land, and offices with their attendant prestige and salary to bring renegade Romans back to the fold; during his wars against the Normans one of the keys to Alexios's ultimate success was his recruitment of the traitor Bryennios.[26] In his 1122 campaign against the Pechenges, John II used the lull in fighting over the winter to bribe elements of the nomads to his side and thereby substantially weakened the opposing force. In the general engagement that followed at Berroia (Veria in Macedonia), Byzantine forces crushed the remainder.[27]

Diplomatically the strategy of divide and conquer—or perhaps more aptly in this instance "divide and thwart"—was most spectacularly achieved late in the empire's history during the reign of Michael VIII, whose agents helped to foment revolt on the island of Sicily among the subjects of its king, Charles of Anjou (1266–85), who planned a powerful expedition against Byzantium. Charles had seized the kingdom of Sicily by conquest in 1266 and had papal backing for further expansion. Charles's success had come at the expense of Manfred of Sicily (1258–66) the last Hohenstaufen king of Sicily. Manfred's daughter Constance (d. 1302) married Peter III (d. 1285). Michael VIII thus found in Peter a natural ally, and following the liberal dispersal of Byzantine gold throughout the island, a revolt broke out in Palermo on March 30, 1282. Weeks later, a strong Aragonese fleet whose announced target was Muslim Tunis appeared off the western coast of Sicily. The episode of the so-called Sicilian Vespers rising (named for the prayer at sunset marking the start of the night vigil of the Easter Monday holiday) sparked war between Aragon and the French that lasted for twenty years and crushed Charles's designs on the empire.[28]

Espionage and Intelligence

Strategic Intelligence

Though they suffered their share of failure, the Byzantines often excelled at collecting intelligence and were generally superior to their enemies in espionage activities. From Diocletian onward the state maintained close to the emperor's person a cadre of secret police, *agentes in rebus*, who watched over imperial officials and those suspected of treachery; such agents served as couriers and held passes that allowed them to freely use the imperial post system. These operatives conducted sensitive missions and embassies vital to the interest of the state until the seventh century, when officers under the *logothete* of the dromos (head of the imperial post) assumed their duties.

Prior to the outbreak of hostilities, the Byzantines relied on a network of spies and scouts for advance warning of enemy intentions. Members of embassies dispatched to foreign lands and permanent "secret friends" of the emperor in the courts and entourages of neighbors passed information to Constantinople. In these exchanges, merchants played a vital role. Spies were ideally to live among the lower strata of society and lead unexceptional lives so as to blend in with the population; fluency in the enemy's language, but few family ties, were prerequisites for agents, many of whom were merchants who passed and received intelligence in the marketplace.[29] On the eastern front, Muslim raiding armies gathered in August in the border emirates to wage jihad; at the start of the raiding season the Romans sent merchants across the passes. No doubt some of these were legitimate businessmen in imperial service while others were professional spies. These men visited the target population to collect news of enemy preparations, assess the mood of the enemy, and estimate the stores of materiel gathered and the quality and number of soldiers on campaign.

As noted previously, the Romans also maintained networks of spies throughout the courts of enemies and potential enemies. Peaceful contacts, such as trading and embassies, provided cover under which such agents could collect and pass on intelligence. At times, the Roman state was well informed of what was happening inside the political centers of their enemies. Justinian and his empress Theodora were abreast of the fast-moving developments inside the Ostrogothic kingdom of Italy—the emperor was quickly aware, for example, that his ally, Queen Amalasuntha, had been deposed and imprisoned not long after the event. Her removal and eventual murder provided the pretext on which the Romans would declare war. Agents of this type continued to be employed. In addition to the Bulgar nobles betrayed in 766 during the reign of Constantine V, Byzantine plants within the caliphate passed regular intelligence to imperial agents.[30]

Battlefield Intelligence

Said Nikephoros II, "It is imperative first to find out the number of the enemy host and above all what equipment they have, by means of spies, deserters, and prisoners."[31] The late eleventh-century book of advice by the general Kekaumenos stresses that without a network of informants in hostile territory, a campaign was bound to fail.[32] Just prior to the march into enemy country, generals were instructed to send "defectors" with misinformation about the route of travel and targets. On the eve of the North African campaign of Justinian, the Vandal king Gelimer imprisoned Roman merchants in Carthage and threatened to kill them because he alleged they had urged the emperor to war against the Vandals.[33] When the imperial army landed in Sicily, the historian Prokopios, then Belisarios's secretary, met a merchant who was probably a Roman spy; the man's servant informed them that the Vandal fleet and army had recently departed to quell an uprising in Sardinia.[34]

The emperor Leo recounted that the Byzantines maintained permanent spies in Cilicia who observed the movements of the emirate's armies; the Muslims there were both seaborne and land raiders. When spies reported the Cilician fleet's sailing, the strategoi of the neighboring themes were ordered to attack by land so as to take advantage of the absence of the enemy troops. Conversely, when the Arabs marched on a land raid, the Byzantine fleet was informed and ordered to attack the shore.[35]

The handbooks stress the need to surprise the enemy. Strategic surprise could be achieved by avoiding enemy agents, by disinformation, and by unexpected marches. The *Strategikon* warns that to avoid enemy spies armies should take little-used routes and march through uninhabited areas that were less likely to be under surveillance.[36] Commanders were instructed to divulge targets to no one, not even their inner councils, but to spread word via prisoners and deserters that they intended to attack locations other than the true target.[37] About a week before imperial raiders embarked on their mission, spies who operated in the targeted theaters reported to army camps; if agents reported quiet in the region, then fast, light raiding columns swooped in to plunder.[38] Ahead of the main army *doukators* and light, specialist cavalry troops called *trapezites* or *tasinarioi* preceded the main force as scouts. Doukators located and determined the composition and strength of enemy formations, assessed battlefield conditions, and located pasture, water, and suitable encampment sites. Trapezites light cavalry, the ancestors of modern hussars, rounded up enemy prisoners for interrogation, scouted enemy formations, and ravaged the countryside to pressure the inhabitants. They prepared the battlefield for advancing army units, and when the Byzantines retreated from a raid, the trapezites practiced scorched earth to deny the enemy any use of the evacuated regions. Nikephoros II Phokas ordered trapezites to destroy the cropland and vines of cities targeted for siege; this ravaging prevented the enemy from storing up supplies and decimated enemy morale so that strongholds were less likely to endure a siege.[39] These practices led to success in attaining strategic surprise—while the Muslims believed the army to be occupied in Bulgaria, Basil II mounted his infantry on mules and in an astonishing two weeks of forced marches pressed across Anatolia. When he descended into Syria the shocked Fatimid army of Egypt fled.[40] When in 1156 Manuel I Komnenos wished to chastise the fractious Armenian prince Thoros and his ally, Reynault, prince of Antioch, for continually harassing imperial holdings in Cilicia, Manuel avoided detection during his march across Asia Minor and caught the Armenians and Latins unprepared; they quickly capitulated.[41]

Battlefield intelligence was generally well conducted, though there were cases of serious breakdowns in the high command, such as the failure in 708 in which khan Tervel of Bulgaria ambushed the expeditionary army of Justinian II. In 1176, Kilij Arslan's Turks surprised and destroyed the northern army of Andronikos Vatatzes on the road to Amaseia, then the sultan's troops mauled the forces of Manuel Komnenos in the pass of Tzivritze on the route to Ankara.[42] Most commanders were careful, however, and avoided being surprised by attacks. In the spring of 586, prior to the battle of Solachon, the spies of general Philippikos detected the approach of a large Persian expeditionary force. Suspecting a Sunday attack to catch the Romans in their religious services, the general sent scouts to determine enemy movements and as a result the Persians' attempted surprise failed and the Romans inflicted a heavy defeat on the enemy. Nikephoros II Phokas ordered scouts to be dispatched in all directions as an army moved; when on the march, the Macedonian-era army sent a company of 100 light horse to the rear of the column to scout for shadowing foes and to avoid any potential ambush; they were supported in the rear guard by archers and infantry.[43] Scouts and spies were assigned to each tagma of the cavalry units described in the *Strategikon*; they worked ahead and on the flanks of the armies and patrolled in relays at regular intervals to transmit intelligence to the main army and set up observation posts with messengers to alert commanders to enemy stratagems.[44] During the 971 campaign against Sviatoslav in Bulgaria, the general Bardas Skleros ordered the doukator John Alakaseos to reconnoiter and determine the whereabouts and strength of the Rus'. The next day Alakaseos's messengers informed Bardas that the enemy was nearby, intelligence that Bardas used to set an ambush to the rear of the advancing Rus' army.[45]

Counter-intelligence was a constant concern, and despite the fortified nature of Roman marching camps, spies were able to infiltrate. The *Strategikon* ordered silence to be maintained in the camps, so that lurking agents could be more easily detected. Leo repeated this advice, as well as the trick of having soldiers enter their tents at the sounding of a trumpet: those left outside the tents would be spies and captured. If spies were bold enough to enter the soldiers' tents they would be recognized and seized.[46] In order to confound enemy battlefield scouts, multiple banners were used to trick the enemy into thinking more units were present than actually were; units and the depth of lines were varied, because uniformity made it easy for the enemy to accurately ascertain troop numbers.

TACTICS

For a military establishment that survived and changed over a millennium, tactical flexibility was embraced as critical for survival. The Byzantines might be defeated even twice or three times by an enemy, but they viewed no foe as invincible and learned from their mistakes. Based on the principle preached in the *Strategikon* of understanding their own weaknesses, the willingness to adapt and learn from the enemy was a major contributing factor to the longevity of Byzantium.

Early Period Tactics

In the fifth century Vegetius envisioned a battlefield formation comprised of three divisions, with a center and two flanking wings. Heavy infantry formed the center and provided the anchor of the force and often its primary striking power. Units were drawn up in two or three lines, with elite troops held in reserve in the second line so that they could be moved to support any portion of the line that wavered or to counter enemy encirclement or flanking maneuvers. Heavy cavalry *clibanarii*, mailed and armed with lances, protected the flanks of advancing footmen, while horse archers and light cavalry skirmishers rode on the wings of the battle line; these light cavalry units harassed and broke up the wings of enemy formations. The enemy center, where the best units were expected, had to be broken by the advance of heavy infantry massed in either a block or a wedge formation. The heavy cavalry formations Vegetius envisioned were vulnerable to attack from enemy infantry units and missile troops, thus they were often deployed in mixed formation, that is with light infantry carrying darts, bows, slings, and javelins that could soften the opponent and support retreating cavalry.

By the sixth century the hybrid cavalry, carrying lance, sword, and bow described by Prokopios were difficult to match on the battlefield, as his famous and oft-repeated description attests:

> But the bowmen of the present time go into battle wearing corselets and fitted out with greaves which extend up to the knee. From the right side hang their arrows, from the other the sword. And there are some who have a spear also attached to them and, at the shoulders, a sort of small shield without a grip, such as to cover the region of the face and neck. They are expert horsemen, and are able without difficulty to direct their bows to either side while riding at full speed, and to shoot an opponent whether in pursuit or flight. They draw the bowstring along by the forehead about opposite the right ear, thereby charging the arrow with such an impetus as to kill whoever stands in the way, shield and corselet alike having no power to check its force.[47]

While such hybrid horse archer-lancers (*hippotoxotai*) may have been less heavily armed than the clibanarii or *cataphracti* described by Vegetius, and some certainly were not as well equipped as Prokopios's ideal elite, some were outfitted as Maurice envisioned in his model cavalry; in the battle waged against the Moor Antalas by John Troglita, the Roman commander Geiserith was an imposing figure:

> Girt in shining armor, he bore towering weapons. With his whole body covered in steel, he was a glittering vision, for he had adorned the armor plates with a mesh of gold. And he wore a golden helmet dazzling with inlaid steel whose peak and crest he had decked with a horse's mane. He drew in a belt that gleamed with bejeweled knobs and a sword in an ivory sheath adorned his side. He wore greaves, which a Parthian hide bound with many gold fittings on his legs.[48]

Throughout early Byzantine history cavalry occupied primarily an offensive role. Horsemen provided both frontal assault troops and outflankers who used speed to attempt to encircle enemy lines. The best and heaviest cavalry were therefore stationed in the front two ranks and on the right and left edges of the moira. In battle cavalry broke up enemy infantry formations and sought to drive away light cavalry and infantry skirmishers who threatened them and their Roman infantry complement, who were nearly always present in the field. Unsupported they were not a match for Sasanian heavy cavalry, as two episodes from the sixth century demonstrate. In the defeat at Callinicum on the Euphrates, Roman cavalry fled in the face of the Sasanian cavalry; to resist them, the horsemen dismounted and formed up with the infantry in a phalanx and defended themselves effectively against repeated charges. Even the heaviest cavalry of the day therefore could be defeated by disciplined and well-arrayed spearmen.

Frontal Assault, Outflanking, and Envelopment

In a frontal assault on an enemy formation, cavalry drew up in close formation and advanced at the trot. When the hekakontarch ordered the charge, the front lines, comprised of dekarchs and pentarchs—the most experienced and best equipped troops—leaned forward, covered their heads and necks with their shields, and galloped forward, spears held at shoulder height. The mounted archers in the third through fifth files and beyond opened fire. If the enemy line was longer than the Roman front, the flank guards (*koursores*) extended the formation to match the foe, if shorter, the flankers fanned out into the crescent formation and enveloped their adversaries. If they failed to outflank or break the enemy center, the cavalry retreated to re-form behind the cover of the second line, which usually comprised infantry. If repeated charges failed, the second line advanced to close quarters. The cavalry withdrew to the rear of the second line to regroup, ideally supported by a third Roman line. The opening of ranks to allow retreating horsemen to filter through the infantry was a difficult maneuver that demanded great discipline on the part of both the horsemen, who could not lose cohesion and run headlong into their own troops, and the infantry, who needed to form wide alleys at regular intervals to allow passage while maintaining their formations.[49] At Adrianople, fleeing Roman cavalry collided with the infantry and shattered the Roman lines; the same probably also occurred at Yarmuk.

Roman armies generally operated with a mix of infantry and cavalry; to assume that infantry were tactically irrelevant by the sixth century is incorrect. Although the bulk of the *Strategikon* deals with cavalry tactics of the new model army of Maurice, Book XII outlines infantry composition, formations, and battlefield actions. Among the recommendations that stand in sharp contrast with the previous era of the late Roman army of Vegetius is that, if possible, half the infantry force should comprise archers or, barring this, one third. The Battle of Taginae, where there were 8,000 foot archers in Narses's army, is the kind of prior experience on which this doctrine is grounded. In the Italian campaigns of Justinian, archers provided the Romans with a decided tactical advantage, and in the battles against the cavalry armies of the Persians and Avars their benefits were enormous; even if they were not stout enough to resist direct attacks these troops were capable of wounding and unhorsing enemy riders and thus breaking enemy formations and effectiveness.[50]

In Maurice's army, foot soldier ranks formed a phalanx sixteen men deep with heavy and experienced soldiers in the four ranks at the front and rear of the formation. Heavy and light troops were usually mixed in the phalanx but sometimes fought in separate units. Likewise, there were cases when the heavy infantry formed the middle eight ranks of the army. This implies that skirmishers and light troops were to front and rear and thus opened the action, with the heavy troopers rotating forward as the armies closed to hand-to-hand fighting.[51] As accounts of fourth- to sixth-century combat indicate, the infantry generally formed the center of the army, with the cavalry stationed on the wings, and the horsemen often had flanking guards comprised of heavy and light footmen to screen them against sudden side attack and ambushes or particularly powerful onslaughts of enemy horse. When the signal came to advance, the infantry front moved forward and formed the *foulkon* to protect the face of the line from enemy missiles. When within range the archers behind fired and the men of the first line threw their darts or spears. They then drew their spathas and moved to close combat while the second line supported them with their spears and those behind sustained arrow fire.

The infantry needed to show a high level of drill. Maurice demanded the foot be capable of splitting the formation in half with the rear troops wheeling about to meet attack from the rear and thus form the double phalanx with two fighting faces. The close support of cavalry, with the combined-arms approach of missile troops closely integrated in the files, all indicate a well-disciplined, professional infantry force.

The Dark Ages

During the Dark Ages, tactics and professionalism changed and the battle record of the Romans from the seventh to ninth centuries is uninspiring. They did, however, prove capable of defense of major strongpoints, notably Constantinople when the stout walls and artillery served as a force multiplier and rendered the superior quality of veteran Muslim soldiers of limited advantage. In the mountains of Anatolia, cantonments of professional troops remained and some of these were undoubtedly infantry. However, there is little evidence for the persistence of heavy infantry units as frontier warfare came to be dominated by light cavalry, probably supported by substantial numbers of light troops. The Romans still maintained some drill and discipline even among the thematic troops dispersed through the countryside, but the strategy of attritive war with its avoidance of decisive battle underscores Byzantine tactical weakness. Defeat at the hands of Arab armies and by numerically weaker Bulgar forces in 678–79 suggests that tactical capabilities of Roman forces weakened. The reliance on ambush from the mid-seventh century and the practice of evading large-scale confrontation accompanied a decline in equipment and battlefield tactical capabilities. Nevertheless battlefield units were trained, though it seems thematic soldiers drilled mainly in the wintertime and likely this drill varied by region and the abilities of the local commander. As Haldon has noted, Byzantine armies still drew up ordered battle lines, worked in clearly delineated units under a recognizable command structure, and were generally superior in numbers to the Bulgars and Slavs in the Balkans, though they seem inferior to campaign armies of the caliphate. Archery, especially horse archery utilizing the Hunnic release and strong composite bow, largely vanished, depriving the empire of one of its major tactical advantages. The main force for tactical offense seems to have been light horse lancers.[52]

Middle- and Late Period

By the ninth century the emergence of professional campaign mercenary tagmas recruited for campaigns and as standing units in the themes increased, and tactics improved as the Byzantines recovered economically and militarily. The mid-tenth-century treatise called the *Sylloge taktikon* mentions the *menavlion* pikemen; their role as heavy defensive troops equipped to defeat the strongest cavalry of the day indicates that infantry had returned to a dominant place in the battle line.[53] The integration of 100 heavy-armed pikemen among the 1,000-man taxiarchies demonstrates adaptation to an increased threat from heavily horse units. The menavlatoi were drawn up in gaps between the front line infantry, where they could rush ahead of the main front and meet enemy cavalry charges intended to strike and break up Byzantine infantry units.

Nikephoros Ouranos's treatise of the early eleventh century, the *Taktika*, indicates further refinement to the combined arms approach mixing heavy infantry, archers, light infantry, and menavlatoi. On the battlefield, the Byzantines utilized the hollow square comprised of infantry men seven deep; through this "marching camp" concept Roman cavalry sheltered within the square deployed to meet enemy attacks on the battlefront or flanks. This formation was not new, but its revival by the Byzantines shows how refined their military prowess had become by the tenth century. Twelve infantry taxiarchies of 1,000 men—400 heavy infantry, 300 archers, 200 skirmishers, and 100 menavlatoi—comprised the square, with gaps wide enough to permit the charge and withdrawal of light and heavy cavalry and support troops and baggage train sheltered in the corners of the square. In broken or rugged terrain, the Romans deployed in a narrower fronted rectangular formation that permitted the same tactics of swift, responsive cavalry egress and withdrawal to the shelter of backing footmen. The marching square made enemy envelopment nearly impossible, since the square had a double face, with pikemen stationed at the front and behind, and light infantry and cavalry support within the shelter of the phalanx which were free to engage any quadrant that came under attack.[54]

According to the *Sylloge*, combat began by cavalry maneuver through the gaps in the square:

> The cavalry are the first to begin battle by moving out through the largest intervals. ...Should they put the enemy to flight, they pursue them with all their might, with the infantry divisions trailing behind. In case they are defeated, they turn to go back to the infantry units once again. They either take their place inside the infantry units by coming in through the intervals—that is, inside the vacant place where they were before—or outside, on the wings

of the infantry units, and on both its flanks they fight alongside the infantry formation.[55]

The 200 light infantry, armed with sling, javelin, or bows, blocked enemy attack on the intervals in the square. On the front and rear lines of the square, two ranks deep, stood the menavlatoi; those in the rear could be rushed to the front to double the depth of the pike formation to four deep. They were supported by the light infantry who plugged the gaps as the enemy deployed to assault. Once the enemy cavalry committed to an assault on the infantry spearmen, the menavlatoi received the charge with their pikes and the light infantry skirmishers moved to strike the flanks of the enemy kataphraktoi.[56] A vital change to the composition of this force arose under Nikephoros Phokas, who quadrupled the number of menavlatoi in the square to 1,200 men with a corresponding decrease in the regular heavy-armed infantry phalangites.[57]

As the tenth century progressed and the enemy adapted their tactics, the Byzantines responded first by increasing the number of pikemen, as noted, but also in pinning the menavlatoi to the infantry line, rather than forward of the formation as the *Sylloge* suggested. Another response was a further deepening of the infantry formation; once the enemy angle of attack was determined, the menavlatoi moved from the rear as before, but every second file moved laterally into the adjacent file, which made the formation twice as deep, including six ranks deep of pikemen, with little loss of breadth.[58] This tactical maneuver offered a dense and impressive front to opposing cavalry, but retained the mix of skirmishing troops and flexible response of Phokas's reformed army.

The double line of cavalry deployment of the *Strategikon* was revived and modified in the tenth century. The *Sylloge tacticorum* attests that, as in Maurice's day, the standard cavalry deployment remained that of three front-line units and four units in the second, where the commander stationed himself; this host moved with flank guards and skirmishers along its sides, with an additional third line of horse followed by a rear guard, the *saka* (an Arab term). The new kataphraktoi heavy cavalry deployed in wedge formation on the front line, behind the light prokoursatores (skirmishers) arrayed in open order who ideally numbered 500, 110 to 120 of which were mounted archers. The regular cavalry, in *banda* of 50 men, grouped into tactical formations of 500 riders, 100 across and five deep. As in Maurice's day, these men were composite cavalry, with the front ranks bearing lances and those behind serving as mounted archers, with the last line also carrying lances, providing the ability to turn about and present a front of lancers no matter from which direction the enemy threat appeared.

Outflankers stationed on the right, as in the sixth century, now supported the kataphraktoi cavalry, heavy armed and armored riders with barded and shod animals whose equipment made them a much weightier striking force than their predecessors. Flank guards moved to their left, their role was to stave off attack from the enemy right that threatened the kataphraktoi and the regular cavalry stationed behind. The kataphraktoi assembled in a wedge formation, twelve rows deep, with the front row comprised of twenty men and each subsequent line adding four men, so that sixty-four men stood in the last line; a smaller wedge of ten men in front with four additional men stationed in each line so that the rear line contained fifty-four was also used. The kataphrakt wedge mirrored the composite makeup of the regular cavalry formation; the first four ranks carried iron maces, and from the fifth line to the twelfth the wedge comprised a mix of troops; lancers occupied the edge of the formation, with mace or sword bearers inside them, and the core of the unit filled with 150 mounted archers. The two 500-strong regular cavalry units stood on either side of the kataphrakt wedge at intervals that allowed these flanking units to support the heavy horsemen but also for advance of units from behind, or the retreat of units to the safety of the second and third lines.

McGeer traces battle tactics which Nikephoros Phokas and Basil II's general Nikephoros Ouranos envisioned when on the offensive in enemy territory. In the first scenario, the Byzantine mixed infantry and cavalry army confronts a foe with a similar composition of horse and foot. Once scouts reported the location and disposition of the enemy, the prokoursatores moved ahead of the infantry square and its supporting cavalry to attack; if the prokoursatores drew the main weight of the enemy force against them, the general sent two regular cavalry troops to their aid, then thrust forward with the supporting second line of cavalry. If the prokoursatores found themselves pressed by the bulk of the enemy formation, they withdrew to the safety of the infantry and additional cavalry forces deployed from the center of the square to attack, followed by the supporting infantry. When the opposing force fled, the prokoursatores returned to the attack.

Should the enemy phalanx strike in good order against the Byzantine square, the Roman commander ordered the kataphrakt wedge and its cavalry escort to assault the front of the enemy infantry. Swift-moving enemy infantry often tried to deny the Byzantines the ability to deploy their heavy cavalry wedge through the square to the front of the line, whereupon the commander ordered his kataphraktoi through the intervals in the side of the square to attack the opposing spearmen in the flanks. All of these movements were coordinated with supporting archery and missile fire from the light units and close reinforcement from the infantry.

In the second scenario, Roman cavalry operate as a vanguard and seek contact with the enemy. The prokoursatores once more open the engagement, probing the enemy formation and attempting to rout them if they see disorder. In the event the enemy holds firm in good order, the general identifies the enemy commander and his picked troops and the Roman wedge moves forward, slowly and silently. The measured, quiet advance of the iron wall of heavy lancers and mace-wielding kataphraktoi had a tremendous psychological effect on the enemy infantry, who faced the prospect of a devastating cavalry charge. As the kataphraktoi came into archery range of the enemy, their heavy armor protected them from missile fire and their own horse archers returned fire; the ensuing charge aimed for the heart of the enemy infantry line and the opposing general, whose death or flight would seal a Roman victory. In the event the enemy's heavy horsemen moved to strike, the Roman general dispatched three units of regular cavalry to surround and destroy them. If the kataphraktoi failed to rout the enemy, the general detached two of the regular cavalry taxiarchies to the front and remained with elements of the second and third line to react to the battle as it unfolded.

The tactics of the tenth century—sharp discipline, and mixed battle formations of heavy and light infantry fighting in close coordination with light and heavy cavalry units, including horse archers and the heaviest armored and equipped lancers of the day, the kataphraktoi—represent the peak of Byzantine tactics. The army of the tenth century was a nearly unstoppable offensive force whose constant campaigning expanded the empire's borders in the east into Syria and in the west to the Danube, a recovery of territory and prestige unmatched in history.

The decline of the thematic armies, whose service obligations were increasingly commuted to cash payments to the state throughout the eleventh century, led to a drastic decline in the defensive and offensive position of the military. By the time of the Battle of Mantzikert in 1071, the emperor Romanos IV found that most of the theme units had degraded to an unserviceable status. Mantzikert, like most subsequent Roman warfare, was fought with a cobbled together host of professional mercenaries, both Byzantine and foreign. The defeat at Mantzikert and subsequent loss of the heart of Asia Minor in the decades that followed due to civil war and Seljuk Turkish aggression meant that Alexios Komnenos possessed nothing like the army of his predecessors. His forces were professional, but the multiplicity of ethnic groups and lack of standard drill meant that the tactical mettle of the armies of the tenth century could not be entirely duplicated. The army of Manuel Komnenos was, however, professional and capable of sustained defensive and offensive operations. It relied on the same mix of heavy and light armed infantry and cavalry units, but their tactical flexibility and discipline did not match those of the tenth century. Heavy infantry persisted, however, as an important tactical component of the armies of the Komnenoi down to the defeat at Myriokephalon, and kataphraktoi were also present, but overall, the decline in state revenues, attrition, and the increasing reliance on foreigners had a deleterious effect on the tactical capabilities of the Byzantine army.[59]

As Haldon argues, the history of Byzantine tactics in a developed form ends with the Komnenoi. The subsequent sack of Constantinople and the loss of the field army and state apparatus needed to support it resulted in a poor-quality army engaged in civil and defensive wars; tactically the avoidance of decisive open-field engagements was paramount and instead ambushes and harassment were used to fight generally superior enemy forces. Western tactics dominated, with infantry of varying quality supporting knights, shock cavalry whose charges were intended to break up enemy infantry formations. Infantry and cavalry continued to campaign together, with cavalry remaining the dominant offensive arm. The infantry probably resembled the more lightly armored forces of the seventh to ninth centuries than the tenth-century phalangites of Nikephoros Phokas's reformed army. Archers provided skirmishing troops; they were only lightly armed and armored. In 1345, at the Battle of Peritheorion, the emperor John

Kantakouzenos divided his forces into three tagmata, with kataphrak-toi on the left, the emperor and heavy cavalry in the center, and Turkish allied horse archers stationed on the right flank. In 1305 at the Battle of Apros between imperial forces and the Catalan Company, the Byzantines arrayed in five divisions in two lines, a vanguard and a main battle force; the composition of the divisions was based largely on eth-nic affiliation, which usually determined the tactics of mercenary units in the first place.[60]

Siege Warfare

The ability to overcome fortified cities and fortresses was a large part of the Roman art of war. By the fourth century, imperial forces had longstanding experience against opponents who possessed developed engineering skills, especially in the east, where cities of great antiquity were commonly walled and protected by other passive defenses, such as ditches and moats. The Romans utilized a range of siege machinery which required specialists to build, operate, and maintain them. Most of these weapons were developed by Hellenistic engineers in the cen-turies prior to the rise of Rome. However, though the basic principles of defeating walled targets remained the same, the means used to break walls changed considerably from the fourth to the twelfth century.

Vegetius noted that in siege warfare the first assault was often the most likely to succeed, since inexperienced defenders could be terrified by displays of arms and the appearance of siege machinery. In order to take cities, the Romans either starved the city into submission, or found a way over the top of the walls using machines or earthen ramps or under them with mines. Before the targeted city was besieged, the Byzantines prepared the battlefield by constant raids to destroy the crops and economic base of the land around the town and thus deny its inhabitants food and other supplies. Direct attack efforts in which Roman troops attempted to breach gates or walls were difficult, time-consuming, and expensive in terms of time, materiel, and lives. Throughout their history, the Byzantines preferred to rely on traitors, dissension within the city, or starvation when taking enemy cities. Only when other measures failed was an assault planned. Since the *Strategikon* does not deal with siege warfare, we have manuals discussing siege warfare only from the late ninth- or early tenth-century *Taktika* of emperor Leo VI, who indicates that at the opening of hostilities, easy terms were to be offered in order to cause doubt and dissension among the citizens; if a prompt surrender was not forthcoming, the general placed under guard the major and postern gates and organized rotations for workers and attackers. Daily attacks, Leo cautioned, wore out the army and though fighting was to be sustained around the clock, only a portion of the besieging force was in action at a given time. Attacks round the clock were necessary to deprive the enemy of sleep, which destroyed morale and made mistakes on their part more likely. If the town had flammable houses, fire darts or pots filled with incendiaries were cast over the walls with trebuchets to burn the houses and spread panic.

Throughout their history the Byzantines, like many ancient armies and their advanced neighbors such as the Persians and Arabs, tunneled to undermine the foundation of walls, an ancient practice that was the most common way of defeating fortifications. As the tunnels were dug, props supported the tunnel ceiling and eventually the hollow spot was created as stones were removed from the wall. Countermining by the enemy was a constant danger and could best be avoided by digging deep mines. In his *Taktika*, the great general Nikephoros Ouranos (d. after 1007) noted,

> The men of old, in their conduct of siege warfare, constructed many devices, such as rams, wooden towers, scaling ladders with various features, as well as tortoises and all kinds of other things which our generation has never even seen. It has, however, tried all these devices and discovered that of all of them, the more effective way, the one the enemy cannot match, is undermining the foundations.[61]

In besieging cities, the Byzantines employed many devices, especially the traction trebuchet, introduced sometime in the sixth century from the east, probably Persia. The traction trebuchet was effective against many walls and had the advantages of its cheapness to produce and ease of operation. Leo's *Taktika* mentions the general use of the traction trebuchet, which seems to have been the most common stone-thrower used through the middle period. In practice, however, battering down fortification walls was rarely done; instead, Nikephoros Ouranos recommended general assaults using ladders, combined with *laisai*, siege pavilions woven from vine stalks or other woody plants, that provided refuges to workmen, archers, and staff slingers who bombarded the battlements and offered covering fire to men advancing with rams and hammers against gateways and weak points along the wall. In assaults, the commander divided his forces into three teams, one of which prosecuted the attack while the other two rested inside the lasai.[62] Nikephoros envisioned direct, sharp attacks of relatively short duration in which artillery, missile fire, and ladder assault was combined with undermining efforts that would collapse the fortification walls.[63] These aggressive, frontal assault tactics differed considerably from earlier practices of long investment and starvation and demonstrate the unique situation of the tenth century, when Byzantine capabilities and confidence were at a high point. The later adoption of the counterweight trebuchet, noted above and discussed further in Chapter 7 below, indicates a groundshift in Roman siege tactics; with the employment of this device even the most impressive Near Eastern fortifications could be pounded to rubble. John II Komnenos made the counterweight trebuchet the main weapon of his seize-and-hold policy of fortress taking throughout Anatolia.

When facing a siege, the general was instructed to see first to the provisioning of the city or fortress to be invested by the enemy. Water and food were to be strictly rationed, and those who entered the fortified refuge had to bring four months' provisions with them. Enemy armies encamped round fortified strongpoints in a circle in order to cut off supplies in communication, and Nikephoros noted that this made certain sectors prone to lax discipline and carelessness; he urged night attacks by Roman infantry against these elements. If the terrain did not permit the enemy to encircle and they encamped in one location, the commander was instructed to destroy enemy horses and food stocks, as well as to deny them provisions and shelter through scorched earth tactics—crops and Roman villages that could shelter the enemy were burned. Night ambushes and harassment would not only wear down the besiegers, but also distract them so that supplies and reinforcements could be inserted into the invested fortress or city.

This brief overview of strategy and tactics has shown that the Byzantines maintained longstanding practices gained by innumerable encounters with a range of enemies. Rarely did the Romans deviate from the strategic concepts of limited warfare, the pillars of which were the general avoidance of decisive battle, harassment, and attrition of the enemy. Wars were planned and fought with the aim of defeating the enemy, but the aim of victory was to secure peace in the short or long term. Wars were considered defensive wars even during the aggressive posture of the empire in the tenth century, when offensive operations allowed the recovery of former territories. Byzantine tacticians adopted enemy practices readily when these had proven effective, and though they suffered numerous defeats, the stabilization of the eastern frontier especially hinged on the successful implementation of lightning warfare conducted by light cavalry, defense of strongholds, and guerrilla tactics. The shift of the 950s was again decisive, with the return of heavy units, complex mixed formations, and the capacity for skilled battlefield maneuver that rendered well-led field armies indomitable. The failure to maintain the level of material commitment and aggressiveness ultimately led to the collapse of the eastern and western fronts under sustained pressure by new, more capable enemies.

SIX

ENEMIES OF BYZANTIUM

OVER THE MILLENNIUM OF ITS EXISTENCE, the Byzantines faced a vast array of peoples who threatened its territory and people. Several of these proved militarily superior and dealt heavy defeats on the empire. In the end, however, the Byzantines generally gained the upper hand, often through decades or even centuries of defense, stabilization, assimilation, and counterattack. The Byzantines learned a great deal from their enemies; indeed the ability to adapt to the challenges posed by opponents was one of the great pillars of Byzantine military success.

GERMANIC PEOPLES

The Gothic tribal confederacies posed the most serious challenge to the late antique Roman state of any Germanic group. The Goths comprised coalitions of tribal groups, mostly from the east Germanic peoples who by the third century A.D. inhabited a vast swathe of territory from the Oder and Vistula rivers to the southern steppes of Russia, the Crimea, and the Carpathian basin. East Germanic peoples had posed a significant threat to the eastern provinces of the Roman state from the third century. In 267, Goths and Heruls burst through the Danubian defenses and ravaged Thrace and much of the Balkans, sacking Athens before the emperor Claudius Gothicus dealt them a stinging defeat in 269. Following their defeat by the Huns, large groups of

Goths migrated south to the Danube where they were admitted as suppliants to Roman territory. Their provisioning was bungled due to corruption, and an underdeveloped transportation response led to starvation among the Goths and rebellion that culminated in the armed confrontation at Adrianople. At the end of the sixth century, after its recovery from the Goths, the empire had to concede the loss of most of Italy to the newly arrived Lombard confederation, whose grip on the peninsula spread throughout the seventh century. The Byzantines also entered sporadic conflicts with the Franks from the sixth century and even fought against Charlemagne (801–10) for control of the Istrian and Dalmatian coasts.

Organization

The Goths were organized in decimal units with major groupings of "hundreds" (hundafaþs) as were their Germanic relatives, the Anglo-Saxons and their Roman neighbors, whose centurions were well known to the eastern Goths. Gothic mercenaries served in the Roman army throughout the late third century, and by the time of the emperor Constantine, Gothic elements were settled in Transdanubia. By the fourth century Gothic military organization had evolved at least in part under the influence of Roman practice. Gothic tribal raiders crossed into Roman territory and proved a sufficient nuisance to attract the interest of Constantine, who waged multiple campaigns against them. By now the Goths probably included and coexisted alongside elements of several ethnic Iranians (Sarmatians), Slavs, Romano-Dacians, and Getae. The remains of a commonly articulated material culture from the second through fifth centuries (the Chernyakhov culture) indicate broad contact and exchanges; such adaptations were not always peaceful and the transferal of knowledge from one people to another certainly included warfare. According to Maurice, the "fair-haired races," especially the Lombards, grouped themselves not into numerically ordered units but according to kin group.

Methods of Warfare

The Goths fought as both cavalry and infantry. Until the last few decades, historians have viewed the Goths as primarily a cavalry army and attributed to this their shattering victory over the infantry legions in 378 at Adrianople. Their numbers were probably never as numerous as some Roman authors would have us suppose—Heather estimates that in sixth century Italy and Gaul there were about 15,000 Gothic elite males.[1] When the Gothic king Theodoric reigned over the united Gothic territories in Spain, Gaul, and Italy, his Gothic subjects numbered about 200,000 people.[2] However, although we have few contemporary sources, the majority of Goths seem to have often fought as infantry spearmen and swordsmen. Certainly the Goths served in large numbers in the legions as infantry. At Adrianople the Goths had perhaps 5,000 cavalry and probably twice as many infantry. According to Vegetius, the Goths possessed numerous archers, who fought on foot. In the sixth century, Prokopios provided a clearer picture of the Gothic army, which fielded a large cavalry component who fought in massed formations as lancers, while the infantry seem to have been mainly skirmishers armed with javelins and archers. Other infantry fought as spearmen and swordsmen equipped with a spatha and carrying shields. Given the high casualty rate caused by Roman archery among the Goths, it is doubtful that they were more heavily armored than their Roman foes. In fact, the Goths closely resembled their late Roman counterparts.

Byzantine Adaptation

Since after Adrianople the empire was too weak to destroy the Gothic confederacies, the Romans sought to neutralize them by treaty. The emperor Theodosius recruited numerous Goths into the Roman army, as an expedient means to replenish the devastated ranks of the eastern field forces, but also as a way to weaken the Goths, whose presence in the Balkans created a state of emergency. Theodosius recruited numerous Gothic federates who fought loyally for him and of whose lives the Roman high command was apparently none too careful—a contemporary panegyrist acclaims the emperor for using barbarian to fight barbarian, thus bleeding both of them. Nonetheless the Goths formed a sizable but not dominant portion of the eastern field army. By 400 A.D. the Gothic warlord Gainas dominated imperial politics in the capital of Constantinople, but his unpopular policies led to his downfall and a riot of citizens who trapped and massacred 7,000 of his Gothic troops. The Gainas affair marked the apogee of Gothic influence in the imperial center; the Romans countered Germanic elements in the army by recruiting Isaurian highlanders from Asia Minor. Finally, the last major elements not assimilated or settled within the Roman Balkans or Asia Minor were sent to Italy under Theodoric the Amal. Justinian renewed the Gothic conflict, invading Italy and conquering it. In 554 the Roman general defeated a Frankish-Alemanni force at Volturnus through his combined arms approach—horse archery again proved a major Roman tactical advantage over the Frankish infantry force. Though the Byzantines lost most of Italy to the Lombards in the later sixth and early seventh centuries, they created the exarchate of Ravenna with several dukes under its control to check the Lombard advance. The exarch held joint civil and military power and, as viceroy of the emperor, was free to respond to crisis without direct orders from Constantinople. These reorganizations helped the Byzantines maintain territory in portions of Italy until 1071.

PERSIANS

The most sophisticated, rich, and militarily threatening power that the Romans faced in the early part of their existence was the empire of Sasanian Persia. Founded after victory in a civil war in 226 A.D., the Sasanian dynasty ruled territory stretching from Central Asia to the Persian Gulf and Mesopotamia. Their propaganda declared dynastic ties to the Achaemenid Persian Empire destroyed by Alexander the Great and consequently the rights to the former Persian territories of Asia Minor, Egypt, and the Mediterranean coast. While the Sasanians acted on these grand claims on only one occasion, during the mighty conflict that raged with Rome in 603–28, clashes over strategic borderlands and satellite peoples were frequent. The frequency and intensity of these conflicts rose from a simmer to a steady boil by the sixth century, culminating in the Persian conquest of most of the Roman east in the following century.

Organization

The Sasanian shah Kosrow I (531–79) reformed the Persian military and in doing so created several Roman-style structures. Kosrow divided the empire into four army districts in which he stationed army corps under the command of four *spahbeds* (field marshals). Along the border, the king established margraves, *marzbans*, who administered sensitive border districts and commanded the frontier forces stationed there. The Eran-ambaragbed, "minister of the magazines of empire," was, like his Roman counterpart, the praetorian prefect, in charge of arming and equipping the troops. The general (*gund-salar*) led individual field armies on campaign; sometimes under the authority of the *spahbed*. By the sixth century the army was largely professionally recruited and paid; there was a professional infantry commander in charge of standing guard units, but in the sixth century the Persians apparently continued to rely on conscripts for a large portion of their rank-and-file infantry. Mailed cavalry units and the royal guard formed the crack troops of the empire; these were generally drawn from the Persian nobility or from aristocratic allied families, such as the Hephthalites and Armenians, with whom the Persians had close contacts.

Methods of Warfare

The proportion of infantry to cavalry in the Sasanian army is unknown, but the Persians relied to a large degree on heavy horsemen, who could both shoot the bow and strike with heavy lances. The Persians favored direct massed cavalry assaults to break up enemy formations; the shock of their horsemen proved decisive against the Romans on several occasions. Normally the Sasanians drew up their forces in three cavalry lines. The Sasanians occasionally employed elephants in combat, but though they made a great psychological impression, they were not an important part of their military. The left of the Persian line was traditionally manned by left-handed archers and lancers who could thus strike effectively across the face of the enemy formation (right-handed mounted archers especially had difficulty shooting to their right). The left of the host formed the defensive anchor, whose role was to avoid enemy flanking maneuvers and to support the offensive right of the formation, where were stationed the best noble cavalry. The Sasanian right typically tried to outflank the enemy left, though the heavily armed kataphracts, covered from head to toe in mail and bearing lances, could be used in frontal assaults on infantry and cavalry groups. Behind the center line of regular cavalry were stationed the infantry formation, which supported the cavalry and sheltered retreating horsemen in case their attacks failed. In addition to their archery and horsemanship, the Sasanians were outstanding siege engineers. From the fourth through seventh centuries they seized some of the best defended and most powerfully built Roman fortress cities.

Byzantine Adaptation

The Sasanians and Byzantines knew one another well and there was considerable exchange of military knowledge and practice across the frontiers. Militarily, each side came to resemble the other. In early twentieth-century excavations at Dura Europus, a Roman frontier city on the middle Euphrates taken by Sasanian assault in the year 256 archaeologists discovered the remains of at least nineteen Romans and one Sasanian attacker. The Sasanian wore chain mail, carried a jade-hilted sword, and wore a pointed ridge-type helmet with a prominent center piece whose rivets joined the two lobes of the helmet together.[3] Such gear was typical in Roman armies by the third century. In 533 at the battle of Dara, Belisarios countered Sasanian superiority by limiting their cavalry and playing to their psychological sense of superiority. In subsequent battles he used the Sasanians' wariness of his stratagems to force their withdrawal by aggressive posturing. The Persians, used to the traps and feigned retreats of their nomad enemies, could be made too cautious by aggressive maneuvers. They could be thwarted by the commander's well-chosen battlefield that cut off the Persians' ability to place their weaker elements on protective rough ground. The poor soldiers among the Sasanians did not fight with spear and shield, but seem to have been mainly skirmishers and archers. They were therefore susceptible to Roman cavalry charges delivered over level ground. The Romans thus relied on stratagems, strategic maneuver, tactical coordination, and discipline to defeat the Persians. When Roman commanders selected the battlefield, they were able to neutralize or defeat these stubborn eastern opponents.

NOMADS

Throughout its existence, the empire confronted a vast array of steppe nomad military powers. The Byzantines fought major wars against the Huns, Bulgars, Avars, Khazars, Hungarians, Pechenegs, and Cumans and numerous minor conflicts with a host of other groups. Nomads were generally bent on plunder of imperial territory and rarely sought to settle on lands south of the Danube, only a small portion of which were suitable for the transient, cattle-herding life of pastoralists. However, both the Huns and Avars posed existential threats to the empire, as they sought to dominate the lands south of the Danube and to destroy the Roman power that contained them north of the river. Nomadic confederations formed under charismatic leadership or during periods of environmental or physical stress. Maurice stressed in the *Strategikon* that nomads typically fought in kin-based tribal or extended family groupings, and this contributed to the nature of their tactics.[4]

Organization

Nomadic society was based on nuclear families and wider, extended kinship ties. Like other tribal societies, blood relation or imagined genealogical connections helped to smooth political dealings and allow for larger groupings or "super tribes" that made massive nomadic military enterprise possible. The Huns under Attila formed an effective monarchy and Maurice stressed that the Avars, unlike many nomads, possessed a kingship. Undoubtedly the power of the central figures within a hierarchy during the Hunnic and Avar episodes of Byzantine history bolstered the barbarians' military effectiveness. After they settled north of the Danube in the late sixth century, the Avars conquered and coopted elements among the Bulgars, Slavs, and Hunnic and Germanic peoples in Transdanubia. The Byzantines portray a grim fate for those whom the Avars conquered, especially the Slavs who served as hard laborers and pressed soldiers during the siege of Constantinople in 626. According to Maurice, the Avars arranged themselves by tribe or kin group while on the march. Their social structure made them vulnerable to desertions and divisions within the ranks, which the Byzantines sought to exploit.

Methods of Warfare

Steppe nomads fought primarily as lightly armed horse archers. Speed and surprise were cornerstones of their strategic and tactical success. Their ability to swarm and the firepower they brought to bear could break up enemy formations and drive the enemy from the field. In the fourth century, when the Romans had little experience dealing with the tactical swarming attacks, war cries, strange appearance, and mobile horse archery of the Huns, these nomads struck terror into the hearts of many soldiers and won numerous victories across the length of the empire. In addition to horse archers, the Huns and Avars deployed heavier lancers who bore a resemblance to the Sasanian hybrid cavalry, armed with bow, sword, and lance. The *Strategikon* notes that the Avars carried a lance strapped on their back which freed them to operate their bows. In addition to the lance and bow, Avar warriors carried swords; they seem to have been more heavily armed than their Hun predecessors, as Maurice noted that they wore chain mail coats. The Avars wore long coats of mail or lamellar split at the crotch, with panels on each side to protect the leg. The famous Nagyszentmiklós Treasure includes a gold plate depicting what is probably an Avar or Bulgar warrior wearing such a coiffed mail coat, splinted greaves, helmet, and carrying a pennoned lance.

Byzantine Adaptation

The Byzantines relied on diplomatic means to buy off and deflect Hun designs on imperial territory. The defensive posture of the empire throughout the fifth century precluded decisive confrontations against a superior enemy in the open field, and the massive defenses of Constantinople shielded the eastern territories from Hun penetration and conquest, though most of their European possessions were ravaged and slipped from Byzantine control. Although our sources provide no insight into the exact mechanisms of the adoption of steppe nomad tactics and equipment, the Byzantines recruited Hunnic horse archers into their armies and probably from these and deserters derived the knowledge of horseback archery. By the sixth century, the hybrid horse archer and lancer cavalry among the armies of Justinian were the most important tactical elements within the Roman army. The Byzantines adopted the stirrup from the Avars and this provided Roman cavalry with a more stable fighting platform. Maurice's *Strategikon* notes that the thonged Avar lance and Avar-type tents and riding cloaks were also adopted directly from their steppe enemies. Lamellar cavalry armor also became more prominent in the panoply of Roman soldiers in the sixth and seventh centuries and this, too, indicates that the Byzantines borrowed extensively from nomads. The use of the feigned retreat, while known to classical armies, was a common steppe nomad tactic that the Byzantines perfected under steppe influence and employed throughout their history. The adoption of nomadic equipment, tactics, and strategy were among the most important adaptations of the Byzantine army and proved critical to the long-term survival of the empire.

ARABS

By the time of the rise of Islam in the early seventh century, the Romans possessed extensive military experience with the Arabs. Arab scouts and light troops had served as guides and auxiliaries almost from the beginning of Roman rule in the Near East. By the sixth century, the Roman system of paying subsidies to allied tribal confederations to maintain law and order along the frontier from the Red Sea to the Euphrates was integral to the governance of the eastern provinces.

The powerful Christian tribal confederation of Ghassan, which included both settled and tribal elements, largely managed the eastern periphery of the empire, and despite the general hostility of Greek-speaking elites to their Arab allies, these clients were both effective and reliable. Ghassanid auxiliaries defeated their Persian-sponsored counterparts and provided valuable light cavalry raiders and skirmishers to the eastern field armies on campaign in Syria and Mesopotamia. At the Battle of Yarmuk in 636 the Ghassanids fought alongside their Roman masters and though many subsequently converted to Islam and remained in Syria, a sizable group migrated to Roman territory. The Muslim Arab victors at Yarmuk overran the whole of Syria, Mesopotamia, and eventually wrested Egypt, Libya and North Africa from Roman control. Muslim Arab attempts to conquer Constantinople and thereby destroy the remnants of the Roman Empire unfolded in the epochal sieges of the seventh and early eighth centuries in which the empire emerged battered but intact. With the overthrow of the Umayyad dynasty and shift of the locus of Muslim government to Mesopotamia, the threat to the existence of the Roman state diminished, and as the Abbasid caliphate unraveled politically, the Byzantines mounted a sustained counterattack to recover lost territories in the east.

Organization

Arab armies of the conquest were organized along tribal lines, though it is uncertain if these were grouped into units of 10–15 soldiers called 'arifs known from just after the conquests. Muslim Arab armies were recruited mainly from Arabic-speaking family and tribal groupings. But soldiers were also raised from among Byzantine and Sasanian deserters, as well as non-Arab clients (mawali) dependent on regional Arab lords.[5] Larger tribal groups fought under the banners of their tribal sheikhs in army groups of varying strength, usually numbering 2,000–4,000 men. On rare occasions, as at Yarmuk, combined commands could field as many as 30,000 or 40,000 soldiers. In 661, the Battle of Siffin was fought between the Syrian forces under Mu'awiya and the Iraqi Arabs led by the Prophet's cousin and son-in-law 'Ali, said to have comprised 150,000 and 130,000 men, respectively; these numbers are inconceivable and could probably safely each be reduced by a factor of ten.[6] During the Umayyad era, when the Syrian army provided the main prop to the caliph's authority, armies of 6,000 Syrian troops are commonly mentioned and these may represent standard field force groupings, not dissimilar in size and equipment from their Byzantine neighbors.[7] In 838, the caliph al-Mu'tasim (d. 842) led an army of up to 80,000 men against Amorium, a number that represented a large force and among the largest the Byzantines ever confronted.[8]

Methods of Warfare

Although the commonly held perception of early Muslim armies today is of swift-moving horsemen mounted on Arabian chargers, the armies of the conquest era were mainly infantry forces fighting as spearmen and archers. Arab archery was particularly deadly to both the Byzantine and Persian forces encountered during the first campaigns of the conquest. Early Muslim armies generally lacked heavy cavalry, and they eagerly accepted the Sasanian horse who deserted to their ranks following the initial encounters in Mesopotamia. Infantry continued to form an important part of Arab armies up to the end of their military encounters with the Byzantines. Nikephoros Phokas noted that the Arab raiders who penetrated the Byzantine borderlands included a mix of cavalry and infantry; like their Roman counterparts, the infantry formed a *foulkon*, a dense mass of infantry spearmen, and supported the cavalry who formed the major offensive wing of Arab armies. Regular Arab cavalry fought primarily as lancers, while missile support was provided by foot archers. The Arabs never mastered horseback archery and instead relied on Turkic troops to provide mobile fire. The light cavalry encountered by the Byzantines in their reconquest of northern Syria and Mesopotamia were Bedouin light horse riding swift Arabian mounts. Nikephoros advised to keep them at bay with archery rather than chase them, since even the best Byzantine horses, encumbered as they were with heavily equipped fighting men, would not be able to catch them and the danger of being cut off and overwhelmed was a persistent peril of pursuit. Well led and generally possessing superior numbers, training, and equipment, the Arab armies of the early medieval period repeatedly exposed Byzantine weaknesses. Decisive engagements nearly always ended with Arab victories; only when the empire recovered somewhat economically and demographically while the caliphate began to fragment did the initiative return to the Romans.

Byzantine Adaptation

Given the asymetrical nature of the encounter between the Byzantines and Arabs after the initial clashes of the early and mid-seventh century, Byzantine commanders responded in the only way they could, via a strategy of defense coupled with limited, punitive raids to keep the enemy from settling in the strategic Anatolian highlands and to maintain the appearance of Byzantine power among the populations of the border lands. Imperial troops, seriously degraded through the loss of many men in the defeats in Syria and Egypt, underpaid, poorly equipped, and scattered throughout the provinces, were scarcely a match for caliphal field armies. The Byzantines often found themselves paying tribute to convince the Arabs not to attack them—a humiliating concession that drained both the fisc and morale. But the sieges of 674–78 and 717–18 revealed that without achieving naval dominance the Arabs had to conquer the Anatolian plateau if they were to achieve their objective of outright conquest of the Christian empire. Yet, due to their organization of the themes, whose armies could shadow and harass Muslim raiding columns and sometimes defeat them, the Romans made penetration of their territory hazardous. Stubborn Byzantine forces, although no match for grand caliphal campaign armies, often held their own against raiding columns and themselves raided exposed regions when Arab field forces were engaged elsewhere. By the tenth century, the centuries of incessant warfare had helped to create a warrior caste among the frontiersmen of the eastern marchlands who would remake the Byzantine army based on their experiences fighting the Arabs. Their combined arms approach and their use of psychological terror, scorched earth, and incremental advancement of imperial territory by sieges marked the apogee of the practice of Byzantine arms in the medieval east.

BULGARS

The Turkic Bulgars appeared in the sixth century, first as a rump of the so-called Old Bulgarian Empire, the Kutrigurs, defeated by Belisarios outside Constantinople in 559, settled north of the Danube and were absorbed by the Avars. Following the collapse of Avar power in the eighth century, new Bulgar arrivals and existing elites in Transdanubia gradually formed the Bulgar khanate, which adopted Slavic language and customs. Given their cultural origins in the Eurasian steppe, it is unsurprising that throughout the medieval period the Bulgarian social elite fought mostly as heavy armed cavalry lancers. Bulgaria formed the most important state to the north of the empire. Though there were long stretches of peace between the two peoples and even alliance, Byzantine-Bulgar relations were strained by their fundamental conflicting goals—both empires sought to dominate the Balkans and each considered the presence of the other unacceptable. Thus the Bulgars sought to capture Constantinople or subjugate the Byzantines militarily, while the latter sought to contain or even annex Bulgaria outright.

Organization

Initially the Bulgars organized themselves along the lines of most steppe empires, with "inner" and "outer" tribes whose power relationships were articulated through marriage alliances, genealogies, and material exchange. Beneath the outer tribes in the pecking order were subject groups like Slavs, Greeks, and the mélange of Avar, Hunnic, and Germanic remnants that rendered the rich cultural matrix of the Danube basin. The khan stood at the pinnacle of an increasingly sophisticated hierarchy that developed under steppe and Byzantine influence. Senior "inner" nobles, called *boilas* (often Anglicized as "boyar"), and junior "outer" nobles, *bagains*, formed the elite of the Bulgar state and provided both the military leadership and elite troops of the khanate. The Bulgars matched their Byzantine foe with a strong hierarchical military organization with the khan in overall command while his leading generals, the *tarqan*, commanded his administrative regional center and presumably took the center of the battle line as well. The *targan's* subordinates included *komites* (sing. *komes*), after Byzantine usage, who commanded the wings of the army.[9] The highest-ranking Bulgar nobles were heavily equipped cavalry with barded mounts and relied on heavy household cavalry and lighter armed horse archers as did their steppe nomad ancestors.

Methods of Warfare

The Bulgars employed mass conscription to fill out the ranks for their armies. Fear was the main tool used to compel men to enlist and show up equipped for the occasion. Khan Boris Michael (d. 907) ordered that men who arrived for muster without proper equipment or unprepared for campaign were to be executed, as were those who deserted before or during battle.[10] The rank and file included many Slavs who fought as light infantry, carrying shields and javelins. Bulgar cavalry resembled both their Byzantine enemy and other steppe nomads. The Bulgars were expert in their use of terrain, relying on ambush and surprise in their confrontation with the enemy.[11] They demonstrated a high level of strategic planning, strong discipline, and military cohesion, and on numerous occasions were able to confront and defeat imperial field armies, as they did at Varbica in 811 when they trapped a large force led by the emperor Nikephoros I and destroyed it by hemming the Byzantines against a wooden palisade and surrounding it. The emperor himself was killed and his heir mortally wounded. The Bulgars were intimately acquainted with Byzantine military strategy and tactics and, unlike the fragmented Arab emirates to the east, formed a more unified foe unbowed by the shock of repeated defeats.

Byzantine Adaptation

The Byzantines dealt with the Bulgars via a full range of economic, diplomatic, and military strategies. Trade was limited by treaty to designated zones and monitored by imperial officials. Spies were maintained at the Bulgar court at Pliska; the Bulgar khan Telerig (768–77) tricked the emperor into revealing the identity of Byzantine agents among the Bulgars by the ruse of his promised defection, then slaughtered those in the pay of the empire.[12] Byzantine failures against the Bulgars were often due to weakness in strategic and battlefield intelligence that resulted in the surprise of imperial field forces. Experienced and cautious commanders found warfare in Bulgaria perilous. Thus, in the ongoing dispute over control of lands in Thrace and Mesembria on the Black Sea coast, the emperor Nikephoros II Phokas mounted a brief campaign in which he found the the Bulgars' skillful use of the mountainous terrain and difficulties of supply and communication hard to overcome. Nikephoros therefore induced Sviatoslav I of Kiev to invade Bulgaria; the Rus' captured scores of Bulgarian towns and fortresses and overwhelmed Bulgar resistance, which led to a direct confrontation between the Rus' and their new Bulgar subjects and Byzantium. John I Tzimiskes's defeat of the Rus' at Dorostolon in 971 opened the way for Byzantine annexation of Bulgaria. The subjugation of Bulgaria took decades, however, with persistent and arduous campaigning by the emperor Basil II, who reduced each quarter of the Bulgar state through sieges and attrition, finally grinding down Bulgar resistance. Bulgaria provided another test for Byzantine strategies of attritive warfare: imperial forces used sieges, scorched earth, and incremental capture-and-hold methods to gradually expand their bases of operations and finally wear out a formidable, skillful, and disciplined opponent. Although the empire possessed a dominant position in Bulgaria by the death of Basil II in 1025, serious resistance continued to the death of the Bulgarian tsar Peter II in 1041. Byzantine control of Bulgaria, won over decades of bitter warfare, lasted for nearly a century and a half.

NORMANS

The Normans arrived in the Byzantine world not as enemies, but as valued mercenaries esteemed for their martial prowess. The settlement of Scandinavian raiders created the duchy of Normandy, when the region was ceded to their war leader Rollo (d. ca. 931) by the Carolingian king Charles the Simple (898–922). Rollo's descendants mingled with the local French population to create the Normans, a people thoroughly Christian, doggedly militaristic, and unfailingly expansionistic. Norman soldiers entered Italy around the start of the eleventh century where they served as mercenaries for various Lombard princes. By the 1050s large numbers of "Franks," as the Byzantines called them, had served as mercenaries in Byzantine armies from Syria to Bulgaria, and Normans served as part of the standing garrison of Asia Minor.[13] In the 1040s the Normans began the conquest of south Italy, establishing several counties in the south and finally invading and conquering Sicily from the petty Muslim dynasts there by 1091. Since the late 1050s the Normans had challenged Roman interests in Italy and Robert Guiscard led a Norman invasion of the Byzantine Balkans in 1081. In the ensuing conflict the Normans defeated Alexios I Komnenos, who expelled them only with great difficulty. Two more major Norman invasions followed over the next century, and the Norman kingdom of Sicily remained a threat to imperial ambitions in the west and to the imperial core until the Hauteville Norman dynasty failed in 1194. By this time all hope for the Byzantine recovery of south Italy and Sicily had vanished, thanks to Norman power.

Organization

The Normans served under captains who rose to prominence due to birth or their fortunes in war. Minor nobility like Tancred of

Hauteville, who founded the dynasty that would conquer much of Italy and Sicily, was a minor baron in Normandy and probably the descendant of Scandinavian settlers. The warriors who carved out territory within Byzantine Anatolia seem to have been either petty aristocrats or simply successful soldiers. One such Norman was Hervé Frankopoulos, who in 1057 led 300 Franks east in search of plunder and territory. After initial successes around Lake Van, he was delivered to the emperor and eventually pardoned. Thus, Norman companies were of no fixed numbers, and it seems that each baron recruited men according to his wealth and status. Norman lords in Italy raised the core of their army from men to whom they distributed lands and wealth in exchange for permanent military service. Lords were required to provide fixed numbers of troops, either knights or infantry sergeants. Other Normans served for pay and plunder, including conquered lands to be distributed after successful occupation of enemy territory. The Normans that the Byzantines encountered were a fluid group—some fought for the empire and then against it; their interests were pay and personal advancement rather than any particular ethnic allegiance. In this the Normans who warred against the Byzantines resembled the later free companies of the late medieval period—variable in numbers, generally following a capable, experienced, and charismatic commander, and exceptionally opportunistic. As a warlord's success grew, so did his resources. Thus Robert Guiscard rose from the leader of a band of Norman robbers to be Count and then Duke of Apulia and Calabria; in 1084, following his defeat of Alexios at Dyrrachium, Guiscard marched on Rome with thousands of infantry and more than 2,000 knights, a far cry from the scores or hundreds with which he began his career.[14]

Methods of Warfare

The bulk of the Norman fighting forces were infantry, but they formed a largely defensive force that operated in support of the cavalry. Norman infantry fought generally as spearmen—the Bayeux Tapestry shows many Normans on foot wearing the nasal helm and mail hauberks, but it is unlikely that the majority were so armed. Most were probably unarmored and relied on shields for protection like most of their counterparts throughout Europe. Light infantry archers fought with little or no armor, and missile troops played a role in their Balkan campaigns as well—the Byzantine commander George Palaiologos suffered an arrow wound to his head in battle at Dyrrachium in 1082, but generally the Byzantines relied on superior Turkish archery in order to unhorse the Normans and immobilize the knights.[15] Norman knights wore heavy mail hauberks and mail chausses with in-pointed mail foot guards, which Anna Komnene noted slowed the Norman cavalry down when they were unhorsed.[16] These mounted men carried lances and swords. The weight of their mail made them relatively safe from the archery of the day. Norman knights usually decided the course of battle; it was the shock cavalry charge delivered by the Norman knight that delivered victory in battle after battle. Unlike the Turks and Pechenegs with whom the empire regularly contended and whose weaponry was lighter and who relied on mobility, hit-and-run tactics, and feigned retreat, the Normans preferred close combat. They fought in dense, well-ordered ranks and exhibited exemplary discipline.[17] In an era when infantry were generally of questionable quality, most foot soldiers throughout Europe and the Middle East could not stare down a Norman frontal cavalry charge. Norman horsemen punched holes in opposing formations and spread panic and disorder that their supporting troops exploited. By the end of the eleventh century, Norman prowess on the battlefield yielded them possessions from Syria to Scotland.

Byzantine Adaptation

The Byzantines avidly recruited Normans into their armies. Though critics have unfairly blamed the medieval Romans for not adapting their warfare in light of the new western techniques and technologies to which they were exposed, fully equipped and well-trained kataphraktoi could match the skill and shock power of the Norman knight. What the Byzantines of the Komnenoi era lacked were the disciplined heavy infantry of the Macedonian period and combined arms approach of mounted and dismounted archery that could blunt enemy attack and cover infantry and cavalry tactical operations. Alexios I relied on Turkish and steppe nomad auxiliaries and patchwork field armies assembled from mercenaries drawn from the empire's neighbors. As with other intractable foes, the Byzantines relied on a combination of defense and offense—the Normans were contained in the Balkans allowing space for an imperial recovery and the time to muster new forces following the heavy defeat late in 1081 of the Roman army at Dyrrachium on the Adriatic. Alexios allied with southern Italian nobles and the German emperor Henry IV (1084–1105) who menaced the Norman flanks. The death of Robert Guiscard in 1085 removed the most serious threat to Byzantine rule since the seventh century, but Guiscard's son, the redoubtable Bohemund, renewed war against the empire in 1107–8. Alexios had learned from his twenty years of dealing with the Norman adversary and returned to the traditional Byzantine strategies of defense, containment, and attrition. The Byzantines relied on their Venetian allies to provide naval squadrons on the Adriatic that interfered with Norman shipping and resupply, and Alexios's forces blocked the passes around Dyrrachium; the emperor forbade his commanders to engage in a large-scale confrontation with the Normans. In the skirmishes and running battles against Norman scouting and foraging parties Byzantine archers shot the enemy mounts from beneath their riders and then cut down the beleaguered knights. Hunger, disease, and lack of money undid Bohemund, who was forced to sign a humiliating treaty and return to Italy.[18] Thus the ages-old Byzantine principles of indirect warfare proved triumphant against a stubborn and superior enemy.

SEVEN

THE BYZANTINE ARMY AT WAR

THROUGHOUT THEIR HISTORY the Byzantine art of war may be seen in numerous campaigns and individual engagements. Though some have been well studied, contemporary sources describe many more encounters with the enemy in the barest terms, or make no mention of them at all. In what follows, we will view the Byzantine army at war via studies of major campaigns, individual battles, and siege warfare.

CAMPAIGNS: THE VANDAL WAR

In 406 the East Germanic Vandals and their tribal confederates, including Germanic Suebi and Iranian Alans, crossed the Rhine. After an initial defeat at the hands of the Franks, the Vandals enlisted Alan support and smashed their way into Gaul, plundering the countryside mercilessly as they advanced into the south. In the early 420s Roman pressure forced the Vandals into southern Spain where the newcomers faced a Roman-Gothic alliance; this threat the Vandals managed to defeat, but there could be no peace. Under their fearless and brilliant war leader Geiseric (428–77), whose fall from a horse had made him lame, the Vandals sought shelter across the Mediterranean; their long exodus led as many as 80,000 of them to Africa where, they believed, they could shelter themselves from Roman counterattack. They commandeered ships and ferried themselves across the straits to Tangiers, in the Roman province of Mauretania Tingitana.

There the local dux had few men to oppose Geiseric, who swept him aside and, after a year's plundering march, in 410 reached the city of Hippo Regius (modern Annaba in Algeria). There one of the great luminaries of Christian history lay dying: Augustine of Hippo, bishop of the city and church father. The Vandals stormed the city and spread death and sorrow, but Augustine was spared the final horror; he died on August 28, 430, about a year before the Vandals returned and finally overcame the city. By then Vandal aggression had prompted a large-scale imperial counteroffensive led by count Boniface. In 431 an imperial expedition from the east led by the generalissimo Aspar joined forces with Boniface but suffered defeat and had to withdraw in tatters. The future eastern emperor Marcian (d. 457) served in the expedition and fell into Vandal hands. He helped broker the resulting peace, which recognized Vandal possession of much of Roman Numidia, the lands of what is now eastern Algeria. The Romans licked their wounds but could in no way accept barbarians in possession of one of the most productive cornlands and who threatened the richest group of provinces of the whole of the Roman west. In 442 the emperor Theodosius II dispatched a powerful force from the east with the aim of dislodging the Vandals. It too was defeated and in 444 the Romans were forced to recognize Vandal control over the provinces of Byzacena, Proconsularis, and Numidia, the regions today comprising eastern Algeria and Tunisia—rich districts with vast farmland and numerous cities. In 455 the Vandals sacked Rome, the second time the great city had suffered sack in fifty years, having been plundered by Alaric in 410. The eastern emperor Marcian had his own problems to deal with, namely the Huns, and therefore sent no retaliatory expedition.

Instead, Constantinople finally responded in 461 in conjunction with the capable western emperor, Majorian (457–61), but Majorian's crossing to Africa from Spain was frustrated by traitors in his midst who burned the expeditionary ships and undid the western efforts. By this time the Vandals had established a powerful fleet and turned to piracy; they threatened the Mediterranean coastlands as far as Constantinople itself. In 468 the emperor Leo I launched another massive attack against Vandal North Africa under the command of his brother-in-law Basiliskos; Prokopios records that the expedition cost the staggering sum of 130,000 lbs. of gold. The expedition began promisingly enough. Leo sent the commander Marcellinus to Sardinia, which was easily captured, while another army under Heraclius advanced to Tripolis (modern Tripoli) and captured it. Basiliskos, however, landed somewhere near modern Hammam Lif, about 27 miles from Carthage. There he received envoys from Geiseric who begged him to wait while the Vandals took counsel among themselves and determined the course of negotiations. While Basiliskos hesitated, the Vandals assembled their fleet and launched a surprise attack using fire ships and burned most of the anchored Roman fleet to cinders. As his ship was overwhelmed, Basiliskos leaped into the sea in full armor and committed suicide.

The stain on Roman honor from the Basiliskos affair was deep; rumors abounded of his incompetence, corruption, or outright collusion with the enemy. The waste of treasure and the loss of life was so severe that the eastern empire made no more effort to dislodge the Vandals and to recover Africa. As the fifth century deepened and the Hunnic threat receded, the east settled into an uneasy relationship with the former imperial territories of North Africa, trading and exchanging diplomatic contacts, but never allowing the Vandals to think that Africa was rightly theirs. The emperor Zeno established an "endless peace" with the Vandal foe, binding them with oaths to cease aggression against Roman territory. Upon the death of Geiseric, his eldest son Huneric (477–84) ruled over the Vandals; he is remembered as a cruel persecutor of Catholics in favor of the heretical form of Christianity, Arianism, practiced by the Vandals and Alans. Huneric's son with his wife Eudoxia, the daughter of the former western emperor Valentinian III, was Hilderic, who claimed power in Africa in 523. Under Hilderic, relations with Constantinople warmed considerably. Hilderic himself had a personal bond with Justinian from the time the latter was a rising talent and force behind the throne of his uncle, the emperor Justin (518–27), and in a policy designed to appease local Africans and the empire, Catholics were left unmolested; many Vandals converted to the orthodox form of Christianity. The Vandal nobility found their situation threatened, as one of the key components of their identity, Arianism, was under attack; assimilation and disintegration, they reasoned, were sure to follow. When, in 530, Hilderic's younger cousin Gelimer overthrew the aged Vandal king it was with the support of the majority of the elites. Hilderic died in prison as Justinian monitored events from Constantinople with dismay. Roman diplomatic attempts to restore Hilderic failed. But Justinian was unable to act because war with Persia had commenced and his forces were tied down in Syria. By 532, Justinian sealed peace with Persia, freeing his forces and their young general Belisarios, the victor in 530 over the Persian army at Dara, to move west.

On the heels of the signing of the peace with Persia in 532, Justinian announced to his inner circle his intentions to invade the Vandal kingdom. According to a contemporary witness and one in a position to know, the general Belisarios's secretary Prokopios, the news was met with dread. Commanders feared being selected to lead the attack, lest they suffer the fate of prior expeditions, while the emperor's tax collectors and administrators recalled the ruinous expense of Leo's campaign that cost vast amounts of blood and treasure. Allegedly the most vocal opponent was the praetorian prefect John the Cappadocian, who warned the emperor of the great distances involved and the impossibility of attacking Africa while Sicily and Italy were in the hands of the Ostrogoths. Eventually, we are told, a priest from the east advised Justinian that in a dream he foresaw Justinian fulfilling his duty as protector of the Christians in Africa, and that God himself would join the Roman side in the war. Whatever the internal debates and the role of faith, there was certainly a religious element to Roman propaganda; Catholic bishops stirred the pot by relating tales of Vandal atrocities against the faithful. Justinian overcame whatever logistical and military misgivings he possessed through belief in the righteousness of his cause.

It could not have been lost on the high command in Constantinople that Justinian's plan of attack was identical to Leo's, which was operationally sound. Imperial agents responded to (or more likely incited) a rebellion by the Vandal governor of Sardinia with an embassy that drew him to the Roman side. Justinian supported another revolt, this one by the governor of Tripolitania, Prudentius, whose Roman name suggests he was not the Vandal official in charge there. Prudentius used his own troops, probably domestic bodyguards, armed householders, and Moors, to seize Tripoli. He then sent word to Justinian requesting aid and the emperor obliged with the dispatch of a force of unknown size under the tribune Tattimuth. These forces secured Tripoli while the main expeditionary army mustered in Constantinople.

The forces gathered were impressive but not overwhelming. Belisarios was in overall command of 15,000 men and men attached to his household officered most of the 5,000 cavalry. John, a native of Dyrrachium in Illyria, commanded the 10,000 infantry. Foederati included 400 Heruls, Germanic warriors who had migrated to the Danubian region from Scandinavia by the third century. Six hundred "Massagetae" Huns served—these were all mounted archers and they were to play a critical role in the tactics of the campaign. Five hundred ships carried 30,000 sailors and crewmen and 15,000 soldiers and mounts. Ninety-two warships manned by 2,000 marines protected the flotilla, the largest seen in eastern waters in at least a century. The ability of the Romans to maintain secrecy was astonishing, for strategic surprise was difficult to achieve in antiquity; merchants, spies, and travelers spread news quickly. Gelimer was clearly oblivious to the existence of the main Roman fleet; apparently an attack in force was inconceivable to him and he saw the Roman ambitions confined to nibbles at the edge of his kingdom. The Vandal king sent his brother Tzazon with 5,000 Vandal horse and 120 fast ships to attack the rebels and their Roman allies in Sardinia.

It had been seven decades since the Romans had launched such a large-scale expedition into western waters, and the lack of logistical experience told. John the Cappadocian economized on the biscuit; instead of being baked twice, the bread was placed near the furnaces of a bathhouse in the capital; by the time the fleet reached Methone in the Peloponnese, the bread was rotten and 500 soldiers died from poisoning. The water was also contaminated toward the end of the voyage and sickened some. After these difficulties, the fleet landed in Sicily near Mount Aetna. In 533 the island was under the control of the Ostrogothic kingdom of Italy, and through diplomatic exchanges the Ostrogoths had been made aware of the Roman intentions of landing there to procure supplies and use the island as a convenient springboard for the invasion. Prokopios reports the psychological effect of the unknown on the general and his men; no one knew the strength or battle worthiness of their foe, which caused considerable fear among the men and affected morale. More terrifying, though, was the prospect of fighting at sea, of which the vast majority of the army had no experience. The Vandal reputation as a naval power weighed heavily on them. In Sicily, Belisarios therefore dispatched Prokopios and other spies to Syracuse in the southeast of the island to gather intelligence about the disposition of the Vandal navy and about favorable landing spots on the African coast. In Syracuse, Prokopios met a childhood acquaintance from Palestine, a merchant, whose servant had just returned from Carthage; this man informed Prokopios that the Vandal navy had sailed for Sardinia and that Gelimer was not in Carthage, but staying four days' distance. Upon receiving this news, Belisarios embarked his men at once and sailed, past Malta and Gozzo, and anchored unopposed at Caput Vada (today Ras Kaboudia in east-central Tunisia). There the high command debated the wisdom of landing four days' march or more from Carthage in unfamiliar terrain where lack of provisions and water and exposure to enemy attack would make the advance on the Vandal perilous. Belisarios reminded his commanders that the soldiers had openly spoken of their fear of a naval engagement and that they were likely to flee if they were opposed at sea. His view carried the day and they disembarked. The journey had taken three months, rendering it all the more remarkable that news of the Roman expedition failed to reach Gelimer.

The cautious Belisarios followed Roman operational protocol; the troops established a fortified, entrenched camp. The general ordered that the dromons, the light, fast war galleys that had provided the fleet escort, anchor in a circle around the troop carriers. He assigned archers to stand watch onboard the ships in case of enemy attack. When soldiers foraged in local farmers' orchards the next day, they were severely punished and Belisarios admonished the army that they were not to antagonize the Romano-African population, whom he hoped would side with him against their Vandal overlords.

The army advanced up the coastal road from the east toward Carthage. Belisarios stationed one of his boukellarioi, John, ahead with a picked cavalry force. Ahead on the army's left rode the 600 Hun horse archers. The army moved 80 stadia (about 8 miles) each day. About 35 miles from Carthage, the armies made contact; in the evening when Belisarios and his men bivouacked within a pleasure park belonging to the Vandal king, Vandal and Roman scouts skirmished and each retired to their own camps. The Byzantines, crossing to the south of Cape Bon, lost sight of their fleet, which had to swing far to the north to round the cape. Belisarios ordered his admirals to wait about 20 miles distant from the army and not to proceed to Carthage where a Vandal naval response might be expected.

Gelimer had, in fact, been shadowing the Byzantine force for some time, tracking them on the way to Carthage where Vandal forces were mustering. The king sent his nephew Gibamund and 2,000 Vandal cavalry ahead on the left flank of the Roman army. Gelimer's strategy was to hem the Romans between his forces to the rear, those of Gibamund on the left, and reinforcements from Carthage under Ammatas, Gelimer's brother. The plan was therefore to envelop and destroy the Roman forces. Without the 5,000 Vandal troops sent to Sardinia, the Vandal and Roman armies were probably about equal in strength. Around noon, Ammatas arrived at Ad Decimum, named from its location at the tenth milestone from Carthage. In his haste, Ammatas left Carthage without his full complement of soldiers and arrived too early by the Vandals' coordinated attack plan. His men encountered John's boukellarioi elite cavalry (fig. 7.1). Outnumbered, the Vandals fought valiantly; Prokopios states that Ammatas himself killed twelve men before he fell. When their commander perished, the Vandals fled to the northwest back toward Carthage. Along their route they encountered penny packets of their countrymen advancing toward Ad Decimum; the retreating elements of Ammatas's forces panicked these men who fled with them, pursued by John to the gates of the city. John's men cut down the fleeing Vandals in great number, bloody work far out of proportion to his own numbers. About four miles to the southeast, the flanking attack of the 2,000 Vandal cavalry under Gibamund encountered the Hunnic flank guard of Belisarios. Though they were outnumbered nearly four to one, the 600 Huns had the advantage of tactical surprise, mobility, and firepower. The Vandals had never experienced steppe horse archers; terrified by the reputation and the sight of them, Gibamund and his forces panicked and ran; the Huns thus decimated the second prong of Gelimer's attack.

Belisarios had still not been informed of his lieutenant's success when at the end of the day his men constructed the normal entrenched and palisaded camp. Inside he left the baggage and 10,000 Roman infantry, taking with him his cavalry force and boukellarioi with the hopes of skirmishing with the enemy to determine their strength and capabilities. He sent the four hundred Herul foederati as a vanguard; these men encountered Gelimer's scouts and a violent clash ensued (fig. 7.2). The Heruls mounted a hill and saw the body of the Vandal army approaching. They sent riders to Belisarios, who pushed forward with the main army—Prokopios does not tell us, but it seems that this could only have been the cavalry wing, since only they were drawn up for action. The Vandals drove the Heruls from the hill and seized the high point of the battlefield. The Heruls fled to another portion of the vanguard, the boukellarioi of Belisarios, who, rather than hold fast, fled in panic (fig. 7.3).

Gelimer made the error of descending the hill; at the bottom he found the corpses of the Vandals slain by John's forces, including Ammatus. Upon seeing his dead brother, Gelimer lost his wits and the Vandal host began to disintegrate. Though Prokopios does not mention it, there was more in play; the string of corpses on the road to Carthage informed the king that his encirclement plan had failed and he now faced a possible Roman encirclement. He could not be certain that a Roman force did not bar the way to Carthage. Thus, as Belisarios's host approached, the Vandal decision to retreat to the southwest toward Numidia was not as senseless as Prokopios claimed. The fighting, which could not have amounted to much more than running skirmishing as the Vandals withdrew, ended at nightfall (fig. 7.4).

The next day Belisarios entered Carthage in order; there was no resistance. The general billeted his soldiers without incident; the discipline and good behavior of the soldiers was so exemplary that Prokopios remarked that they purchased their lunch in the marketplace the day of their entry to the city. Belisarios immediately started repairs on the dilapidated city walls and sent scouts to ascertain the whereabouts and disposition of Gelimer's forces. Not much later his men intercepted messengers who arrived from Sardinia bearing news of the defeat of the rebel governor at the hands of the Vandal general Tzazon. Gelimer and the Vandal army, which remained intact, were encamped on the plain of Bulla Regia, four days' march south of Carthage. The king sent messengers to Tzazon in Sardinia, and the Vandal army there returned and made an uncontested landing west of Carthage and marched overland to Bulla Regia where the two forces unified. Belisarios's failure to intercept and destroy this element of the Vandal force when it landed was a major blunder that Prokopios passes over in silence.

Once Gelimer and Tzazon unified their forces, they moved on Carthage, cut the main aqueduct, and guarded the roads out of the city. They also opened negotiations with the Huns in Roman service, whom they enticed to desert, and they attempted to recruit fifth columnists in the city to help their cause.

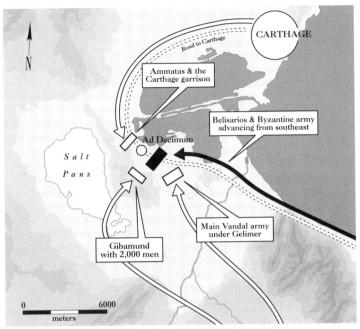

Fig. 7.1. The Vandal encirclement plan, after Cplakidas, 2012.

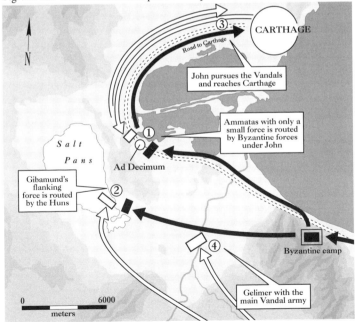

Fig. 7.2. The Battle of Ad Decimum, phase 1, after Cplakidas, 2012.

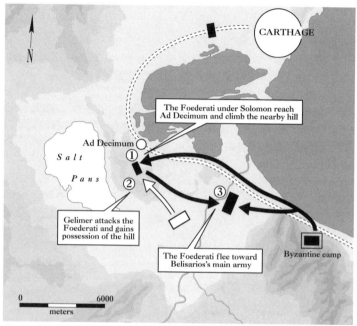

Fig. 7.3. The Battle of Ad Decimum, phase 2, after Cplakidas, 2012.

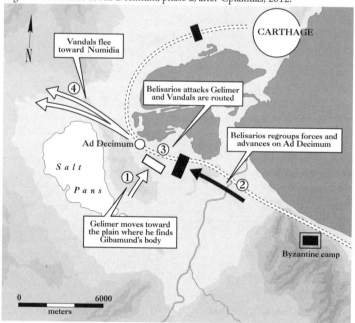

Fig. 7.4. The Battle of Ad Decimum, phase 3, after Cplakidas, 2012.

The two armies encamped opposite one another at Tricamarum, about 14 1/2 miles south of Carthage. The Vandals opened the engagement, advancing at lunch time when the Romans were at their meal. The two forces drew up against one another, with a small brook running between the front lines. Four thousand five hundred Roman cavalry arrayed themselves in three divisions along the front; the general John stationed himself in the center, and Belisarios came up behind him with 500 household guards. The Vandals and their Moorish allies formed around Tzazon's 5,000 Vandal horsemen in the center of the host. The two armies stared one another down, but since the Vandals did not take the initiative, Belisarios ordered John forward with picked cavalry drawn from the Roman center. They crossed the stream and attacked the Vandal center, but Tzazon and his men repulsed them, and the Romans retreated. The Vandals showed good discipline in their pursuit, refusing to cross the stream where the Roman force awaited them. John returned to the Roman lines, selected more cavalry, and launched a second frontal assault. This, too, the Vandals repulsed. John retired and regrouped and Belisarios committed most of his elite units to a third attack on the center. John's heroic final charge locked the center in a sharp fight. Tzazon fell in the fighting and the Vandal center broke and fled, joined by the wings of the army as the Romans began a general advance. The Romans surrounded the Vandal palisade, inside which they took shelter along with their baggage and families. In the clash that opened the battle of Tricamarum in mid-December 533, the Romans counted 50 dead, the Vandals about 800.

As Belisarios's infantry arrived on the battlefield, Gelimer understood that the Vandals could not withstand an assault on the camp by 10,000 fresh Roman infantry. Instead of an ordered retreat, though, the Vandal king fled on horseback alone. When the rest of the encampment learned of his departure, panic swept the Vandals, who ran away in chaos. The Romans plundered the camp and pursued the broken force throughout the night, enslaving the women and children and killing the males. In the orgy of plunder and captive taking, the cohesion of the Roman army dissolved completely; Belisarios watched helplessly as the men scattered and lost all discipline, enticed by the richest booty they had ever encountered. When morning came, Belisarios rallied his men, dispatched a small force of 200 to pursue Gelimer, and continued to round up the Vandal male captives. The disintegration of the Vandals was clearly complete, since the leader offered a general amnesty to the enemy and sent his men to Carthage to prepare for his arrival. The initial pursuit of Gelimer failed, and Belisarios himself led forces to intercept the king, whose existence still threatened a Vandal uprising and Moorish alliances against the Roman occupiers. The general reached Hippo Regius where he learned Gelimer had taken shelter on a nearby mountain among Moorish allies. Belisarios sent his Herul foederati under their commander Pharas to guard the mountain throughout the winter and starve out Gelimer and his followers.

Belisarios garrisoned the land and sent a force to Sardinia which submitted to Roman control and sent another unit to Caesarea in Mauretania (modern Cherchell in Algeria). In addition, the general ordered forces to the fortress of Septem on the straits of Gibraltar and seized it, along with the Balearic Islands. Finally he sent a detachment to Tripolitania to strengthen the army of Prudentius and Tattimuth to ward off Moorish and Vandal activity there. Late in the winter, facing deprivation and surrounded by the Heruls, Gelimer negotiated his surrender and was taken to Carthage where Belisarios received him and sent him to Constantinople.

Roman victory was total. The Vandal campaign ended with a spectacular recovery of the rich province of Byzacium and the riches of the African cities and countryside the Vandals had held for nearly a century. Prokopios is reserved in his praise for his general, Belisarios, and for the performance of the Roman army as a whole, laying the blame for Vandal defeat at the feet of Gelimer and the power of Fortune, rather than crediting the professionalism or skill of the army commanders and rank and file. The Romans clearly made several blunders—chief among these the failure to intercept Tzazon's reinforcing column, and Belisarios's inability to maintain discipline in the ranks upon the plundering of the Vandal encampment at Tricamarum. On balance, though, the army and the state had performed well enough. The work of imperial agents in outlying regions of Tripolitania and Sardinia distracted the Vandals and led them to disperse their forces. Experienced Roman soldiers who had just returned from years of hard fighting against the Persians proved superior to their Vandal enemy in hand-to-hand fighting. Indeed, they had proved capable of meeting and destroying much larger enemy contingents. Belisarios's leadership, maintenance of morale, and (apart from the Tricarmarum incident) excellent discipline accompanied his cautious, measured operational decisions that conserved and protected his forces. Roman losses were minimal in a campaign that extended imperial boundaries by more than 50,000 square kilometers (19,300 square miles) and more than a quarter million subjects. The empire held its African possessions for more than a century until they were swept under the rising Arab Muslim tide in the mid-seventh century.

THE EASTERN CAMPAIGNS OF NIKEPHOROS PHOKAS, 964–69

Nikephoros II Phokas rose to the office of domestikon ton scholon, replacing his father in command in 954. His elevation reflected both his reputation and the desire of his sovereign, Constantine VII, to wage war aggressively against the Muslims. The eastern emirates were a perpetual threat to the empire. Since the reign of Basil I, however, the Romans had made considerable gains in the east, destroying the heretical state of the Paulicians and striking against the raiding emirate of Melitene in a series of campaigns that culminated in the 934 sack of the city and the destruction of one of the most important Arab bases (see below) by John Kourkouas. Since the eighth century Muslim holy warriors (ghazis) flocked to Melitene or Tarsos in Cilicia to join the jihad against the Byzantines. Once Kourkouas destroyed one prop of the holy war, Nikephoros set his sights on the southern flank of the empire.

The emirate of Tarsos was one of the frontier bastions of Islam (thugur). Tarsian raiders attacked the frontier zone incessantly, and launched major invasions throughout the ninth and tenth centuries. The caliph al-Ma'mun used the city as a staging ground from which to invade Byzantium in 833, a prelude to the massive campaign his successor al-Mu'tasim launched from Tarsos in 838 that ruined the vital Byzantine city of Amorium. Major raids launched from Tarsos in 862 and 878 penetrated Cappadocia and captured several fortresses. The expedition of 878–79 consisted of 3,000 ghazis whom the Byzantines defeated at Herakleia in Cappadocia. In 894, the Muslims of Tarsos mounted another expedition in force as far as Pisidia in Anatolia. In 931, the emir Thamal al-Dulafi led a raid to Amorium and captured a huge number of slaves—women and children—who fetched 136,000 gold dinars in the slave markets. During the governorship of Thamal the frontier fortresses of Adana, Massisa (Yakapınar in Cilicia), and Mar'ash (ancient Germanikeia, modern Kahramanmaras in southeastern Turkey) were repopulated and garrisoned.[1] When Sayf ad-Dawla rose to power in the northern Syrian city of Aleppo, he coordinated his jihad activities with the emir of Tarsos—in 950, Sayf (whose name means "Sword of the State") led a large army into Anatolia that included some 4,000 men from Tarsos. The Byzantines badly mauled this force and the raid ended in disaster.[2]

In the tenth century, Tarsos was populous and rich. It had extensive trade connections and was well situated in the midst of the lush, well-watered Cilician plain. Although the city lay on level ground, it was large and as impressively defended as any city of the Levant. The Kydnos River flowed by the city, providing plenty of water. A near-contemporary Muslim writer, Tarsusi, noted the city had a double wall, the inner wall was of great height and strengthened by one hundred towers and crenellations offering protection to archers and to artillery—traction trebuchets and bolt casting machines. Five gates pierced each wall—those on the outer wall were iron-sheathed wood while those inside were solid iron. The inhabitants of the city included many full-time warriors and seasonal ghazis; its population was fervent in its pursuit of the jihad and had a reputation as skilled horsemen and well-trained warriors. Even boy volunteers were given weapons appropriate for their size and age when the city came under threat. According to Tarsosi, the city had 34,000 houses, two-thirds of which domiciled ghazi warriors who made Tarsos their home in fulfilling their jihad vows. Ibn Hawqal, the Muslim geographer who visited the city before its conquest by the Byzantines, wrote around 988 that the ghazis who packed the city came from all corners of the Muslim world, from places as far-flung as North Africa, Yemen, and Kerman in eastern Iran. Ibn Hawqal's assertion that Tarsos fielded 100,000 cavalry is probably off by a factor of ten, but it nonetheless remained a menace with which Nikephoros wanted to deal once and for all.[3]

In August 963, Nikephoros Phokas seized power in a bloody coup, assuming protection over the young boy emperors Basil and Constantine. The following year, Nikephoros dispatched John Tzimiskes against the Muslims of Cilicia. Tzimiskes arrived on the warm Cilician plain in December 963 or January 964, which meant he led his Cappadocian troops through the mountain passes in bitter winter; this out-of-season attack probably surprised the Muslims. Near Adana the forces of Sayf ad-Dawla, emir of Aleppo and champion of the border wars and struggle against the Christian Romans, appeared. The Tarsian army numbered 15,000; the number of Byzantine troops is unknown. During what became known as the battle of the Mountain of Blood, the Cilician Muslims first routed a section of the Byzantine army—it is uncertain whether this was a feigned retreat, but either Tzimiskes's ambush force or his reserve cut the pursuing Muslim force in half. Consequently 4–5,000 Muslims took refuge on a steep hilltop, inaccessible to cavalry. Tzimiskes dismounted his cavalry and, along with the infantry, fought his way to the summit, massacring every Muslim defender there.[4] This act of extreme brutality certainly lay outside the bounds of the normal conduct of war between the two powers. It shocked and demoralized the Muslims of Cilicia, and the people of Adana abandoned their town and fled to nearby Massisa (ancient Mopsuestia). John's annihilation of his enemy also deprived Sayf, who was sick and near the end of his life, of precious veteran troops and paved the way for the Byzantine assault on their main target, the city of Tarsos itself. Tzimiskes then moved toward Massisa, 20 km (about 12 1/2 miles) east, another one of the thugur cities. Like Tarsos, Massisa was splendidly fortified, and the Roman general assaults on the circuit failed; after a siege of three months, Tzimiskes abandoned the operations as the summer season began. Already a famine gripped Cilicia because of the war and the Romans could not forage enough supplies to feed themselves or their horses. Before he withdrew, Tzimiskes smashed through the defenses of al-Mallun, the port of Massisa, then pillaged and burned his way to Tarsos. Muslim reinforcements from Khurasan (eastern Iran and regions beyond) arrived in large number, but they encountered a devastated countryside and were unable to find enough provisions to maintain themselves—most drifted back home before the invasion of the emperor in the following year.

In November 964, Nikephoros II Phokas himself led an army of Romans along with Iberian (from the Caucasus) and Armenian allies into Cilicia. The emperor's aim was the capture of Tarsos and the destruction of the raiding emirate. Nikephoros divided his forces in two and put his brother Leo in charge of the force sent against Tarsos. Leo's forces were apparently driven from the walls of Tarsos by stubborn defenders. Meanwhile the emperor himself moved against Massisa, another strongly fortified city bifurcated by the Pyramos (today the Ceyhan). The siege dragged on for many months. Finally, in

July 965, the historian Leo the Deacon records that Nikephoros inspected the walls of the city and instructed his sappers where to dig, and that in one night they removed enough earth to completely undermine a tower. This seems unlikely; it must have taken many days to mine sufficient material from underneath the foundations. At dawn on July 13, the Byzantines fired the wooden props beneath the tower, which collapsed with considerable loss of life among the defenders.[5] The Romans then stormed the gap and seized half the town. The main battle took place when the Byzantines forced the bridge between the main city and the major suburb of Kafarbayya and drove the Muslim inhabitants out, seizing thousands of prisoners and huge spoils.

Nikephoros then swung the giant maw of his army to the east, against steadfast Tarsos. The Romans encamped around the city and besieged it, cutting down the orchards and destroying the food and fodder throughout the plain. The Tarsians, fractious as ever, decided to challenge the imperial host in the open field. Nikephoros arrayed his army:

> The emperor himself led out from camp the bravest and most robust soldiers and arranged the divisions on the battlefield, deploying the ironclad horsemen in the van, and ordering the archers and slingers to shoot at the enemy from behind. He himself took his position on the right wing, bringing with him a vast squadron of cavalrymen, while John Tzimiskes . . . fought on the left. . . . When the emperor ordered the trumpets to sound the charge, one could see the Roman divisions move into action with incredible precision, as the entire plain sparkled with the gleam of their armor. The Tarsians could not withstand such an onslaught; forced back by the thrusts and spears and by the missiles of the [archers] shooting from behind, they immediately turned to flight. . . . They were overwhelmed by a terrible cowardice.[6]

After driving the Tarsians from the field, the emperor settled in for a siege and as the citizens began to starve, they sued for peace. Most departed for Antioch in Syria under a Roman escort, and Nikephoros moved against the remaining cities of Muslim Cilicia, capturing all of them. With Tarsos destroyed and Melitene in imperial hands, the two most important border emirates were dismantled and the Romans possessed a clear path to Syria.

In 966 the emperor returned to the field and plundered northern Mesopotamia. Passing via Melitene, Nikephoros ransacked through the territory of the city of Amida (Diyarbakir), pillaged Dara, Nisibis, and Mayyafarakin (today Silvan in eastern Turkey), then turned south along the Euphrates River, arriving at the Syrian city of Membij, not far west of the river, in October. The citizens of Membij spared their city by handing over a holy tile with a miraculous image of Christ's face on it. The Byzantines then turned south toward Aleppo, where Sayf ad-Dawla resided. Sayf offered to pay tribute to Nikephoros, but the emperor scorned the offer and instead ravaged his way toward Sayf, who fled southward. Nikephoros wasted the land along the route to Antioch, then returned to Roman territory to face the Bulgarians. In 967 Sayf ad-Dawla died and the Muslims lost a vigorous and capable defender whose effectiveness in his last years was blunted by dynastic strife and ill health. Nikephoros only returned to Syria in 968, when he once again descended into Mesopotamia, and plundered as far south as the coast of Lebanon, seizing cities and fortresses and immense plunder as he went. Antioch fell to a Roman force in October the following year and Aleppo arranged tribute during December 969 or January 970. In the deep of the chilly night of December 11 the brilliant commander John Tzimiskes crept through the imperial palace and into his sleeping uncle's bedchamber and struck him down. Phokas, who was fifty-seven years old, had overseen a dramatic overhaul of the Byzantine army, under intense discipline and with tremendous battlefield effectiveness. It was this sharp instrument that Tzimiskes turned at the throats of his neighbors and passed on to his successor, Basil II, who would accomplish the conquest of Bulgaria and push the frontier to the Danube for the first time since the days of Justinian.

The Battle of Kleidion, 1014

The empire reached its largest medieval territorial extent under Basil II, who is considered by many to have been the greatest Byzantine emperor. While the view of Basil as a perfect sovereign who was wise in counsel and indomitable in war is largely a function of his effective propaganda, his campaigns against Bulgaria led to the annexation of vast territories in the Balkans and carried Byzantium to the apex of its medieval prestige and glory. He proved to be the bane of the Bulgars, in particular, and though the statement of the historian Skylitzes that he campaigned annually against them is exaggerated, Basil vigorously pursued their subjugation. Since the seventh century, when the Bulgars first settled between the Danube and the Balkan Mountains, the Byzantines and Bulgars had fought one another for control of the region. Severe clashes were interspersed with periods of simmering peace. In 708 Justinian II suffered defeat at Bulgar hands at the first Battle of Acheloos, but Bulgar allies played a critical role in staving off the Muslim attack on Constantinople in 717–18. Although imperial forces scored several important victories throughout the eighth century, the emperors could neither dislodge the Bulgars from their homeland, nor bring them under Byzantine political domination. In 811, the major expedition of the emperor Nikephoros I, the largest in centuries, met with disaster—the Bulgars destroyed the army, killed the emperor, and mortally wounded his heir. Though periodic conflicts followed, peaceful relations between the two powers dominated the ninth century, when the Byzantines were increasingly focused on the east and the Bulgars faced Frankish expansion and threats from the steppe.

Upon his ascent to the throne, the khan Simeon (893–927) pursued hostilities with Byzantium in the hopes of becoming emperor of a unified Byzantine-Bulgar realm. In 917, at the second Battle of Acheloos (Anchialos), Simeon's forces ambushed and crushed the divided military command of Leo Phokas assisted by the fleet of Romanos Lekapenos. Simeon warred against the Romans for the rest of his reign and hostilities continued under his son and successor, Peter I (927–69), who suffered from the Byzantine-Kievan Rus' alliance negotiated by Nikephoros Phokas. The invasion of Sviatoslav, prince of Kiev culminated in heavy Bulgar defeats in 968 and 969. Under John Tzimiskes, the Byzantines drove out their former Rus' allies after their victory at the Battle of Dorostolon in the summer of 971. From this point on the Byzantines claimed rule over Bulgaria, but it would take decades of hard fighting for the empire to wear down their opponents and establish peace.

Following his suppression in 979 of the attempted usurpation of the Anatolian military magnate, Bardas Skleros, the young Basil II (he was just twenty-one at the time) sought to win his spurs against the Bulgars. Basil led a large imperial army northwest and struck Serdica (modern Sofia) and thus cut the Bulgar kingdom in half. The historian Leo the Deacon was present during the expedition in which Basil sieged Serdica for about three weeks but could accomplish nothing, allegedly due to the inexperience of his soldiers and the incompetence of the senior commanders. Clearly Basil was in large measure to blame—in all likelihood he excluded from the campaign seasoned veterans of the eastern wars who had fought for Tzimiskes a decade prior; perhaps these men had backed Bardas Skleros in his rebellion and consequently were stricken from the rolls. Whatever the case, as the army withdrew the Bulgars ambushed the Byzantines and routed them in a defile near present Ihtiman, in western Bulgaria. The imperial forces suffered heavy losses and withdrew. Little was accomplished in the war with the Bulgars since Basil, as a consequence of his internal military policies, faced renewed opposition from the Anatolian magnate families.

Only in 1001–5 could the emperor return to the theater. He made great gains, capturing Serdica in 1001 and besieging Vidin in the northwest of the kingdom at the confluence of the Sava and Danube rivers.[7] In subsequent years Basil methodically campaigned, reorganized the political landscape by establishing Byzantine administrators, and undermined Tsar Samuel (997–1014) by dislodging his followers. In 1005 the Byzantine diplomatic offensive yielded the greatest of the low-hanging fruit of Bulgaria with the handover of Dyrrachium on the Adriatic by the influential Chryselios family who had previously acknowledged the overlordship of Samuel. Basil's efforts in 1001–5 returned to imperial control the major trans-Balkan road, the ancient Via Egnatia, and provided the Byzantines a coherent strategic front on Bulgaria's southern flank.[8]

No sources detail action between 1005 and 1014, but when we next see the emperor in action, in 1014 at Kleidion, Basil faced a Bulgar army that blocked the passage of his army as it marched from the valley of the Strymon River in eastern Thrace to the valley of the Axios (Vardar). Samuel's men had built a series of ramparts that blocked the trunk road between lofty mountains that led from Thessaloniki to Niš. Basil's troops repeatedly assaulted the Bulgar earthworks, but the enemy repulsed these attacks and hurled missiles at the Byzantines from above. Basil was about to give up and depart for Roman territory when Nikephoros Xiphias, Basil's senior commander and active campaigner with the emperor since 1001, hatched a plan: Basil's forces would continue to attack the Bulgar wooden palisades while he picked infantry and led these troops to the south. Xiphias's men pushed

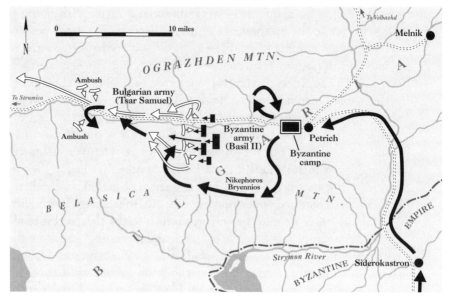

Fig. 7.5. The Battle of Kleidion, 1014.

through the heavily wooded mountains and, via unknown trackways made their way to the Bulgar rear (fig. 7.5). On July 29, Xiphias fell upon the Bulgars from the heights behind them. Samuel's men broke and fled as the Byzantines dismantled the makeshift fortifications. A vast number of Bulgars, said by contemporary sources to number as many as 15,000, were taken prisoner. The historian Skylitzes states that the emperor blinded these men and sent them back to Samuel with one-eyed leaders for each hundred men.[9] Blinding was a treatment reserved for rebellious subjects, and this incident, apocryphal or not, shows Basil's determination to bring to heel the Bulgar state and reflects the view of the emperor and those who later retold the story: the lands from Thrace to the Danube belonged to the empire. Although the final annexation of Bulgaria came in 1018 only after four years' hard campaigning, the incorporation of the Bulgar realm within Byzantium was given its final impetus by the victory at Kleidion.

THE BATTLE OF SEMLIN, 1167

Manuel I Komnenos (1143–80) preserved a similar lion's image as his predecessor. Like Basil II, he was an indefatigable soldier and statesman who energetically rose to meet every challenge to his empire. These were numerous and came from all quarters. Manuel had to deal not only with the renewed Norman threat from Sicily and various Balkan powers in the west, but the arrival of the Second Crusade (1145-49) as well. Manuel has been blamed on more than one occasion, unjustly, for the stupendous failure of the Crusade, which included the luminous princes of the Europe, including Holy Roman Emperor Conrad II (1138-52) and Louis VII of France (1137-80). The Second Crusade was launched in response to the fall of the most exposed crusader enclave in Frankish Outremer, the county of Edessa that had been established by the crusader adventurer Baldwin of Boulogne in 1098 but which fell in 1144 to the forces of Imad al-Din Zengi (1127-46), atebeg of Mosul and the main protagonist in the counter crusade launched by Muslim forces in Syria. Manuel also faced encroachment in the east by the Seljuk sultanate of Rum, the political entity that thrived on the Anatolian plateau in the old heartlands of former Byzantine Asia Minor, feasting on the carcass of the old Byzantine heartland following the civil wars that rived the empire following the Battle of Mantzikert in 1071. No fewer than five usurpers or warlords had subsequently challenged Michael VII (1071-78), either directly or by carving out independent petty states from the trunk of former imperial lands, greatly eroding the strategic position of the empire and allowing the Turks to settle extensively across the plateau.

In 1144 Manuel contained the fractious prince of Antioch, Raymond of Toulouse (1136-49), who had to acknowledge Byzantine overlordship and give up claims to Cilicia in the face of mounting danger from Zengi. The young emperor skillfully played his hand, exercising a show of force to awe the Antiochian Franks while avoiding direct confrontation with Zengi, who was a useful lever against the Franks in the east. With his hands free, Manuel turned his forces against the Sultanate of Rum, Masud (1116-56); this expedition defeated the Seljuks at Akroinon (Afyon) and pressed on to plunder the environs of Masud's capital of Konya. Having made a show of his zeal against the infidel, Manuel signed a treaty and hurried to receive the western emperor Conrad and his 20,000 Germans. Despite Manuel's relationship with Conrad (he was married to Conrad's sister-in-law Bertha of Salzburg), Byzantine-German dealings were tense. The emperor had the German army ferried across the Bosphoros as quickly as possible. On the dusty high plains of Anatolia, the two German columns met separate but similar fates, being ambushed and routed with heavy losses along the route to Konya.

In the meantime, the Norman Roger II of Sicily (1130–54) had taken advantage of the pandemonium of the Second Crusade to seize Corfu and pillage the mainland cities of Thebes and Corinth where the imperial silk works were plundered and their Jewish weavers removed to Sicily. In 1148 the emperor raised a powerful army comprised of the combined forces of the eastern and western tagmas and foreign mercenaries, as well as a combined Byzantine and Venetian fleet. The historian Choniates numbers this force in the tens of thousands; among them the historian Kinnamos numbered five hundred triremes and one thousand horse transports and supply ships.[10] Before the emperor could cross to Corfu he had to deal with a Cuman (the Cumans were Turks of the Kipchak tribal confederacy) raid across the Danube. Since the loss of Asia Minor, Greek holdings south of the Danube formed the economic core of the state and every threat from the north had to be dealt with swiftly. Late in 1148 the emperor unleashed his attack against the city of Kerkyra, on Corfu, and penned the Norman garrison in the citadel, which he sieged. The attempts on the citadel by Byzantines and their Venetian allies, who fought from siege towers erected on ships, failed when the siege ladders broke under the weight of the troops and plunged them into the sea. The Roman general, Stephanos Kontostephanos, died when the defenders cast a particularly well-aimed trebuchet round and smashed the siege engine he was supervising.

Roger II sent his admiral, George, against Thrace and Constantinople and a portion of the Byzantine squadron pursued the Sicilian vessels, preventing them from doing much damage to the rich suburbs of the capital. Roger had also forged an alliance with the Germans, Serbs, and Hungarians, who were aware that the emperor's forces were tied down in the Ionian Islands. Roger's diplomacy served the interest of Byzantium's neighbors, who chafed under the domination of their powerful neighbor and sought to expand their territories at the expense of the Romans.

By 1149, Manuel's alliance with Conrad II checked Roger II in Italy, where the German emperor had an interest in maintaining a presence and support for the papacy, which was generally opposed to Sicilian ambitions. The emperor thus momentarily abandoned his efforts against the Sicilians and returned to the Balkans, leading a campaign against the župan (count) of Serbia, Uroš II (1145–62), who was supported by Hungary. Manuel attacked Ražanj, 55 kilometers northeast of Niš and pillaged the environs. The emperor took numerous captives and continued his raid in force through the Nišava and Morava valleys. The Serbs defeated a stay-behind detachment and Manuel returned the following year, when his forces advanced up the Drina River where they encountered a Hungarian force allied with the Serbs. This turned out to be the vanguard of a much larger Hungarian army that intended to link up with Uroš Serbs and surround Manuel. The Hungarians and Serbs abandoned the river crossing at the sight of the imperial banner and Manuel personally led the charge that broke their formations—Kinnamos reported the wild chase in which the emperor in his zeal to capture the župan outstripped his supporting troops and fought a series of hand-to-hand engagements with the Hungarians. The Hungarian commander Bagan landed a sword blow across the emperor's cheek, but Manuel's heavy chain-mail mask deflected the blow, and Manuel cut off the Hungarian's hand and took him prisoner.[11] Not long after the battle on the Drina, Uroš II sued for peace and became a vassal of Manuel.

In 1162, the death of King Géza II (1141–62) presented the opportunity for Manuel to interfere in his neighbor's realm. After a failed attempt to install an uncle of the reigning monarch, King Stephen III (1162–73), on the throne, the emperor reached a compromise whereby Géza's youngest son Béla would live at the court in Constantinople and succeed Stephen as king. Béla married one of Manuel's daughters, solidifying a Byzantine dynastic alliance. But Stephen continued to resist Byzantium in the Balkans, allying with the Holy Roman Empire under Frederick I Barbarossa (1155–90), Serbia, and the Russian principalities of Gallicia and Kiev. In violation of the treaty, Stephen designated his own son as his successor. In 1164, Stephen III and Duke Vladislav II of Bohemia marched to confront Manuel, who was stationed with his army on the Danube. Stephen agreed to cede to the empire the rich region of Syrmia, which was a family holding of Prince Béla, in exchange for the empire withdrawing its support for Stephen III's uncle, also named Stephen, who had been fighting with Byzantine assistance to claim the throne. Later in the year, Stephen III seized Sirmium, a blatant act of war against the empire.[12]

Manuel dislodged Frederick I Barbarossa from his Hungarian alliance, and pulled onto his side the Russian principality of Kiev, as well as Venice. Stephen's forces busied themselves with the siege of Zeugminon (part of modern Belgrade, Serbia), which they seized by April 1165. Manuel led his forces northward in June 1165 and laid siege to Zeugminon. Manuel's troops stormed the city on their third attempt and plundered the place mercilessly. In the meantime, Manuel's general John Doukas had cut through Serbia and subdued the coastal cities and fortresses of Dalmatia, which Stephen III had also ceded as part of Béla's holdings. In 1166 the Hungarians defeated Byzantine forces in Dalmatia and at Sirmium.

The Battle of Sirmium, July 8, 1167

Manuel responded with the dispatch of his nephew, Andronikos Kontostephanos at the head of a strong Roman army, about one-third of which were mercenaries or allied foreigners. Roman scouts captured a Hungarian who revealed that the enemy force numbered 15,000 knights, bowmen, and light infantry.[13] The Byzantine army was probably about equal in numerical strength. Kontostephanos drew up his marching order with Cuman and Turkish horse archers and a handful of western knights in the vanguard. Behind came three divisions of Byzantine regular cavalry and kataphraktoi, followed by units of allied Turkish and western mercenary cavalry. The last line comprised a mixed formation of Roman infantry and archers alongside a battalion of armored Turks, presumably also infantry.

Dénes, count of Bács, commanded the combined Hungarian-German force. Dénes drew up his mailed knights in the front, with infantry support to the rear (fig. 7.6). The historian Choniates noted that the Hungarian battle line was drawn up in a single, dense mass, in the shape of a tower; the cavalry fronted this deep formation.[14] The Hungarian lancers presented an awesome sight—their horses wore frontlets and breastplates (these must have been padded or mail, since plate horse armor was uncommon in Europe prior to 1250) and carried riders mailed from head to foot. In short the Hungarian forces featured the best of modern western arms and equipment. They faced a lighter Byzantine force arrayed with the Turk and Cuman horse archers in the

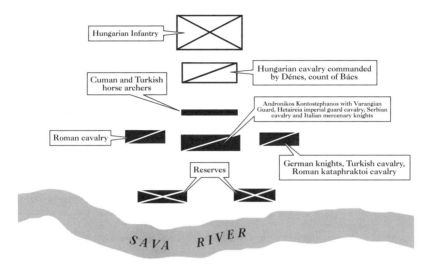

Fig. 7.6. The Battle of Sirmium, disposition of forces.

front of the formation. Behind, Andronikos divided his army into three divisions. On the left he stationed the regular Roman cavalry. In the center stood Andronikos, commanding elements of the Varangian Guard, Hetaireia imperial guard cavalry, Serbians, probably mailed cavalry, and Italian mercenary knights. The Roman right consisted of the third element of the line of march, with German mercenary knights and Turkish cavalry and Roman kataphraktoi cavalry. Behind the right and left wings of the army Andronikos stationed supporting troops, which presumably were mainly regular cavalry and infantry flank guards and outflankers who could also support the wings when pressured. That two of these supporting battalions were cavalry seems to be indicated by how the battle unfolded.

Andronikos opened the battle by sending ahead the Turk and Cuman horse archers and presumably the light infantry as well (fig. 7.7). They were instructed to send an arrow storm into the Hungarian cavalry and thus break up the formation. In the face of a Hungarian charge Andronikos instructed them to fan out to left and right and thus sweep to the side of the Byzantine force. The Byzantine left broke in the face of the Hungarian charge and fled toward the river Sava, but two battalions stood fast—these were likely the flank guards stationed behind the left wing. Dénes led a general charge into the Byzantine

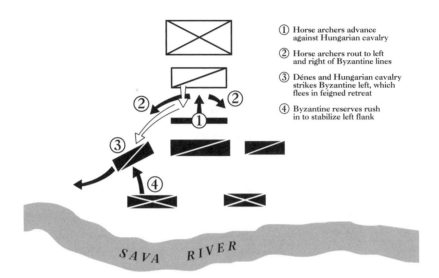

① Horse archers advance
   against Hungarian cavalry

② Horse archers rout to left
   and right of Byzantine lines

③ Dénes and Hungarian cavalry
   strikes Byzantine left, which
   flees in feigned retreat

④ Byzantine reserves rush
   in to stabilize left flank

Fig. 7.7. The Battle of Sirmium, phase 1.

center, hoping to kill Andronikos; those in the center of the Roman
formation sustained the heavy cavalry charge. The Byzantine right
attacked the flank of the Hungarian cavalry formation, Andronikos's
men in the center of the line drew their iron maces and pressed forward
for close combat, and the "routed" Byzantine left that had feigned flight
returned to strike the Hungarian right flank (fig. 7.8). This envelopment broke the Hungarians, and thousands perished or were captured
in the ensuing rout. Kinnamos reported that 2,000 cuirasses were taken
from the dead, and countless shields, helmets, and swords came into
Roman hands from the great number of fallen. The Battle of Sirmium
was the greatest victory of Manuel's reign; it demonstrated that tactical
skill and great discipline were still to be found in the armies of the
Komnenoi, as were commanders who were able to conceive and execute
complicated battlefield maneuvers. As a result of Sirmium, Hungary
became a client, and upon the death of Stephen III in 1172 Manuel
easily installed his protégé Béla on the Hungarian throne, which
remained at peace with the empire until 1180.

The campaigns of Manuel against Hungary that culminated in the
Battle of Sirmium demonstrate that, when properly led, the Byzantine
army remained the finest in eastern Europe, capable of defeating heav-

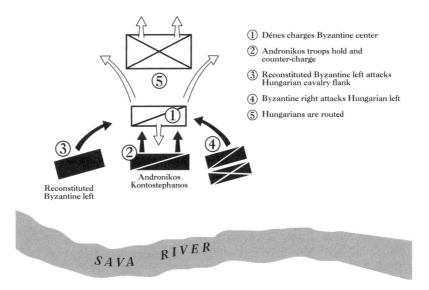

Fig. 7.8. The Battle of Sirmium, phase 2.

ily armed and armored western knights. But these actions also show that the strategic situation of Byzantium had deteriorated significantly—with the coalescence of larger, more organized, and economically vibrant states on all sides, the empire faced extreme challenges to its territorial integrity. While Belisarios's decisive victory over the Vandals a half millennium in the past had brought Africa under imperial control and established a peace that was largely maintained for a century, the "decisive" victory of Manuel at Sirmium delivered only twenty years of peace. In light of the capabilities of his enemies, it is small wonder that Manuel generally preferred attritive campaigns and small-war actions that wore down his foes and made enemy aggression too costly for them, rather than risking his limited forces in all-or-nothing engagements on the battlefield. In this sense, his failures are more telling than his numerous minor successes, since the emperor removed neither Sicily nor Hungary nor the Seljuks from their menacing positions along the frontiers. Instead, Manuel had to settle for a largely defensive posture in the territory he inherited from his father John.

Siege Warfare

The most famous sieges in Byzantine history were defensive rather than offensive operations. Over its millennial existence as capital of the Byzantine state, Constantinople endured dozens of sieges; only two, the Fourth Crusade of 1204 and the Ottoman siege of 1453, were successful in breaching the massive defenses of the capital, which were established in the fifth century to counter the Hun threat and to expand the defended area of the city. The massive land walls cut the peninsula of the old city of Byzantion from the Golden Horn in the north to the Sea of Marmora in the south, a distance of about 6 kilometers (just under 4 miles); the curtains, whose remains are visible today, are largely the work of the early fifth century; they were completed in nine years, between 404–5 and 413. In 448 an earthquake leveled much of the defenses and exposed the city to attack by Attila the Hun, whose forces bore down on the capital. The praetorian prefect Constantine supervised a Herculean refortification effort that employed thousands of workmen, who repaired or rebuilt long stretches of the wall and fifty-seven damaged towers in just sixty days. The land walls of Anthemios included a 20 meters wide moat up to 10 feet deep whose inner side was crowned by a crenelated parapet 1.5 meters high. A terrace 20 meters wide separated the parapet from the outer wall. The outer wall was constructed of limestone ashlars broken by bands of bricks, each course bonded to a rubble and mortar core, 2 meters thick at its foundations, and rising to a height of about 9 meters; along its length stood more than seventy loop or squared towers (fig. 7.9), each rising to a height of about 14 meters. A courtyard 20 meters across separated the outer from the inner wall. Courses of well-cut limestone ashlars broken by bands of brick that helped to protect the stone from the expansion and contraction caused by weather and earthquakes, formed the shell of the 4.5–6 meters thick rubble-cored wall. The inner wall rose to a height of 12 meters; it was crowned by battlements and strengthened by ninety-six massive towers along its length. The breadth of the four-layer defenses was more than 225 feet, making it nearly impossible for enemies to use engines or mine the walls. The walls of Constantinople thus represented the pinnacle of late Roman defensive engineering and a defensive masterpiece.

The Avar-Sasanian siege of 626 was remembered by the defenders of the city in apocalyptic terms, with divine intervention on the part of the Virgin Mary and the saints saving the capital, whose defense was directed by the Patriarch Sergios. The Byzantines defeated a series of attacks on Constantinople from 667 to 673 launched by Mu'awiya, the governor of Syria; here more worldly defenses secured the safety of the citizens. By 671 at the latest, the Byzantines had developed "Greek fire," the enigmatic substance that burned on water (see Chapter 7) and equipped dromons (light warships with a single bank of oars) with the projection tubes and cooking materials needed to prepare and cast the substance. According to the chronicler Theophanes (d. 817–18), the Romans used Greek fire to burn the ships and crews in 672, and by 673 the enemy fleet withdrew.[15]

Fig. 7.9. An isometric drawing of one of the massive squared towers built along the length of the wall surrounding Contantinople's side facing the land.

From Muslim quarters, the greatest challenge to the empire and the city came with the sustained assaults across the years 717–718, when internal upheavals in the empire complicated the defensive efforts. Leo, the strategos of the Anatolikon theme, usurped power in 717. In 716, the Muslim army led by Maslama, the brother of the caliph Sulayman, traversed Asia Minor and sacked a number of cities and forts on its route of march. The Muslim force camped at Abydos on the Hellespont and waited for Leo to turn over the city, which he refused to do. The Arabs crossed over to the Thracian side of the straits and dug a trench the length of the peninsula and behind it erected a dry stone wall. The massive Arab force was there to stay. Inside the city, it is doubtful that Leo had more than 15,000 men at his disposal, given how depleted the army had become and the practicalities of supplying and billeting any force larger than this.

The Arab fleet arrived in September 717—Theophanes states it was a massive fleet of 1,800 vessels of all kinds—but as they passed through the straits, Leo unleashed the Greek fire from his galleys on the large transports and sent many to the bottom.[16] The naval confrontation cost the Arabs considerable men and the loss of vital supplies. The winter of 717 was bitter and deep; the invaders lost thousands of camels, pack mules, and cavalry horses. In the spring two large Arab relief fleets bearing corn, weapons, and other supplies arrived, one from Egypt of 400 vessels, and a second from North Africa comprised of 360 ships. These large fleets feared to approach the capital due to the Greek fire ships, and they anchored on the Asian side of the straits in a sheltered bay. When the emperor learned of their location, he dispatched dromons and biremes with Greek fire siphons against them and destroyed them. The failure to resupply the besieging land army was devastating, but the Bulgar allies of the empire, who hemmed in the Muslims in Thrace and prevented their foraging, were the death blow. The field forces of the caliphate starved in their encampment, eating their pack animals and suffering from the disease that inevitably descended on the malnourished. A Bulgar attack in force killed thousands. On August 15, 718, a year after their siege began, the defeated Muslims embarked on their transports and sailed through the straits. Most of the ships were scattered or destroyed in a series of storms in the Aegean. The capital and the empire were saved.

Since Byzantium was on the defensive during most of its history, offensive siege operations were less common than defensive engagements. Offensive sieges were always important components of strategy, designed to weaken enemy strongpoints, capture people or plunder, or permanently recover territory. Especially from the later ninth century, when the empire was on the offensive first to regain lost territories from the Arabs and then later across multiple fronts to recover territories lost to the Hungarians, Turks, Arabs, and Bulgarians, the Byzantines frequently besieged cities and fortresses. With their development of the counterweight trebuchet, Roman capabilities to break cities reached their pinnacle.

A momentous event in the revival of imperial military fortunes was the capture of the capital and heart of the raiding emirate of Crete by Nikephoros Phokas, who was domestikos ton scholon during the reigns of Romanos I Lekapenos (920–44), Constantine VII (945–59), and Romanos II (959–63). Crete had fallen into Arab hands around 824, when Andalusian Arab refugees attacked and settled the island under their leader Abu Hafs. They made their capital Chandax (modern Heraklion), from whence they raided and engaged in piracy throughout the Aegean and eastern Mediterranean. The island, astride the major communications routes of the empire, posed a major threat to Byzantium's shipping and the Aegean isles. Unsurprisingly the empire struggled mightily to drive out the Muslims. Michael II (820–29) launched two attacks against the Cretans in 825–26. Both invasions met with defeat. Again in 866 the Muslims destroyed another sizable imperial expedition. In 911 a major fleet was prepared, consisting of 177 warships carrying 5,937 soldiers. In 949, the empire equipped a fleet of 128 vessels and 4,186 men; it too ended in failure. Romanos II (959–63) appointed Nikephoros Phokas as domestikos ton scholon of the east to assault Crete once more. Our sources do not record the invasion force size but likely it was similar to the earlier attempts of 911 and 949, thus around 5,000 men and over 150 warships. On July 13, 960, Nikephoros landed at Almyros, not far west of Chandax, and took the enemy by surprise.[17] Leo the Deacon provides an account of the landing of the Byzantine army on Crete in which the transports, provided with ramps, permitted the swift disgorgement of fully armed men who immediately formed three closely ordered detachments, surprising the Cretans.[18] The Romans drove them from the beach after a short, sharp encounter. However, the majority of sources make no mention of this fight, which in all likelihood occurred a day or two after the landing. An uncontested landing is more likely— such surprise was vital to Byzantine chances for success in avoiding a risky sea engagement or an opposed landing, as prior engagements had shown. Given the network of spies maintained by the Muslims, the frequency of shipping, and the fast spread of news, keeping secret the equipping and target of such a large flotilla was another impressive feat. In all likelihood, disinformation about the target for the expedition (possibly suggesting the Levantine coast) and the knowledge of past Byzantine failures may have been enough to convince the Cretan Muslims that they had nothing to fear.

Phokas's men apparently met scant resistance—there was probably a skirmish not long after his forces disembarked, and within three days he had created a fortified camp. In the face of the powerful Byzantine fleet and its fireships, the Muslim navy apparently withdrew. Leo the Deacon mentions a detachment under the Thrakesian theme commander Pastilas, who led his army on a foraging expedition in the countryside. Pastilas's men lost discipline: after they plundered and got drunk on local wine, an Arab force ambushed them and inflicted heavy losses. Pastilas himself fought valiantly, even after his horse was killed under him, but his death in the fray caused his men to panic and flee.[19]

Nikephoros entrenched his forces around Chandax. The city had a high wall of packed earth and a double moat that rendered attack difficult. The Roman general therefore constructed a palisade between the city and the sea and cut it off from any possibility of maritime resupply. The Byzantine fleet patrolled the coastal waters, wary of a Muslim relief force from one of the major Mediterranean powers, Syria, Egypt, or North Africa. Although 'Abd al-Aziz, the emir of Crete, sent calls for help to rulers throughout the Mediterranean, no Arab reinforcements arrived. Phokas sent strong detachments around the island to subdue the numerous fortresses and cities and these missions proved successful. In the meantime, Leo the Deacon reports a night battle between Phokas and Muslim forces on the island but this is not confirmed by other sources. According to Leo's account, local Christians informed the domestikos of a large enemy force lurking nearby that intended a surprise attack on the besieging Romans. Phokas led his troops on a night march and, when he located the enemy, had his soldiers sleep through the day, then at night he surrounded the hilltop on which the Muslims were encamped and annihilated them; he ordered his men to display some of the severed heads of the fallen before the battlements and for others to be cast over the walls with trebuchets.[20] By the end of 960 Chandax was isolated and most of the island was under Roman control. Nikephoros had launched several frontal assaults, supported by traction trebuchet bombardments, but these direct attacks failed. The Byzantines settled down for a long siege that lasted throughout the autumn of 960 and into the winter of 960–61.

The winter of 960–61 was savage. Both the besiegers and besieged suffered terribly from the cold and from lack of provisions. There seems to have been a dearth of supplies within the empire, and the stormy weather made seaborne resupply of the imperial army difficult. Phokas worked hard to bolster his men's morale and requested additional provisions from Constantinople—despite the winter the ships arrived with supplies from the capital. Just as prescribed in the military handbooks, Phokas began to mine the walls of Chandax.[21] By the night of March 6, 961, a large section had been compromised and the wooden props were fired, probably at dawn on March 7, when the Byzantine troops stormed through the gaping holes in the circuit. Fierce street fighting broke out, and the Byzantines massacred the Muslim inhabitants of the city until Phokas finally got his troops under control and ended the slaughter.[22]

Over the course of his reign the emperor John II Komnenos campaigned with a large siege train that included trebuchets, and we see his armies in city-taking operations throughout the east. Throughout the 1130s the Armenian Prince Leo, whose people had moved into Cilicia in what is today southeastern Mediterranean Turkey, seized imperial holdings there. The rich Cilician plain and its cities remained a cornerstone of Byzantine strategy, viewed as key for eastern communications with Antioch, over which the empire claimed lordship, and with the Levantine seaboard to the south. In 1136–37 Leo threatened Seleukia, an important imperial port, and John II responded with a large-scale counterattack. In 1137 the emperor crossed the Anatolian plateau and descended through the Cilician Gates, seizing Adana and Tarsos. John then moved east against Anazarbos, which was once more a strongly fortified and flourishing city. Choniates describes the place as having a high citadel on a bluff (the remains of which one can see today) and a strong curtain wall protected by artillery. John dispatched two battalions of Turkish mercenaries to test the Armenian defenders, who sallied to meet them and forced the Turks to withdraw. Several taxiarchs of imperial troops rushed forward to support the Turkish vanguard; together they drove the Armenians inside the walls. The Romans then invested the city, erecting their huge stone-throwing machines behind wooden lattice works. The Armenian defenders conducted a stubborn defense, using traction trebuchets mounted on the walls to cast stone and red-hot iron pellets at the Roman besiegers. An Armenian sortie burned the Roman heavy artillery.

John immediately ordered the engines repaired and surrounded their positions with earthworks and clay bricks. The counterweight machines could operate from behind these dugouts, while the Armenian red-hot iron pellets struck the defenses harmlessly. The empire's trebuchets smashed the walls while the defenders despaired of relief and, as the breaches across the curtain wall grew, the Armenians surrendered. After the fall of Anazarbos, the emperor led his forces to the fortress town of Baka (unlocalized), a citadel perched on a high bluff and garrisoned by a strong Armenian force commanded by a certain Constantine. John first attempted to negotiate surrender, but after being rebuffed, the emperor again set his machines to work. The scene of initial resistance then the destruction of the defensive works by Roman artillery was repeated throughout John's campaign into Mesopotamia and northern Syria, where he reduced a number of Muslim fortresses and cities and then, after a two-year campaign, retired to his own territory. Since Nikephoros II Phokas's day nearly two centuries prior, when the reduction of an impressive defensive work using artillery was unheard of, Byzantine siege tactics had changed considerably. Now, artillery bombardment inevitably brought about surrender or a successful assault, since the trebuchet "city breakers" rendered a decisive advantage to the besiegers.

EIGHT

THE BYZANTINE ART OF WAR

The Byzantine Empire's existence spanned more than a millennium from the establishment of the new capital, Constantinople, in the east until its final capture by the Ottoman Turks on May 29, 1453. Over the course of its history, the empire fought innumerable wars against a host of different enemies who sought to destroy, plunder, or settle within its borders. Though the Byzantines suffered numerous defeats, their military record is one of the greatest in European and Asian history, maintaining the security of a state that endured continuous challenges to its territory and existence. The massive shock of the Persian conquests of the seventh century, followed by the miraculous imperial recovery led by the emperor Heraclius, who lived to see his gains unravel at the hands of the Muslim enemy, were contests similar to those that had destroyed the western Roman Empire. Despite the defeats and the loss of the greater share of their population, territory, and fiscal resources, the Romans in the eastern Mediterranean fought on for another seven centuries—a feat unparalleled in the military annals of western Eurasia and Europe.

STRENGTHS

The strengths of the empire's military apparatus and fighting men were many. A system of discipline and drill inherited from Rome waxed and waned throughout the history of the Byzantine state. On balance, however, the cultural values of relying on a core of professional soldiers, trained under officers who themselves were usually the product of the military institutions in which they served, meant that lessons from the battlefield could be absorbed and learned from. Numerous defeats show that individual commanders and armies and their execution of strategy and tactics often did not meet the ideals expressed in the military handbooks, yet aspects of the ideal armies based on expert leadership, caution, and flexibility were achieved to varying degrees. As the handbooks repeatedly stress, even when the outcome of battle seemed to favor the Romans, many factors could undermine the effort and steal victory from them. They had learned these lessons through numerous failures and military breakdowns on fields stained with Roman blood from Adrianople to Yarmuk—engagements where the Romans probably outnumbered and outclassed their enemy, but nonetheless suffered tremendous defeats. The caution instilled by these lessons, and Roman knowledge of their own forces' limits and the extreme difficulty of replacing skilled fighting men, shaped the behavior of most commanders. The Byzantines learned early that, deprived of the resources of the unified Roman Mediterranean, they would often be outnumbered. They therefore adapted to the realities of the military parity or superiority of their enemies. Conservation of forces became a central pillar of Byzantine military doctrine, one that proved to be a key to their tremendous endurance in warfare and critical to the survival of Byzantine civilization.

The high point of military culture, when the Byzantine state was at its most bellicose and militarily successful, occurred during the Cappadocian interlude, when powerful warlords with deep family connections and interests among the border-warrior elites of the eastern frontiers dominated politics: Romanos I, Nikephoros II Phokas, and John Tzimiskes. Nikephoros was truly a revolutionary figure, virtually unknown today, who reshaped the field army into a powerful offensive force without peer in the Mediterranean world. The principles of Byzantine warfare, articulated as early as the sixth century in the *Strategikon* and elaborated and refined against the Muslim foes in the east, demanded patience and indirect confrontation. The defensive depth of the empire, with its frontiers girded by mountainous terrain and the sea, allowed the Byzantine army to harry and wear down determined enemy forces; Roman methods of harassment, disruption of supply, and containment made it difficult for invaders to safely occupy conquered territory. The enduring Byzantine belief in the empire as a state ordained and supported by the Christian God allowed them to absorb shocking defeats that would have broken lesser peoples; it is a testament to the core Byzantine identity that major reverses suffered at the hands of the Arabs, Turks, and Normans did not lead to complete collapse. The Byzantines instead overcame these failures. The Roman abilities to adapt, to learn from the enemy, and to modify their tactics were fundamental to their success. The principles of Byzantine warfare grew from experience gleaned over centuries of confrontation and the confidence that, while the empire was eternal and warfare would always dog the state, no enemy was ordained by God to overthrow them. Only after the fall of Constantinople in 1204 to Christian crusaders was this unshakable faith in Byzantine superiority and destiny eroded. The survival of the Christian Roman Empire as a political and cultural entity over more than a thousand-year span bears ample testimony to the effectiveness of Byzantine strategy and tactics.

WEAKNESSES

In many ways the weaknesses of the Byzantine military were corollaries of its strengths. While the size and topography of the empire, especially the vast area and inhospitable terrain of much of the Anatolian plateau, favored the Roman state, its position astride the meeting point of Europe and Asia rendered it vulnerable to attack from the Eurasian steppe to the north. From the seventh century the Muslim Arab caliphate, animated by a sense of religious destiny unmatched outside of Constantinople, proved a more dangerous enemy than the Sasanians had ever posed, and as Europe awoke from the Dark Ages at the end of the tenth century, the new kingdoms that coalesced around the Mediterranean sometimes gazed upon the riches and opulence of their Christian neighbors with suspicious and greedy eyes. Access to trade routes and the wealth of the east drew many western powers into the Byzantine world, first as adventurers and then as conquerors. As wealth, militarization, and Catholic Christian bigotry increased among the western powers and found their perfect embodiment in the Normans and their successors, the Byzantines found their dominant place in the Balkans and Italy undercut. In the pre-modern era, no state save perhaps China had to sustain conflicts on three frontiers simultaneously, yet this is where the Roman state found itself in the eleventh and twelfth centuries, when steppe peoples, the Catholics of Hungary and Norman Italy, and the Muslim Turks to the east all posed grave challenges to an increasingly beleaguered empire.

Modern critics have been dismissive of obvious Byzantine weaknesses—after Basil II their ability to conduct crushing offensive operations and deliver a knockout blow to opponents when it was most needed was sorely lacking. The Roman predilection for defense and attrition often precluded the types of commanders and soldiers who could meet the challenge of decisive battle. In the eleventh century the Byzantine field army suffered some of its most crippling defeats—at Mantzikert in 1071 and only a decade later against the Normans at Dyrrachium; these battles exposed Roman weaknesses of command and control, but they also destroyed much of the old tagmatic armies and led to an increasing reliance on foreign professionals.

Ironically, while adaptation to the exigencies of warfare was a Byzantine hallmark, their greatest military failures were direct results of an inability to adapt to the new strategic realities of the Mediterranean world. While it would be wrong to see the Norman knight in the revolutionary light that he is often cast, the western mounted warrior was a new phenomenon in eastern warfare and much of his initial success was due to its novelty. The most catastrophic Roman military failing prior to the fall of the empire, the siege of Constantinople in 1204, was dealt by westerners. Not unlike their modern descendants, the Byzantines built their armies to fight the greatest threat; for centuries this had arisen in the steppe lands north of the Danube and the Muslim east. Heavily equipped cavalry had always been a part of Byzantine warfare, but never a dominant one, and the failure to match western knights with equally impressive regiments of kataphraktoi on the scale of their enemies denied the Byzantines the opportunity to end the threat posed by westerners from the eleventh century onward.

Leadership was another area of weakness. In the eleventh century, deepening divisions among the military and civilian aristocracies exposed fractures in society whose existence hindered the effective governance and martialing of resources in a state that had to be on a constant footing for war. The desertion of prominent Byzantine aristocrats to the Normans of Robert Guiscard and Bohemund exposed rifts in elite society on which the state depended and which were never healed, even though the Komnenoi dynasty was able to quell these for more than a century. The increasing fractiousness of the military aristocracy required a vigorous, powerful, and deft ruler at the helm at all times. Threats to the empire from within and without necessitated later Byzantine emperors be superior war leaders who campaigned in person from one end of the empire to another and dealt with the complicated web of foreign and domestic politics in which the empire was embroiled. This need for central control embodied in the person of the emperor developed to the detriment of senior officers, who rarely fought wars with the full confidence and resources of the state in the manner of Belisarios or Nikephoros II Phokas. When Manuel I Komnenos died in 1180 and left his minor son on the throne, no one emerged with the late emperor's talents or energy and the dynasty perished.

WHY DID THE EMPIRE FALL?

After it survived the onslaught of innumerable foes for a thousand years, the Byzantine Empire's fall in 1453 still surprises today. Unlike the earlier fall of the Roman Empire, which has spawned numerous books and an endless number of explanatory theories, the end of Byzantium is today relatively unexplored. Some factors are evident in the decline and fall of the state, namely the rise of a hereditary aristocracy and their takeover of the state and the levers of wealth. Land ownership and upward mobility were constrained and the peasantry largely impoverished during the era of the Komnenoi and after. Earlier scholars have erred in propagating the myth of the robust and happy Byzantine peasantry in earlier eras who formed the backbone of the empire. The truth is that peasants, no matter how well off, were incapable of evading taxation and thwarting the state in the way that aristocrats could. The loss of circulating wealth and the concentration of more and more land into the hands of the powerful starved the state of precious resources and access to manpower it needed to perpetuate itself.

I have noted above that, militarily, the Byzantine high command failed to meet the crusader threat of 1204 that ruined the fortunes of the empire and ensured its destruction. In this moment of crisis, no capable war leader emerged as the empire had produced on countless occasions in the past. This, too, can be partly laid at the feet of the Komnenoi, whose consolidation of power and need for aristocratic support meant fewer chances for advancement from outside this cadre; military men of real ability from humble backgrounds no doubt had limited opportunities under this system.

In tactical terms, the Byzantines suffered from a decline in the quality of local troops. The emergency conditions at the start of Alexios's rule, in which the heavy attrition of the imperial field armies led to reliance on foreign mercenaries, became a permanent feature later in his reign. The main problem with using foreign mercenaries was not their reliability (they generally could be counted on as much as locals) but their cost. Without the Greek professionals to staff the permanent rank-and-file core of the imperial field forces, the pillars of the Byzantine art of war became unsustainable. The loss of local forces meant the disruption of strategy and training regimens. Of course local troops continued to serve in number, but the loss of intensive drill, stamina, and flexibility among local forces coincided with the increased reliance on easily recruited foreign professionals. These men, while capable soldiers, could not be molded into Byzantine soldiers like those who served under Nikephoros II Phokas. By the time the crusaders arrived—jealous of Greek wealth, suspicious of Greek religion and culture, and convinced their mission was just—the Byzantines possessed neither the commander on the spot nor the well-drilled armies of past generations.

When the forces of the Fourth Crusade sacked Constantinople, the nerve center of the empire was ruptured. The parasitical state of the Latin Empire of Constantinople that the Franks formed on the carcass of most former Byzantine lands leached much of the vigor from the Greek elite. The Greek successor states that formed around the Latin Empire were more Greek than Byzantine—led by bickering, petty dynasts who were unable to recover the economic control of the state, nor could they repair the military institutions that were irretrievably broken. The seeds of the fall of the empire in 1453 were therefore sown much earlier, in the social, economic, and military mistakes of the twelfth and thirteenth centuries.

Byzantine Contributions to Warfare

In his classic study of the history of warfare in support of his theory of the indirect approach, military analyst Liddell Hart focused on the battles of Belisarios and Narses in the Gothic Wars. In these campaigns, he saw the articulation of the defensive-offensive strategy that would predominate in the Byzantine military approach throughout its history. Liddell Hart viewed Belisarios's and Narses's cautious method (in which the Byzantines tested opponents, exposed their weaknesses, and then acted decisively to exploit those failings) as early manifestations of the "indirect approach."[1] If one subscribes to his view that frontal assaults were generally bound to fail and in order to succeed other means of attack were required, then from the preceding pages it should be obvious that the Byzantines utilized on numerous occasions this kind of strategy. By understanding their enemy's deficiencies, medieval Roman commanders relied on maneuver to time their engagements with superior foes and were often able to select the battleground where large-scale encounters took place.[2] Fuller, in his analysis of decisive battles in history, saw the generalship of both Belisarios at Tricamarum and Narses at Taginae as moments of Roman brilliance, but followed Gibbon and other early modern historians' grim assessment of Byzantine life by asserting that Italy and Africa would have been better off without Justinian's military intervention. Fuller included the siege of Constantinople of 717–18 among his studies of decisive battles in world history which, combined with the victory of the Frankish leader Charles Martel at Poitiers in 732, marked the high-water mark of Muslim expansion in the Mediterranean world and ensured the survival of the Christian successor kingdoms of the Roman Empire in the west, whose future was their own and not in the hands of the caliph.[3] Although such views are today unfashionable, there can be little debate that Muslim forces, unchecked by Byzantium, would have based themselves in Greece with the real possibility of expansion along the northern shores of the Mediterranean; had the Muslims conquered Byzantium, the fate of the nascent papacy and of Christian Italy and France would have been very different.

In the practice of warfare, a full assessment of the direct legacy of Byzantium within western and eastern traditions is difficult. While the Byzantines certainly influenced their neighbors and those who served in their armies, we have no writings that directly indicate what knowledge was absorbed by Roman allies and enemies and either perpetuated or passed on to others. The relationships between late antique and medieval military handbooks in Greek, Persian, and Arabic have not been studied to appreciate their relationship with one another and the means of transmission of the ideas that they contained. While the Latin military writer Vegetius was known in medieval western Europe, Greek military handbooks do not seem to have traveled outside of the empire and were unknown among westerners before the Renaissance. There was probably much more influence on the Arabic tradition, whose equipment and methods of warfare were often quite close to the Romans' own.

Service in the Byzantine army proved a valuable experience for many westerners and of great historical import. The most famous mercenary known to us was Harald Hardrada (d. 1066) who, following the defeat and death of his half-brother, Saint Olaf, king of Norway (1015–28) at the famous Battle of Stiklestad (1030) traveled to Kiev. Sometime in the early 1030s, Harald journeyed to Constantinople where he and his retinue joined the Varangian Guard. The Norseman won fame and glory, fighting throughout the Mediterranean as far afield as Sicily. During his career Harald gained such an immense quantity of loot that he was able to finance his return home and seizure of the throne of Norway. Some of the plunder may well have equipped the great Norse fleet that assaulted the northern shores of England, where Harald landed in the autumn of 1066. The Norse fought the English army on September 25, and though the Anglo-Saxons defeated them and killed Harald, the old king's attack fatally weakened the Anglo-Saxon host and contributed in no small way to the historic victory of William the Bastard of Normandy at Hastings on October 14. While Harald seemed not to have employed Byzantine tactics, his campaigns and subsequent actions were founded upon the wealth he and his following gained in imperial service.

Certain tactics were passed on to the west via mercenaries who served in Byzantine armies. Theotokis noted that the Normans employed the feigned retreat in their invasion of Sicily in 1061, at Hastings in 1066, and again at Dyrrachium in 1081. Though Theotokis suggests that these tactics were learned by Normans in the east from the Seljuks, by the eleventh century the feigned retreat was such a fundament of Byzantine military doctrine that we probably need look no further. Interestingly, the Norman invasion of Sicily in 1061 took the same invasion route used by the Byzantine general George

Maniakes in his campaign of 1038, which included Norman mercenaries among the imperial soldiery.[4] The Normans who arrived in Italy possessed no clear military organization, but after their service as Byzantine mercenaries, they adopted the 300-man field unit, modeled on the Byzantine *bandon* into which they had been grouped, in order to organize their own battle armies. These Norman units were further based on units of ten, also adopted from the Byzantine military norms.[5]

The Byzantines adapted and refined a number of key battlefield technologies and introduced many other Asiatic modes of warfare to their neighbors. Equipment certainly trickled via confrontation, trade, or mercenary service from Byzantium to their neighbors and allies. The stirrup entered the Roman world via the Avars, and by the time the *Strategikon* was written around the early seventh century the army had adopted this technology. Although Lynn White famously credited the adoption of the stirrup as the first in a chain of events that led to a feudal revolution and the rise of the heavily armored medieval knight, more recent historians have been critical of major elements of his thesis. There is, however, little doubt that the stirrup created a better platform for the mounted warrior and was an important, though probably not decisive, piece of equipment in the history of warfare. Throughout the seventh century, the stirrup likely spread via the Byzantines to several of the surrounding Mediterranean peoples. From the tenth century onward, the warriors of the Kievan Rus' were equipped in a fashion that owed much to Byzantine influence, including their use of the kite-shaped shield. The kite-shaped shield probably spread to the Normans via their service as imperial mercenaries. By the time of the western European return to the military offensive, though, Byzantium had little new to offer them in terms of personal arms.

The Normans adopted other critical Byzantine technologies, especially in the area of logistics and organization. While northern European peoples around the year 1050 had limited knowledge of the large-scale transport of men and supplies by sea, the Byzantines had considerable experience in large-scale naval expeditions, as evidenced by their numerous invasions of Crete, Italy, and Sicily. The fact that in their invasions of Sicily from 1060–64 the Normans used horse transports fabricated in southern ports that were under Byzantine dominion or were culturally Greek argues for an important transferal of knowledge. Bachrach has argued that William the Bastard used men from southern Italy and Sicily to fashion and maneuver his own horse transports prior to his fateful invasion of England in 1066.[6]

Greek Fire

Byzantine adaptations and advances in incendiaries and artillery made a marked impact on warfare in medieval Europe. The most famous Byzantine invention in warfare was "Greek fire" or "liquid fire," the exact composition of which is lost. The aura of the substance as a secret weapon, its decisive role in several famous battles in Byzantine history, and the fact that the recipe for its creation has vanished add to the mystery of Greek fire today. The chronicler Theophanes linked the invention of Greek fire with an individual named Kallinikos, a Syrian from Heliopolis (either today's Ba 'albek in Lebanon or Membij in Syria) which was then under Arab control. According to Theophanes the new weapon was used by the Byzantine navy to destroy the Muslim fleet during the siege of 674–78; the chronicler's notice makes it clear that the weapon was a key part of the Roman victory and was a novel device.[7] Understandably, modern scholars have questioned the timing and novelty of the weapon—incendiary weapons had been used extensively throughout antiquity, including sulfur mixed with pitch that burned on water as well as fire arrows coated in sulfur, resin, asphalt, and pitch mentioned by Vegetius.[8] Greek fire burned on water, which made it all the more terrifying at sea where it was primarily used. The system used to project it created the world's first flamethrower. On ships, bronze or copper cylinders contained the naptha-resin Greek fire compound, which was preheated by a fire fueled by slow-burning flax fibers. A simple force pump pushed the highly flammable mixture into a swiveling projection tip; Haldon's modern experiments show that a light petroleum-based liquid and a simple force pump could effectively deliver a devastating wall of fire, smoke, and heat at a range of up to 15 meters. Everything and everyone downwind of the stream of fire would be charred or rendered unfit for service. In combat, Greek ships pressed close to their opponents, and through tubes projecting from the bow, sides, or stern of the vessel elite squads discharged the flaming mixture onto their enemy's ships (fig. 8.1).[9] Since the liquid did not vaporize upon ignition, the stream of burning Greek fire tended to arch down, which rendered it all the more effective against the low-riding galleys used in medieval Mediterranean warfare.

Fig. 8.1. Byzantine ships using Greek fire on their enemies as illustrated in the twelfth century Skylitzes manuscript. (*Madrid Skylitzes Fol34v.b.*)

Like most new weapons, the psychological shock of Greek fire amplified its effectiveness. In the section of the *Taktika* that dealt with naval warfare, the emperor Leo VI noted the use of "prepared fire with thunder and fiery smoke discharged through siphons, blackening them with smoke."[10] Crews unaccustomed to encountering the naptha firestorm at sea were shocked and overwhelmed by the experience. Roman use of the liquid combustible was critical during the Arab sieges of 674–78 and 717–18. When the fleet of the amir of Tarsos attacked the town of Euripos in Greece in 883, the strategos of Hellas and his troops devastated the Muslim fleet using Greek fire discharged from the fortifications.[11] Greek fire once again proved decisive against the Rus attack of 941, when fifteen mothballed galleys equipped with fire-projecting siphons were pressed into service and destroyed much of the enemy fleet.[12]

Byzantine preparations of Greek fire remained a closely held state secret. Although neighboring peoples captured components of the projection siphons, pumps, and the substance itself, neither the Arabs nor Bulgars were able to duplicate the Byzantine delivery system. When in 812 the Bulgars seized the town of Develtos on the Black Sea, thirty-six bronze cauldrons and siphon systems fell into their hands along with some of the fuel to supply them, but the Bulgars were unable to make use of the weapon.[13] Likewise, although the Arabs managed to utilize a combustible mixture like Greek fire that burned on water, and though they captured ships equipped with the siphons and preparation chambers used to cook the mixture and translated Byzantine military literature that spoke of it, we do not know whether the Muslims were able to duplicate the delivery systems and the precise recipe for making true Greek fire.[14] On one occasion the Muslims did use siphons, as during their attack on Thessaloniki by the renegade Leo of Tripoli, whose men fired from bridges mounted on their ship masts.[15] Muslim Arab forces generally seem to have cast their combustible version of Greek fire in grenades or ceramic pots by hand or from trebuchets. Western peoples had direct experience of the Byzantine use of the weapon; Anna Komnene describes an attack against the Pisans launched by her father Alexios I:

> On hearing this the Emperor ordered ships to be furnished by all the countries under the Roman sway. He had a number built in the capital itself and would at intervals go round in a monoreme and instruct the shipwrights how to make them As he knew that the Pisans were skilled in sea warfare and dreaded a battle with them, on the prow of each ship he had a head fixed of a lion or other land-animal, made in brass or iron with the mouth open and then gilded over, so that their mere aspect was terrifying. And the fire which was to be directed against the enemy through tubes he made to pass through the mouths of the beasts, so that it seemed as if the lions and the other similar monsters were vomiting the fire.[16]

In 1081, the Venetians defeated a Norman fleet off Dyrrachium who were "skilfully blowing the fire which they call Greek and is not extinguished by water, from hidden passages of tubes beneath the waves, cunningly burned between those same waves of the sparkling sea-top a certain ship of ours [of the Normans]."[17] It seems that in the thirteenth century the Angevin kingdom of Sicily used a combustible that they hurled from catapults, but whether they used the siphon systems of Byzantine origin is unclear.[18]

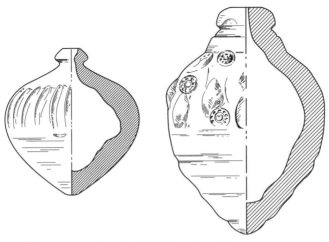

Fig. 8.2. Possible ceramic grenades; after Ettinghausen (1965).

Grenades

In addition to the ship-mounted projecting tubes, the Byzantines delivered Greek fire, as did their Arab enemies, in pottery grenades, tossed by hand or hurled using the small *cheiromangana* (hand trebuchet) or sling staffs. Larger clay vessels were cast using traction trebuchets. Clay spheroconic vessels have been found in large numbers in excavations in Corinth, Hama, and Israel. There is considerable debate about whether these vessels are in fact medieval grenades of the kind that were clearly filled with Greek fire or for other substances, such as mercury or precious unguents, but it seems that ceramic grenades of a type similar to these currently known vessels were used in warfare. Spheroconic terracottas recovered from excavations measure about 8–10 centimeters (fig. 8.2) in diameter and have a strong resemblance to modern grenades; several recovered in Danish excavations of the citadel of the city of Hama in the 1930s appear to have come from a workshop where shells and waxy films present in excavated horizons probably indicate two of the major ingredients for the production of incendiaries—lime and naptha. In conjunction with the spheroconic vessels found there, Pentz has argued persuasively for this complex as a Greek fire grenade manufactory.[19] Whatever the case, textual evidence notes that ceramic firebombs containing Greek fire were a standard part of the Byzantine arsenal.[20]

Fig. 8.3. Manuscript illustration of a hand-held Byzantine flamethrower. (*Codex Vaticanus Graecus 1605*)

Hand-held Flamethrowers

The Byzantines further refined the projection of Greek fire by producing a hand-held infantry siphon operated by an individual soldier. These were typically used on bridges suspended from ship masts, but they were also employed in city defense and in assaults on enemy personnel and fortifications. That the Romans possessed the first firmly attested hand-held flamethrower is evidenced by Nikephoros II Phokas's work, the *Praecepta militaria*, in which infantry units were said to be equipped with small hand trebuchets to cast Greek fire, as well as hand pumps and swivel tubes used to project the substance.[21] A manuscript illustration in Biblioteca Apostolica Vaticana MS. Vat. Gr. 1605, a text on siege warfare attributed to Heron of Byzantion, depicts a soldier on a flying bridge assaulting a city wall with a hand-held flamethrower (fig. 8.3), no doubt projecting Greek fire using a pneumatically powered siphon.[22]

Artillery

The Byzantines did not invent the traction trebuchet, but they were certainly key in its diffusion throughout the Mediterranean world. The traction trebuchet, which originated in China, consisted of a wooden frame supporting an axle on which was mounted a pivoting arm that ended in a sling. A Roman engineer allegedly taught the Avars the secret of manufacturing the traction trebuchet prior to their use of the weapon in the siege of Thessaloniki in 587. By the end of the sixth century the Romans employed small trebuchets on wagons accompanying the baggage train as antipersonnel devices, and utilized larger machines as both offensive and defensive weapons. The latter were mounted on towers of fortresses and cities throughout the empire.[23] A crew hove upon the short end of the beam using suspended ropes, and trained crews using average-sized counterweight trebuchets were able to cast projectiles 80–120 meters, according to the twelfth-century Arab authority al-Tarsusi.[24] Depending on the size of the machine and the skill of the crew, traction trebuchets could propel projectiles weighing as much as 110 kilograms (250 pounds), although smaller, smoothed stones of around 5 kilograms were more common; several of these have been recovered in archaeological excavations.[25] Smaller versions are attested in the Byzantine military handbooks, operated by one or two men and used as antipersonnel weapons that could break up enemy formations on the battlefield.

The traction trebuchet has several advantages over the torsion- and tension-powered artillery machines of the Hellenistic and early Roman periods. A simple machine with few components—Tarver's reconstruction used only about a dozen parts—it was easy to construct and portable, as each component could often be carried by one man for rapid assembly on the battlefield. Unlike the complex and dangerous torsion powered devices it replaced, the traction trebuchet was easy to man and maintain, while its range and effectiveness matched or exceeded earlier stone-throwing devices.

Counterweight Trebuchet

Historian Paul Chevedden has convincingly argued for the Byzantine origins of the counterweight trebuchet, the famous massive piece of siege artillery that marked the apogee of siege weaponry prior to the introduction of the cannon. The first historically attested use of the weapon was during the siege of Nicaea in 1097 during the First Crusade. Anna Komnene noted that during this siege operation, her father had constructed "city-takers" (*helepoleis*) that did not follow conventional design. In the following century, Byzantine armies operated these engines in sieges of Laodicaea in 1104, Mylos, Zeugminon (1165), and Nicaea (1184). The scale of these machines and their destructive power led to a revolution in fortification design around 1200, as engineers attempted to counter the advantage of besieging armies, which for the first time could batter down strong walls and towers. Twelfth-century sources refer in awe to the new artillery, frequently describing them as "huge" or "frightful," a clear indication that a novel and impressively effective form of siege weapon was employed in eastern warfare.[26]

The counterweight trebuchet operates on the same fundamental principles as its traction-powered predecessor (fig. 8.4). However, in place of the pulling crew was a massive counterweight, either fixed, such as a mass of lead or other dense substance, or a wooden coffer filled with rocks or other heavy material. A windlass was used to elevate the box, while the machine was cocked by lowering the beam and its sling-end to ground level; an iron pin inserted where the pulleys used to lower the beam provided

Fig. 8.4. Counterweight trebuchet.

the trigger for the counterweight trebuchet. Knocking out the pin released the arm and allowed the counterweight to fall vertically toward the ground, propelling the massive arm and its payload through an arc of ninety degrees. The addition of heavy counterweight, rigging, and winch technologies allowed for great striking power, as modern reconstructions have shown. The Danish scholar Hansen built a trebuchet with a 2,000-kilogram (4,400 pounds) counterweight that hurled 15-kilogram cement shot 168 meters, while scholars theorize that larger machines with 9-ton counterweights could fire 140-kilogram stones up to 300 meters.

The devastating capabilities of the counterweight trebuchet against masonry fortification structures are widely attested in contemporary medieval sources and in modern reconstructions. As noted above, the emperor John II Komnenos was particularly adept at siege warfare, and his counterweight trebuchets provided the firepower to batter down any fortified position on which the Romans set their sights.

From the Byzantines the crusader armies of western Europe learned of the manufacture and deployment of these heavy artillery devices.

The Normans were the first to make use of them, in 1185 turning counterweight trebuchets against the Byzantines themselves at Thessaloniki. From the Byzantines and crusaders the counterweight trebuchet spread both east and west, to the Muslim Arabs, Turks, and Persians and from there to China where in the thirteenth century the Mongols employed Muslim engineers familiar with the technology. The western Europeans eagerly adopted the device; one of the most famous examples was "War Wolf," the huge machine employed by King Edward I Longshanks during the 1304 siege of Stirling Castle in Scotland. Thus, in a little over a century after its invention by the engineers of Alexios I, the counterweight trebuchet had changed the fundamentals of warfare from one end of the known world to the other.

OVERALL LEGACY

The Byzantine legacy in the history of warfare is difficult to trace. Until the development of modern ideas of strategy following the rise of the centralized state in Europe, the influence of Byzantine developments on strategy and tactics remained informal and indirect. Byzantine handbooks were read and translated within the Islamic states of the Middle East, where they certainly affected the way that commanders thought about and conducted warfare, but no systematic study has ever attempted to trace the strands of medieval Roman influence there or elsewhere. As we have seen, most of the lessons that the Byzantines had to impart in terms of organization, logistics, and the prosecution of military operations took place in the school of the battlefield, where both friend and foe alike learned a great deal about discipline, unit organization, and the movements and maintenance of large bodies of troops. The Normans provide the most obviously affected group: via the imperial armies in which they served or from southern Italians whom they fought or came to rule, the Normans readily adopted many of the strategems and military configurations of their eastern neighbors. According to Anna Komnene, during the First Crusade, when contingents of the western European armies gathered at Constantinople, Alexios I Komnenos held a council of the Latin barons and provided extensive intelligence about the Turks and instructed the crusaders on what to expect in battle, how to form up their own battle lines, how to lay ambushes, and the dangers of pursuing the Seljuks, whose use of the feigned retreat could lure the heavily armed western knights into traps where they could be surrounded and destroyed.[27] How much of his advice the crusaders followed is unclear—certainly the standard narrative of the Battle of Dorylaeum (1097) has the crusaders barely escaping disaster. Given the western bias, no credit for the disposition of any tactical maneuvers that helped them gain the eventual victory would have been afforded their eastern allies.

Among the Turks themselves, Byzantine military methods were transferred in similar ways, both via peaceful contacts as the conquerors of the Anatolian plateau recruited Byzantines from their new territories in their armies and as elite families came into Turkish service. In practical terms we can trace Byzantine influence on the structures of the Ottoman military by the latter's likely adoption of the *pronoia* system of land-supported cavalry units in the form of the Turkish *timar*.[28] Other Byzantine contributions in the form of logistics, the maintenance of imperial transportation networks, and fortifications were probably adopted piecemeal since a full three centuries passed between the formation of the Ottoman state and absorption of Byzantine elements there and the final conquest of the Balkans in the fourteenth and fifteenth centuries.

The Byzantine practice of combined arms is most directly evidenced in the armies of Belisarios and Maurice onward, in which long-range fire, cavalry mobility, and the weight in defense and attack of well-drilled infantry, were present in the best and most successful Byzantine armies. Belisarios further used his elite boukellarioi as officer cadets and special forces in a surprisingly modern manner, reacting to the exigencies of the battlefield. His legacy and those of his successor Narses were felt through the military development of the Frankish kingdom, whose later reliance on cavalry probably grew in part from their experiences in Italy, where their infantry forces proved no match for Roman missile and cavalry units. In the east, the reformed army of the Macedonians revived this combined arms approach of close ordered heavy infantry supporting armored mixed cavalry formations capable of both speed and shock alongside lighter missile troops and artillery that provided ranged attack. These methods, still in force in the eleventh century when the Normans in the south were first exposed to them, parallel later Norman activities in the north, especially the armies of William the Bastard at Normandy, so closely that it is tempting to see Byzantine influence in them. The Norman and Angevin armies continued these traditions of combined arms that sustained the English in their medieval quest for empire through the end of the Hundred Years' War.

The rediscovery of Byzantine tactics in the early modern and modern eras is likewise difficult to trace, but Byzantine theory and practice foreshadowed many of the major tenets of warfare today. Jomini, whose *Art of War* was required reading at West Point among those cadets who staffed the officer corps of the Civil War, merely mentioned Belisarios's expedition among the Vandals.[29] No study exists of the influence of classical thought on the generals of the Civil War, but the American public was so steeped in the tradition that a cartoon of 1864 depicting General George McClellan as a "Modern Belisarius" resonated. In his study of amphibious operations, Vagts viewed the operations of Belisarios in Africa and Italy as the pinnacle of late Roman achievement in the arena, which he viewed as a rare high point in an otherwise dismal period.[30] Students of the concept of maneuver warfare, with its emphasis on spatial mastery and the "indirect approach," could have used one of a number of Byzantine commanders as their inspiration. Indeed, Liddell Hart's "indirect approach" in warfare, which influenced British, German, and later Israeli strategists in World War II the and postwar era, depended in part on his studying Byzantine tacticians like Belisarios and Narses.[31] Liddell Hart's friend and correspondent T. E. Lawrence noted in his classic *Seven Pillars of Wisdom* that he, "like any other man at Oxford," had read of the wars of Belisarios.[32] In fact, with the warfare of our era resembling the small wars fought by Lawrence, it is perhaps time for military planners to revisit the strategy and tactics of the Byzantine art of war.

GLOSSARY

agentes in rebus – early period special agents in imperial service

ala (plural *alae*) – late Roman cavalry unit of 100–500

annona – taxes in-kind used to support officials and soldiers

bandon – unit that varied in number depending on the century and force composition, 50–400 men was common

biarchus – lower rank, possibly junior centurion

boukellarioi – in the early period, private bodyguards usually raised by generals or barbarian chiefs

chiliarch – leader of 1,000

circitor – military rank of uncertain function

clibanarius – see *kataphraktoi*

comes – count

comitatenses – early Byzantine field army or mobile units (contrast with *limitanei*)

comitatus – imperial bodyguard

dekarch – leader of ten men

domestikos   ton scholon – originally commander of the Scholae bodyguards, evolved into marshal commanding eastern or western imperial field armies

dromos – imperial post system

droungarios (*droungar*) – commander of 1,000 men, later commander of bandon of 300–600 men

dux (Greek *doux*, pl. *doukes*) – senior commander; duke

eques – horseman

ethnarch – leader of foreign contingent

foederati – allied foreigners recruited via treaty with their chiefs

foulkon – dense infantry formation

ghazi – Islamic holy warrior

hekacontarch (or *ilarch/kentarchos*) – rough equivalent to Roman centurion, leader of 80–100 men

hippotoxotai – horse archer

kastron - fortress

kataphraktoi – heavy armed and armored cavalry

kentarchos – see *hekacontarch*

kleisourarch – guardian of frontier pass

koursor – scout or skirmishing cavalry

legate (legatus) – Roman commander of a legion

limitanei – troops stationed in frontier regions

magister militum – commander of army division

menavlatoi – infantry armed with menavlion

menavlion – heavy spear/pike

meros – division

pedes – infantry

pentarch – leader of five men

pentecontarch – leader of fifty men

primicerius – palatine guard

pronoia – grant of revenue from state to support a soldier

protectors – group of imperial bodyguards, third to seventh centuries

saka – from Arabic *saqat*, rearguard

spatharios – (pl. *spatharii*) in early period designated a bodyguard, later became a court title

strategos – general

stratopedarches – often equivalent to *strategos*/general

tagma – regiment (pl. *tagmata*) of imperial mobile imperial field regiments in Dark Ages replacing comitatenses; in the later medieval era mercenary regiments

tasinarioi – light cavalry scouts and raiders

tetrarchs – four leaders, called after the rule of four devised by Diocletian, with two senior emperors and two junior colleagues who would accede to the throne after the senior emperors retired

theme (thema) – medieval Byzantine province

tiro – recruit

tourma – a thematic unit or administrative districts

tourmarch – commander of a turma

trapezites – light skirmishing cavalry scouts

tribune – commander of a cohort, later of a vexillatio or bandon

vexillatio – vexillation, an early Byzantine cavalry unit 300 or 600 strong

župan – Serbian ruler of a district, often translated as "count"

NOTES

Abbreviations

Alexiad
  Anna Comnenae Alexias, ed. D. Reinsch (Berlin: de Gruyter, 2001)
  Anna Komnene, *The Alexiad*, trans. E. R. A. Sewter, rev. ed. (London: Penguin, 2009)
Ammianus Marcellinus
  Ammianus Marcellinus, 3 vols., trans. J. C. Rolfe (Cambridge, Mass.: Harvard University Press, 1935)
Anonymous Strategy
  The Anonymous Byzantine Treatise on Strategy, ed. and trans. G. T. Dennis, in *Three Byzantine Military Treatises* (Washington, D.C.: Dumbarton Oaks, 1985): 1–136.
Campaign
  Campaign Organization and Tactics, ed. and trans. G. Dennis, in *Three Byzantine Military Treatises* (Washington, D.C.: Dumbarton Oaks, 1985): 241–328.
Choniates
  Nicetae Choniatae, *Historia*, volume 1, ed. I. A. van Dieten (Berlin: de Gruyter, 1975).
  O City of Byzantium, Annals of Niketas Choniates, trans. H. J. Magoulias (Detroit: Wayne State University Press, 1984)
CJ
  Corpus iuris civilis, ed. P. Krueger, T. Mommsen, R. Schöll, W. Kroll (Berlin: Weidemann, 1954)
  Codex Iustinianus http://uwacadweb.uwyo.edu/blume&justinian/Book% 2012 .asp
CTh
  Codex Theodosianus, ed. Th. Mommsen, *Codex Theodosianus 1.2: Theodosiani libri XVI cum Constitutionibus Sirmondi[a]nus* (Berlin, 1905)—trans. C. Pharr et al., *The Theodosian Code and Novels and the Sirmonidan Constitutions* (Princeton: Princeton University Press, 1952)
De Rebus Bellicis
  Anonymi Auctoris De Rebus Bellicis, ed. R. Ireland (Leipzig: Teubner, 1984)
  A Roman Reformer and Inventor: Being a New Text of the De Rebus Bellicis, trans. E. A. Thompson (Oxford: Clarendon Press, 1952)
EI2
  The Encyclopaedia of Islam, 2nd edition, ed. H. A. R. Gibb (Leiden: Brill, 1954–2002)
IGLS
  Inscriptions grecques et latines de la Syrie, ed. L. Jalabert and R. Mouterde (Paris: Paul Geuthner, 1929)

Kekaumenos
Strategikon, ed. and Italian trans. M. D. Spadaro, *Raccomandazioni e consigli di un galatuomo* (Alexandria: Edizioni dell'Orso, 1998)

Kinnamos
Ioannis Cinnami Epitome rerum ab Ioannine et Alexios Comnenos gestarum, ed. A. Meineke (Bonn: E. Weber, 1836)
Deeds of John and Manuel Comnenus, trans. C. M. Brand (New York: Columbia University Press, 1976)

Leo the Deacon
Leonis Diaconi caloënsis Historiae libri decem et Liber de velitatione bellica Nicephori Augustii, ed. C. B. Hasii (Bonn: E. Weber, 1828)
The History of Leo the Deacon: Byzantine Military Expansion in the Tenth Century, trans. A. M. Talbot (Washington, D.C.: Dumbarton Oaks, 2005)

ODB
The Oxford Dictionary of Byzantium, ed. A. P. Kazhdan and A.-M. Talbot with A. Cutler, T. Gregory, N. P. Ševčenko (New York: Oxford University Press, 1991)

Ouranos
Le "Tactique" de Nicéphore Ouranos (Paris: Les Belles lettres, 1937)
The Taktika of Nikephoros Ouranos, Chapters 56–65, ed. and trans. E. McGeer, in *Sowing the Dragon's Teeth: Byzantine Warfare in the Tenth Century* (Washington, D.C.: Dumbarton Oaks, 1995)

PLRE
The Prosopography of the Later Roman Empire, ed. A. H. M. Jones, J. R. Martindale, J. Morris (Cambridge: Cambridge University Press, 1971–1992)

Praecepta militaria
The Praecaepta militaria of the Emperor Nikephoros II Phokas (963–69), ed. and trans. E. McGeer, in *Sowing the Dragon's Teeth: Byzantine Warfare in the Tenth Century* (Washington, D.C.: Dumbarton Oaks, 1995): 12–60.

Priskos
R. C. Blockley, ed. and trans., *The Fragmentary Classicising Historians of the Later Roman Empire: Eunapius, Olympiodorus, Priscus and Malchus,* vol. 2: *Text, Translation and Historiographical Notes* (Liverpool: Francis Cairns, 1983)

Prokopios, Wars
H. B. Dewing, ed. and trans., *Procopius* (Cambridge, Mass.: Harvard University Press, 1969), vols. 1–5.

Sebeos
The Armenian History Attributed to Sebeos, trans. R.W. Thompson, vols. 1–2 (Liverpool: Liverpool University Press, 1999)

Skirmishing
Skirmishing, ed. and trans. G. T. Dennis, in *Three Byzantine Military Treatises* (Washington, D.C.: Dumbarton Oaks, 1985): 137–240.

Skylitzes
Ioannis Scylitzae Synopsis Historiarum, ed. I. Thurn (Berlin: de Gruyter, 1973)
A Synopsis of Byzantine History, 811–1057, trans. J. Wortley (Cambridge: Cambridge University Press, 2010)

Strategikon
> *Das Strategikon des Maurikios*, ed. and German trans. G. T. Dennis and E. Gamillscheg (Vienna: Verlag der Österreichischen Akademie der Wissenschaften, 1981)
> G. T. Dennis, trans., *Maurice's Strategikon: Handbook of Byzantine Military Strategy* (Philadelphia: University of Pennsylvania Press, 1984)

Taktika (of Leo VI)
> G. T. Dennis, ed. and trans., *The Taktika of Leo VI* (Washington, D.C.: Dumbarton Oaks, 2010)

Theophanes
> *Theophanes Chronographia*, ed. C. de Boor, vols. 1-2 (Leipzig: Teubner, 1885)
> *Theophanes, The Chronicle of Theophanes Confessor, AD 284–813*, trans. C. A. Mango and R. Scott with G. Greatrex (Oxford: Clarendon Press, 1997)

Vegetius
> *Epitoma rei militaris*, ed. M. D. Reeve (Oxford: Oxford University Press, 2004)
> *Vegetius, epitome of military science*, trans. N. P. Milner (Liverpool: Liverpool University Press, 1993)

Chapter One: Historical Overview

1. Michael Kulikowski, *Rome's Gothic Wars: From the Third Century to Alaric* (Cambridge: Cambridge University Press, 2007), 100–105.
2. Warren T. Treadgold, *Byzantium and Its Army, 284–1081* (Stanford, Calif.: Stanford University Press, 1995), 55.
3. Benjamin H. Isaac, *The Limits of Empire: The Roman Army in the East* (Oxford: Clarendon Press, 1990), 169–70.
4. Michael H. Dodgeon and Samuel N. C. Lieu, *The Roman Eastern Frontier and the Persian Wars (AD 226–363): A Documentary History* (London: Routledge, 1991), 170–71.
5. *Ammianus Marcellinus*, XVIII.9–XIX.9.
6. Kulikowski, *Rome's Gothic Wars*, 128.
7. Otto Maenchen-Helfen, *The World of the Huns: Studies in Their History and Culture* (Berkeley: University of California Press, 1973), 441.
8. *Ammianus Marcellinus*, XXXI.4.6.
9. *Ammianus Marcellinus*, XXXI.13.
10. J. D. Howard-Johnston, "Heraclius' Persian Campaigns and the Revival of the East Roman Empire, 622–630," *War in History* 6 (1999).
11. *Sebeos*, p. 67.
12. EI2 "Muta."
13. Fred Donner, *The Early Islamic Conquests* (Princeton: Princeton University Press, 1981), 131.
14. These events cannot be reconstructed with certainty; see Donner, *Early Islamic Conquests*, for the possibilities.
15. Walter Kaegi, *Byzantium and the Early Islamic Conquests* (Cambridge: Cambridge University Press, 1992) is one such effort. More recently, an overview has been pro-

vided by Hugh Kennedy, *The Great Arab Conquests: How the Spread of Islam Changed the World We Live In* (Philadelphia: Da Capo, 2007).

16. *Theophanes*, AM 6237.

17. George L. Huxley, "The Emperor Michael III and the Battle of Bishop's Meadow (A.D. 863)," *Greek, Roman, and Byzantine Studies* (1975).

18. *Theophanes*, AM 6303.

19. *Leo the Deacon*, II.5.

20. *Skylitzes*, p. 444.

21. J.-C. Cheynet, "Mantzikert: un désastre militaire?" *Byzantion* 50 (1980).

22. Marjorie Chibnall, *The Normans* (Malden, Mass.: Blackwell, 2006), 77–81.

23. *Alexiad*, IV.6.

24. John W. Birkenmeier, *The Development of the Komnenian Army: 1081–1180* (Leiden: Brill, 2002), 62–70.

25. Mark C. Bartusis, *The Late Byzantine Army: Arms and Society, 1204–1453* (Philadelphia: University of Pennsylvania Press, 1992), 262–70.

CHAPTER TWO: LEADERSHIP

1. *Taktika* 1 and 2.

2. *ODB*, "Dalassenos," p. 578.

3. *Vegetius*, III.22.

4. *Skylitzes*, pp. 197–198.

5. *Theophanes*, AM 6116.

6. *PLRE*, "Mundus," pp. 903–5.

7. A. H. M. Jones, *The Later Roman Empire, 284–602: A Social Economic and Administrative Survey* (London: Blackwell, 1964), 637.

8. *PLRE*, "Sittas 1," pp. 1161–63.

9. *PLRE*, "Diogenes 2," pp. 400–401.

10. *PLRE*, "Mundus," pp. 903–5.

11. Ioseph Genesios, *On the Reigns of the Emperors*, trans. Anthony Kaldellis (Canberra: Australian Association for Byzantine Studies, 1998), IV.13.

12. Michael Psellus, *Fourteen Byzantine Rulers: The Chronographia of Michael Psellus*, trans. E. R. A. Sewter (New York: Penguin Books, 1966), 35.

13. Bartusis, *The Late Byzantine Army*, 64.

14. Ibid., 210.

15. John F. Haldon, *Warfare, State, and Society in the Byzantine World, 565–1204* (London: UCL Press, 1999), 229; *Skylitzes*, p. 211.

16. *Skylitzes*, p. 233.

17. Savvas Kyriakidis, *Warfare in Late Byzantium, 1204–1453* (Leiden: Brill, 2011), 31.

18. Otto Seeck, *Notitia dignitatum: accedunt Notitia urbis Constantinopolitanae et laterculi prouinciarum* (Berlin: Weidmannos, 1876), 78.

19. Prokopios, *Wars*, I.xiii.

20. *Skylitzes*, p. 296.

21. *Leo the Deacon*, III.2.

22. *Leo the Deacon*, X.1.

23. Birkenmeier, *The Development of the Komnenian Army*, 89.

24. *Choniates*, p. 11.
25. *Choniates*, p. 16; Kinnamos, Bk. 1.8.
26. *Choniates*, p. 20.

CHAPTER THREE: ORGANIZATION, RECRUITMENT, AND TRAINING

1. Jones, *The Later Roman Empire*, 608–36.
2. John F. Haldon, *Byzantine Praetorians: An Administrative, Institutional, and Social Survey of the Opsikion and Tagmata, c. 580–900* (Bonn: R. Habelt, 1984), 143.
3. Jones, *The Later Roman Empire*, 640.
4. Ibid., 633. *De Rebus Bellicis*, V.5.
5. *Vegetius*, III.8.
6. Treadgold, *Byzantium and Its Army*, 91; Jones, *The Later Roman Empire*, 567, 634, 26.
7. Treadgold, *Byzantium and Its Army*, 88–89.
8. Jones, *The Later Roman Empire*, 284–602, 597.
9. Warren T. Treadgold, *The Early Byzantine Historians* (New York: Palgrave Macmillan, 2007), 188.
10. Isaac, *The Limits of Empire*, 209.
11. Jones, *The Later Roman Empire*, 664.
12. Haldon, *Byzantine Praetorians*, 164; Isaac, *The Limits of Empire*, 210. disagrees; Treadgold, *Byzantium and Its Army*, 93, states that these men were removed from the payroll by Justinian.
13. Treadgold, *Byzantium and Its Army*, 94.
14. Ibid., 96.
15. Haldon, *Byzantine Praetorians*, 116.
16. Ibid., 173.
17. A. N. Oikonomides, "Les premières mentions des thèmes dans la chronique de Théophane," *Zbornik radova Vizantoloskog Instituta* 16 (1975).
18. Haldon, *Byzantine Praetorians*, 176.
19. *ODB*, "Anatolikon," pp. 89–90; *ODB* "Armeniakon," 177; *ODB* "Karabisianoi," pp. 1105–6; Hélène Ahrweiler, *Byzance et la mer: la marine de guerre, la politique et les institutions maritimes de Byzance aux VIIe-XVe siècles* (Paris: Presses universitaires de France, 1966), 19–31. Many of the issues surrounding the themes are dealt with in John F. Haldon, "Military Service, Military Lands, and the Status of Soldiers: Current Problems and Interpretations," *Dumbarton Oaks Papers* 47 (1993).
20. *Theophanes*, AM 6159; Jadran Ferluga, "Le Clisure bizantine in Asia Minore," in *Byzantium on the Balkans: Studies on the Byzantine Administration and the Southern Slavs from the VIIth to the XIIth Centuries*, ed. Jadran Ferluga (Amsterdam: A. M. Hakkert, 1976), 73.
21. Treadgold, *Byzantium and Its Army*, 106–8.
22. *ODB*, "Tourmarches," pp. 2100–2101.
23. Treadgold, *Byzantium and Its Army*, 100–105.
24. Haldon, *Warfare, State, and Society in the Byzantine World*, 110. Ibn Khurradadhbih, *Kitab masalik wa al-mamalik* (Arabic), 111, 82 (French).
25. Treadgold, *Byzantium and Its Army*, 103.
26. Haldon, *Warfare, State, and Society in the Byzantine World*, 116.

27. *Byzantine Praetorians*, 191–95.

28. Ibid., 196.

29. Haldon, *Warfare, State, and Society in the Byzantine World*, 111; Treadgold, *Byzantium and Its Army*, 102; Hans Joachim Kühn and Johannes Koder, *Die byzantinische Armee im 10. und 11. Jahrhundert: Studien zur Organisation der Tagmata* (Vienna: Fassbaender, 1991), 73 ff.

30. Haldon, *Byzantine Praetorians*, 280–81.

31. Ibid., 224–26.

32. Treadgold, *Byzantium and Its Army*, 110.

33. Ibid., 106; Haldon, *Warfare, State, and Society in the Byzantine World*, 116.

34. *Skirmishing*, §16.

35. Nicephorus Bryennius, *Nicéphore Bryennios histoire: Introduction, texte, traduction et notes*, trans. P. Gautier, Corpus fontium historiae Byzantinae (Brussels: Byzantion, 1975), 282–83.

36. *Leo the Deacon*, VI.11.

37. *ODB*, "Nikephoritzes," p. 1475.

38. Haldon, *Warfare, State, and Society in the Byzantine World*, 93.

39. Birkenmeier, *The Development of the Komnenian Army*, 28.

40. *ODB*, "Allagion," pp. 67–68.

41. Rodolphe Guilland, *Recherches sur les institutions byzantines* (Berlin: Akademie-Verlag, 1967), 596–600; Mark C. Bartusis, "The Megala Allagia and the Tzaousios: Aspects of Provincial Military Organization in Late Byzantium," *Revue des études byzantines* 47 (1989): 203.

42. Bartusis, *The Late Byzantine Army*, 199.

43. Jones, *The Later Roman Empire*, 616; Cécile Morrisson and Jean-Claude Cheynet, "Prices and Wages in the Byzantine World," in *The Economic History of Byzantium: From the Seventh Through the Fifteenth Century*, ed. Angeliki E. Laiou and Charalampos Bouras (Washington, D.C.: Dumbarton Oaks Research Library and Collection, 2002), 864.

44. John F. Haldon, *Recruitment and Conscription in the Byzantine Army c. 550–950* (Vienna: Verlag der Österreichischen Akademie der Wissenschaften, 1979), 26.

45. Jones, *The Later Roman Empire*, 614.

46. Prokopios, *Wars*, III.18; *PLRE*, "Ioannes 14" vol. 3.A, pp. 635–36; he was an "*optio*," here not a quartermaster, but a picked commander.

47. Marie Theres Fögen, "Lombards," in *Oxford Dictionary of Byzantium*, ed. A. P. Kazhdan (New York: Oxford University Press, 1991), 1249.

48. *Sebeos*, p. 31; Richard G. Hovannisian, *The Armenian People from Ancient to Modern Times* (New York: St. Martin's Press, 1997), 110.

49. Haldon, *Recruitment and Conscription in the Byzantine Army*, 37.

50. Andreas Nikolau Stratos, *Byzantium in the Seventh Century 3. 642–668*, trans. Harry T. Hionides (Amsterdam: Hakkert, 1975), 234.

51. *Theophanes*, AM 6184.

52. Treadgold, *Byzantium and Its Army*, 110.

53. Peter Charanis, "The Armenians in the Byzantine Empire," *Byzantinoslavica* 22 (1961).

54. Jonathan Shepard, "The English and Byzantium: A Study of Their Role in the Byzantine Army in the Later Eleventh Century," *Traditio* 29 (1973): 60.

55. Bartusis, *The Late Byzantine Army*, 192–93.

56. Treadgold, *Byzantium and Its Army*, 155.

57. Morrisson and Cheynet, "Prices and Wages in the Byzantine World," 864.

58. Jones, *The Later Roman Empire*, 623–24, 34.

59. Treadgold, *Byzantium and Its Army*, 150–54.

60. Morrisson and Cheynet, "Prices and Wages in the Byzantine World," 860.

61. Treadgold, *Byzantium and Its Army*, 153–54.

62. Ibid., 146–48.

63. Morrisson and Cheynet, "Prices and Wages in the Byzantine World," 865.

64. Ibid., 862–65.

Chapter Four: Equipment and Logistics

1. Simon James, "The *Fabricae*: State Arms Factories of the Later Roman Empire," in *Military Equipment and the Identity of Roman Soldiers: Proceedings of the Fourth Roman Military Equipment Conference*, ed. J. C. N. Coulston (Oxford: British Archaeological Reports, 1988), 257.

2. Jones, *The Later Roman Empire*, 624–25; Roger S. Bagnall and Raffaella Cribiore, *Women's Letters from Ancient Egypt, 300 BC–AD 800* (Ann Arbor: University of Michigan Press, 2006), Letter 288.

3. Karen R. Dixon and Pat Southern, *The Roman Cavalry* (London: Routledge, 1997), 62.

4. Jones, *The Later Roman Empire*, 835.

5. Haldon, *Warfare, State, and Society in the Byzantine World*, 132.

6. Haldon, "Military Service, Military Lands, and the Status of Soldiers: Current Problems and Interpretations," 17; Haldon, "Some Aspects of Byzantine Military Technology from the Sixth to the Tenth Centuries," *Byzantine and Modern Greek Studies* 1 (1975): 42.

7. Michael Hendy, *Studies in the Byzantine Monetary Economy c. 300–1450* (Cambridge: Cambridge University Press, 1985), 628–30; John F. Haldon, *Byzantium in the Seventh Century: The Transformation of a Culture* (Cambridge: Cambridge University Press, 1990), 232–44. See also R.-J. Lilie, "Die Zweihundertjährige Reform: zu den Anfängen der Themenorganisation im 7. und 8. Jahrhundert," *Byzantinoslavica* 45 (1984): 190–201.

8. Norbert Kamp and Joachim Wollasch, *Tradition als historische Kraft: interdisziplinäre Forschungen zur Geschichte des früheren Mittelalters* (Berlin: de Gruyter, 1982), 254–66.

9. Haldon, "Military Service, Military Lands, and the Status of Soldiers," 17.

10. Haldon, *Warfare, State, and Society in the Byzantine World*, 328, n. 8.

11. *Choniates*, p. 118.

12. *Choniates*, p. 58.

13. Birkenmeier, *The Development of the Komnenian Army*, 178.

14. Walter Kaegi, "Byzantine Logistics: Problems and Perspectives," in *Feeding Mars: Logistics in Western Warfare from the Middle Ages to the Present*, ed. J. A. Lynn (Boulder: Westview Press, 1993), 41.

15. Ibid., 45.
16. S. Thomas Parker, *The Roman Frontier in Central Jordan: Final Report on the Limes Arabicus Project, 1980–1989* (Washington, D.C.: Dumbarton Oaks, 2006), 120.
17. Michael Decker, "Towers, Refuges, and Fortified Farms in the Late Roman East," *Liber Annuus* 56 (2006).
18. *IGLS*, 4.1397.1; 4.1385.
19. Louis Robert, "Noms métiers dans des documents byzantins," in *Charisterion eis Anastasion K. Orlandon 1*, ed. Anastasios K Orlandos (Athens: He en Athenais Archaiologike Hetairea, 1965), 333.
20. Haldon, *Warfare, State, and Society in the Byzantine World*, 150.
21. Constantine Porphyrogenitus, *Constantine Porphyrogenitus: Three treatises on imperial military expeditions*, trans. John F. Haldon (Vienna: Verlag der Österreichischen Akademie der Wissenschaften, 1990), 99.
22. *Praecepta militaria*, II.1–4.
23. John F. Haldon, "The Organisation and Support of an Expeditionary Force: Manpower and Logistics in the Middle Byzantine Period," in To empolemo Byzantio = Byzantium at War (9th–12th c.): International Symposium 4 [of the] Institute for Byzantine Research [Athens, 1996], ed. Nicolas Oikonomides, Kostas Tsiknakes (Athens: Goulandre-Chorn Foundation, 1997), 122–23.
24. Ibid., 116–21.
25. Ibid., 125.
26. P. Grotokowski, *Arms and Armour of the Warrior Saints* (Leiden: Brill, 2010), 193–98.
27. *Strategikon*, I.2.
28. Timothy Dawson, "Kremasmata, Kabbadion, Klibanion: Some Aspects of Middle Byzantine Military Equipment Reconsidered," *Byzantine and Modern Greek Studies* 22 (1998): 42; Grotowski, *Arms and Armour of the Warrior Saints*, 166–70; Taxiarchos Kolias, *Byzantinische Waffen: Ein Beitrag zur byzantinischen Waffenkunde von den Anfängen bis zur lateinischen Eroberung* (Vienna: Verlag der Österreichischen Akademie der Wissenschaften, 1988), 54–57.
29. *Strategikon*, I.2.
30. *Strategikon*, XII.8.1–6.
31. *Ouranos*, 56.139–44; pp. 96–97.
32. Haldon, *Warfare, State, and Society in the Byzantine World*, 128.
33. *Vegetius*, I.20.
34. J. C. N. Coulston, "Late Roman Armour, 3rd–6th Centuries AD," *Journal of Roman Military Equipment Studies* (1990), 147.
35. *Strategikon*, I.2.
36. *Strategikon*, XII.8.
37. *De Rebus Bellicis*, XV.2.
38. Ian P. Stephenson, *Romano-Byzantine Infantry Equipment* (Stroud, Gloucester: Tempus, 2006), 52.
39. On the *zaba* see Kolias, *Byzantinische Waffen*, 37–39; Russ Mitchell, "Archery Versus Mail: Experimental Archaeology and the Value of Historical Context," *Journal of Medieval Military History* 4 (2006).

40. *Ammianus Marcellinus*, XV.i.13.
41. S. M. Perevalov, "The Sarmatian Lance and the Sarmatian Horse-Riding Posture," *Anthropology & Archeology of Eurasia* 41, no. 4 (2003).
42. *Alexiad*, IV.7; Dawson, "Kremasmata, Kabbadion, Klibanion," 46.
43. Ibid., 47; Maria G. Parani, *Reconstructing the Reality of Images: Byzantine Material Culture and Religious Iconography (11th–15th Centuries)* (Leiden: Brill, 2003), 108, pl. 29.
44. Dawson, "Kremasmata, Kabbadion, Klibanion," 47; Haldon, "Some Aspects of Byzantine Military Technology from the Sixth to the Tenth Centuries"; Kolias, *Byzantinische Waffen*, 45–46.
45. Bartusis, *The Late Byzantine Army*, 323–24.
46. *Strategikon*, XII.4.
47. Stephenson, *Romano-Byzantine Infantry Equipment*, 71.
48. Timothy Dawson, "Suntagma Hoplôn: The Equipment of Regular Byzantine Troops, c. 950–c. 1204," in *A Companion to Medieval Arms and Armour*, ed. D. Nicolle (Woodbridge: Boydell Press, 2002), 83.
49. Stephenson, *Romano-Byzantine Infantry Equipment*, 17; Kolias, *Byzantinische Waffen*, 76.
50. Stephenson, *Romano-Byzantine Infantry Equipment*, 27.
51. Dawson, "Suntagma Hoplôn," 83.
52. Ibid., 83–84.
53. Minor M. Markle, III, "The Macedonian Sarrissa, Spear and Related Armor," *American Journal of Archaeology* 81, no. 3 (1977): 324; N. Tarleton, "Pastoralem Praefixa Cuspide Myrtum (Aeneid 7.817)," *Classical Quarterly* 39, no. 1 (1989): 270; Stephenson, *Romano-Byzantine Infantry Equipment*, 80; Marijke van der Veen and Alison Cox, *Consumption, Trade and Innovation: Exploring the Botanical Remains from the Roman and Islamic Ports at Quseir al-Qadim, Egypt* (Frankfurt am Main: Africa Magna Verlag, 2011), 220.
54. G. R. Davidson and Tibor Horváth, "The Avar Invasion of Corinth," *Hesperia* 6, no. 2 (1937): 232–34.
55. M. P. Anastasiadis, "On Handling the Menavlion," *Byzantine and Modern Greek Studies* 18 (1994).
56. *Strategikon*, XII.8.
57. Conrad Engelhardt, *Nydam mosefund, 1859–1863* (Copenhagen: I commission hos GEC Gad, 1865), 81–82, plates VI–VII.
58. Evelyne Godfrey and Matthijs van Nie, "A Germanic Ultrahigh Carbon Steel Punch of the Late Roman-Iron Age," *Journal of Archaeological Science* 31 (2004).
59. Stephenson, *Romano-Byzantine Infantry Equipment*, 92.
60. *Praecepta militaria*, II.
61. Parani, *Reconstructing the Reality of Images*, fig. 104.
62. Bartusis, *The Late Byzantine Army*, 329.
63. Prokopios, *Wars*, VI.xxv.1.
64. *Praecepta militaria*, I.25–26, pp. 14–15.
65. *Strategikon*, XI.3.
66. *Vegetius*, I.17.

67. *Sylloge*, 38.10.
68. Haldon, "Some Aspects of Byzantine Military Technology," 38–39.
69. *Vegetius*, III.14, p. 91.
70. Wallace McLeod, "The Range of the Ancient Bow," *Phoenix* 19, no. 1 (1965): 7–10.
71. Stephenson, *Romano-Byzantine Infantry Equipment*: fig. 26.
72. Bartusis, *The Late Byzantine Army*, 298–99.
73. Ibid., 127–32.
74. *CJ* 85.2: http://webu2.upmf-grenoble.fr/Haiti/Cours/Ak/link_en.htm.
75. Duncan B. Campbell, *Greek and Roman Artillery 399 BC–AD 363* (Oxford: Osprey Publishing, 2003), 21, 36.
76. Prokopios, *Wars*, V.xxi.14–22.
77. Josephus, *Jewish War*, V.270 notes that first-century scorpions (one-armed stone throwers similar to the later *onagers*) cast one talent (about 32 kg/71 lbs.) about 400 meters.
78. Quoted in Paul E. Chevedden, "The Invention of the Counterweight Trebuchet: A Study in Cultural Diffusion," *Dumbarton Oaks Papers* 54 (2000): 74.

CHAPTER FIVE: STRATEGY AND TACTICS

1. "Strategy," *Oxford English Dictionary*. Third edition. http://www.oed.com.
2. *Taktika*, 1§1–3.
3. Haldon, *Warfare, State, and Society in the Byzantine World*, 34. See the recent work on proposing a unfied "Grand Strategy": Edward N. Luttwak, *The Grand Strategy of the Byzantine Empire* (Cambridge, Mass.: Harvard University Press, 2009).
4. *Priskos*, IV.1–2.
5. Francis Dvornik, *Origins of Intelligence Services: The Ancient Near East, Persia, Greece, Rome, Byzantium, the Arab Muslim Empires, the Mongol Empire, China, Muscovy* (New Brunswick, N.J.: Rutgers University Press, 1974), 132–37, 48.
6. Haldon, *Warfare, State, and Society in the Byzantine World*, 67 ff.
7. *Taktika*, 20§37.
8. *Taktika*, 20§47: a repetition of *Strategikon* 8.2.1, which in turn echoed ancient Greek notions of just war, cf. Onasander, 5.1.
9. *Strategikon*, II.18.
10. *Taktika*, 20§72.
11. *Taktika* 20§63.
12. *Taktika* 4§41; 20§160.
13. *Ouranos*, 65.79–85.
14. *Strategikon*, VIII.2.12.
15. Birkenmeier, *The Development of the Komnenian Army*, 112 ff.
16. *Taktika*, 20§112.
17. *Alexiad*, XIV.2.
18. Bartusis, *The Late Byzantine Army*, 345.
19. Ibid., 65.
20. *Strategikon*, Proem.
21. *Anonymous Strategy*, §25, n.1.
22. *Skirmishing*, §22.

23. Treadgold, *Byzantium and Its Army*, 21–23.
24. *Praecepta militaria*, IV.195–203.
25. *Skylitzes*, pp. 66–69.
26. *Alexiad*, VI.1.
27. *Choniates*, p. 10.
28. Steven Runciman, *The Sicilian Vespers: A History of the Mediterranean World in the Later Thirteenth Century* (Cambridge: Cambridge University Press, 1992), 214–87.
29. *Anonymous Strategy*, §42.
30. Dvornik, *Origins of Intelligence Services*, 147–48.
31. *Praecepta militaria*, IV.192–95.
32. *Kekaumenos*, II.24.
33. Prokopios, *Wars*, III.xx.1.
34. Prokopios, *Wars*, III.xiv.7.
35. *Taktika*, 20§131–32.
36. *Strategikon*, I.9; *Taktika*, 19§21.
37. *Ouranos*, 63.12–14.
38. *Ouranos*, 65.165–172.
39. *Skirmishing*, §6; *Campaign*, §21.
40. Yahya-Ibn-Saïd, *Histoire de Yahya-Ibn-Saïd d'Antioche, continuateur de Saïd-Ibn-Bitriq: fascicule II*, ed. René Graffin and François Nau, trans. I. Kratchkovsky and A. Vasiliev, 2 vols., vol. 2, Patrologia Orientalis (Paris: Firmin-Didot, 1932), 442.
41. *Kinnamos*, IV.17.
42. *Choniates*, pp. 58–59.
43. *Skirmishing*, §6; *Campaign*, §10.
44. *Strategikon*, II.11.
45. *Leo the Deacon*, VI.12–13.
46. *Taktika*, 17§89.
47. Prokopios, *Wars*, 1.1.12–15.
48. Flavius Cresconius Corippus, *The Iohannis, or, De bellis Libycis*, trans. George W. Shea (Lewiston, N.Y.: Edwin Mellen Press, 1998), 125.
49. *Strategikon*, III.12–16.
50. *Strategikon*, XII.9; Philip Rance, "Narses and the Battle of Taginae (Busta Gallorum) 552:"Procopius and Sixth-Century Warfare," *Historia: Zeitschrift für Alte Geschichte* 54, no. 4 (2005): 430.
51. *Strategikon*, XII.17.
52. Haldon, *Warfare, State, and Society in the Byzantine World*, 210–17.
53. Ibid., 210–18; Alphonse Dain and Emperor Leo VI, *Sylloge tacticorum, quae olim "Inedita Leonis tactica" dicebatur* (Paris: Société d'édition "Les Belles lettres," 1938), 47.16.
54. *Ouranos*, 56.35–77.
55. McGeer, *Sowing the Dragon's Teeth*, 264.
56. Ibid., 268–70.
57. Ibid., 273.
58. Ibid., 276.
59. Haldon, *Warfare, State, and Society in the Byzantine World*, 224–25.

60. Bartusis, *The Late Byzantine Army*, 253–60.

61. *Ouranos*, 65.139–43.

62. *Ouranos*, 65.110–15.

63. *Ouranos*, 65.105–39.

CHAPTER SIX: ENEMIES OF BYZANTIUM

1. Peter Heather, *The Goths* (Oxford: Blackwell, 1996), 274.

2. Ibid., 236.

3. Simon James, "Stratagems, Combat, and 'Chemical Warfare' in the Siege Mines of Dura-Europos," *American Journal of Archaeology* 115, no. 1 (2011): 76; "Evidence from Dura Europos for the Origins of Late Roman Helmets," *Syria* 63, nos. 1-2 (1986). For additional information on Sasanian helmets, see Stephen V. Grancsay, "A Sasanian Chieftain's Helmet," *Metropolitan Museum of Art Bulletin* 21, no. 8 (1963).

4. *Strategikon*, XI.2.

5. Hugh Kennedy, *The Armies of the Caliphs* (London: Routledge, 2001).

6. Michael Lecker, "Siffin," in *The Encyclopaedia of Islam*, ed. C. E. Bosworth, E. van Donzel, and W. P. Heinrichs (Leiden: Brill, 1997), 552–56.

7. Kennedy, *The Armies of the Caliphs*, 32–34.

8. Warren T. Treadgold, *The Byzantine Revival, 780–842* (Stanford, Calif.: Stanford University Press, 1988), 297.

9. Panos, Sophoulis, *Byzantium and Bulgaria, 775–831* (Leiden: Brill, 2012).

10. Ibid., 77.

11. Ibid.

12. *Theophanes*, AM 6266.

13. Jonathan Shepard, "The Uses of the Franks in Eleventh-Century Byzantium," *Anglo-Norman Studies* 15 (1993): 288–89.

14. Goffredo Malaterra, *The Deeds of Count Roger of Calabria and Sicily and of His Brother Duke Robert Guiscard* (Ann Arbor: University of Michigan Press, 2005), 165–66.

15. *Alexiad*, IV.4.

16. *Alexiad*, V.6.

17. Birkenmeier, *The Development of the Komnenian Army*, 60–61.

18. Ibid., 69–70.

CHAPTER SEVEN: THE BYZANTINE ARMY AT WAR

1. Clifford Edmund Bosworth, "The City of Tarsus and the Arab-Byzantine Frontiers in Early and Middle Abbasid Times," *Oriens* 33 (1992): 274–77.

2. Marius Canard, *Histoire de la dynastie des H'amdanides de Jazira et de Syrie* (Algiers: Imprimeries "La Typo-litho" et J. Carbonel réunies, 1951): 763–70.

3. Bosworth, "The City of Tarsus and the Arab-Byzantine Frontiers," 282.

4. Yahya Ibn Sa'id, I. Kratchkovsky, and A. Vasiliev, *Histoire de Yahya-Ibn-Sa`id d'Antioche, continuateur de Sa`id-Ibn-Bitriq, fasicule 1*, 3 vols., vol. 1, Patrologia Orientalis (Paris: Firmin-Didot, 1924), 95; Canard, *Histoire de la dynastie des H'amdanides de Jazira et de Syrie*, 818–19; *Skylitzes*, 257.

5. *Leo the Deacon*, III.11.

6. *Leo the Deacon*, IV.4.

7. Paul Stephenson, *Byzantium's Balkan Frontier: A Political Study of the Northern Balkans, 900–1204* (Cambridge: Cambridge University Press, 2000), 65.

8. Ibid., 67.

9. *Skylitzes*, 331.

10. *Kinnamos*, III.2; *Choniates*, pp. 45–46.

11. *Kinnamos*, III.9.

12. *Kinnamos*, V.10; Birkenmeier, *The Development of the Komnenian Army*, 119.

13. *Kinnamos*, VI.7.

14. *Choniates*, p. 88.

15. *Theophanes*, AM 6165.

16. *Theophanes*, AM 6209; R.-J. Lilie, "Die Zweihundertjährige Reform: zu den Anfängen der Themenorganisation im 7. und 8. Jahrhundert," *Byzantinoslavica* 45 (1984): 190–201, 128–29.

17. Demetres Tsounkarakes and Euangelos K. Chrysos, *Byzantine Crete: From the Fifth Century to the Venetian Conquest* (Athens: Historical Publications St. D. Basilopoulos, 1988), 64–65.

18. *Leo the Deacon*, I.3.

19. *Leo the Deacon*, I.4.

20. *Leo the Deacon*, I.8.

21. *Ouranos*, 65.20.

22. Tsounkarakes and Chrysos, *Byzantine Crete*, 72.

CHAPTER EIGHT: THE BYZANTINE ART OF WAR

1. B. H. Liddell Hart, *The Strategy of Indirect Approach* (London: Faber and Faber, 1941), 59–62.

2. Ibid., 72.

3. J. F. C. Fuller, *A Military History of the Western World* (New York: Funk & Wagnalls, 1954), 339.

4. Georgios Theotokis, "The Norman Invasion of Sicily, 1061–1072: Numbers and Military Tactics," *War in History* 17, no. 4 (2010): 393.

5. Bernard Bachrach, "On the Origins of William the Conqueror's Horse Transports," *Technology and Culture* 26, no. 3 (1985): 513.

6. Ibid., 514.

7. *Theophanes*, AM 6165.

8. *Vegetius*, IV.18.

9. John F. Haldon, "'Greek Fire' Revisited: Recent and Current Research," in *Byzantine Style, Religion and Civilization: In Honour of Sir Steven Runciman*, ed. Elizabeth Jeffreys (Cambridge: Cambridge University Press, 2006), 314.

10. *Taktika*, 19.59.

11. John H. Pryor and Elizabeth M. Jeffreys, *The Age of the Dromon: The Byzantine Navy ca. 500–1204* (Leiden: Brill, 2006), 620.

12. Ibid., 618.

13. Ibid., 609.

14. Ibid., 609ff.

15. Ibid., 612.

16. *Alexiad*, XI.10.

17. Pryor and Jeffreys, *The Age of the Dromon*, 612.

18. Ibid., 613.

19. Peter Pentz, "A Medieval Workshop for Producing 'Greek Fire' Grenades," *Antiquity* 62, no. 234 (1988).

20. Maurice Mercier, *Le feu grégeois, les feux de guerre depuis l'antiquité, la poudre à canon* (Paris: P. Geuthner, 1952), 84–91.

21. *Praecepta militaria*, I.150–55.

22. Pryor and Jeffreys, *The Age of the Dromon*, 619–20.

23. George T. Dennis, "Byzantine Heavy Artillery: The Helepolis," *Greek, Roman, and Byzantine Studies* 39 (1998): 101.

24. W. T. S. Tarver, "The Traction Trebuchet: A Reconstruction of an Early Medieval Siege Engine," *Technology and Culture* 36, no. 1 (1995): 149.

25. Ibid., 162.

26. Chevedden, "The Invention of the Counterweight Trebuchet," 77.

27. *Alexiad*, X.11.

28. S. Vryonis, "The Byzantine Legacy and Ottoman Forms," *Dumbarton Oaks Papers* 23–24 (1969–70): 273–74.

29. Antoine Henri Jomini, baron de, *The Art of War*, trans. G. H. Mendell and W. P. Craighill (Philadelphia: J. P. Lippincott, 1862), 366.

30. Alfred Vagts, *Landing Operations: Strategy, Psychology, Tactics, Politics, from Antiquity to 1945* (Harrisburg, Pa.: Military Service Pub. Co., 1946), 116.

31. Liddell Hart, *The Strategy of Indirect Approach*, 49–69.

32. T. E. Lawrence, *Seven Pillars of Wisdom* (London: Vintage, 2008), 117.

BIBLIOGRAPHY

Ahrweiler, Hélène. *Byzance et la mer: La marine de guerre, la politique et les insti-tutions maritimes de Byzance aux VIIè–XVe siècles.* Paris: Presses universi-taires de France, 1966.

Anastasiadis, M. P. "On Handling the Menavlion." *Byzantine and Modern Greek Studies* 18 (1994): 1–10.

Bachrach, Bernard. "On the Origins of William the Conqueror's Horse Transports." *Technology and Culture* 26, no. 3 (1985): 505–31.

Bagnall, Roger S., and Raffaella Cribiore. *Women's Letters from Ancient Egypt, 300 BC–AD 800.* Ann Arbor: University of Michigan Press, 2006.

Bartusis, Mark C. *The Late Byzantine Army: Arms and Society, 1204–1453.* Philadelphia: University of Pennsylvania Press, 1992.

———. "The Megala Allagia and the Tzaousios: Aspects of Provincial Military Organization in Late Byzantium." *Revue des études byzantines* 47 (1989): 183–207.

Birkenmeier, John W. *The Development of the Komnenian Army: 1081–1180.* Leiden: Brill, 2002.

Bosworth, C. E. "The City of Tarsus and the Arab-Byzantine Frontiers in Early and Middle Abbasid Times." *Oriens* 33 (1992): 268–86.

Campbell, Duncan B. *Greek and Roman Artillery 399 BC–AD 363.* Oxford: Osprey Publishing, 2003.

Canard, Marius. *Histoire de la dynastie des H'amdanides de Jazîra et de Syrie.* Algiers: Imprimeries "La Typo-litho" et J. Carbonel réunies, 1951.

Charanis, Peter. "The Armenians in the Byzantine Empire." *Byzantinoslavica* 22 (1961): 196–240.

Chevedden, Paul E. "The Invention of the Counterweight Trebuchet: A Study in Cultural Diffusion." *Dumbarton Oaks Papers* 54 (2000): 71–116.

Cheynet, J.-C. "Mantzikert: Un désastre militaire?" *Byzantion* 50 (1980): 410–38.

Chibnall, Marjorie. *The Normans.* Malden, Mass.: Blackwell, 2006.

Constantine Porphyrogenitus. *Constantine Porphyrogenitus: Three Treatises on Imperial Military Expeditions.* Translated by J. Haldon. Vienna: Verlag der Österreichischen Akademie der Wissenschaften, 1990.

Corippus, Flavius Cresconius, and George W Shea. *The Iohannis, or, De Bellis Libycis.* Lewiston, N.Y.: Edwin Mellen Press, 1998.

Coulston, J. C. N. "Late Roman Armour, 3rd–6th Centuries AD." *Journal of Roman Military Equipment Studies* (1990): 139–60.

Dain, Alphonse, and Emperor Leo VI. *Sylloge Tacticorum, Quae Olim "Inedita Leonis Tactica" Dicebatur.* Paris: Société d'édition "Les Belles lettres," 1938.

Davidson, G. R., and Tibor Horváth. "The Avar Invasion of Corinth." *Hesperia* 6, no. 2 (1937): 227–40.

Dawson, Timothy. "Kremasmata, Kabbadion, Klibanion: Some Aspects of Middle Byzantine Military Equipment Reconsidered." *Byzantine and Modern Greek Studies* 22 (1998): 38–50.

———. "Suntagma Hoplôn: The Equipment of Regular Byzantine Troops, c. 950–c. 1204." In *A Companion to Medieval Arms and Armour*, edited by D. Nicolle, 81–90. Woodbridge: Boydell Press, 2002.

Decker, Michael. "Towers, Refuges, and Fortified Farms in the Late Roman East." *Liber Annuus* 56 (2006): 499–520.

Dennis, George T. "Byzantine Heavy Artillery: The Helepolis." *Greek, Roman, and Byzantine Studies* 39 (1998): 99–115.

Dixon, Karen R., and Pat Southern. *The Roman Cavalry*. London: Routledge, 1997.

Dodgeon, Michael H., and Samuel N. C. Lieu. *The Roman Eastern Frontier and the Persian Wars (AD 226–363): A Documentary History*. London: Routledge, 1991.

Donner, Fred. *The Early Islamic Conquests*. Princeton: Princeton University Press, 1981.

Dvornik, F. *Origins of Intelligence Services: The Ancient Near East, Persia, Greece, Rome, Byzantium, the Arab Muslim Empires, the Mongol Empire, China, Muscovy*. New Brunswick, N.J.: Rutgers University Press, 1974.

Engelhardt, Conrad. *Nydam Mosefund, 1859–1863*. Copenhagen: I commission hos GEC Gad, 1865.

Ferluga, Jadran. "Le Clisure Bizantine in Asia Minore." In *Byzantium on the Balkans: Studies on the Byzantine Administration and the Southern Slavs from the VIIth to the XIIth Centuries*, edited by Jadran Ferluga. Amsterdam: A. M. Hakkert, 1976.

Fögen, Marie Theres. "Lombards." In *Oxford Dictionary of Byzantium*, edited by A. P. Kazhdan, 1249. New York: Oxford University Press, 1991.

Fuller, J. F. C. *A Military History of the Western World*. New York: Funk & Wagnalls, 1954.

Genesios, Ioseph. *On the Reigns of the Emperors*. Translated by Anthony Kaldellis. Canberra: Australian Association for Byzantine Studies, 1998.

Godfrey, Evelyne, and Matthijs van Nie. "A Germanic Ultrahigh Carbon Steel Punch of the Late Roman-Iron Age." *Journal of Archaeological Science* 31 (2004): 1117–25.

Grancsay, Stephen V. "A Sasanian Chieftain's Helmet." *Metropolitan Museum of Art Bulletin* 21, no. 8 (1963): 253–62.

Grotowski, P. *Arms and Armour of the Warrior Saints*. Leiden: Brill, 2010.

Guilland, R. *Recherches sur les Institutions Byzantines*. Berlin: Akademie-Verlag, 1967.

Haldon, J. *Byzantine Praetorians: An Administrative, Institutional, and Social Survey of the Opsikion and Tagmata, c. 580–900*. Bonn: R. Habelt, 1984.

———. *Byzantium in the Seventh Century: The Transformation of a Culture*. Cambridge: Cambridge University Press, 1990.

———. *The Byzantine Wars*. Stroud, Glos.: The History Press, 2008.

———. "'Greek Fire' Revisited: Recent and Current Research." In *Byzantine Style, Religion and Civilization: In Honour of Sir Steven Runciman*, edited by Elizabeth Jeffreys, 290–325. Cambridge: Cambridge University Press, 2006.

———. "Military Service, Military Lands, and the Status of Soldiers: Current Problems and Interpretations." *Dumbarton Oaks Papers* 47 (1993): 1–67.

———. "The Organisation and Support of an Expeditionary Force: Manpower and Logistics in the Middle Byzantine Period." in To empolemo Byzantio = Byzantium at War (9th–12th c.): International Symposium 4 [of the] Institute for Byzantine Research [Athens, 1996], ed. Nicolas Oikonomides, Kostas Tsiknakes (Athens: Goulandre-Chorn Foundation, 1997).

———. *Recruitment and Conscription in the Byzantine Army c. 550–950*. Vienna: Verlag der Österreichischen Akademie der Wissenschaften, 1979.

———. "Some Aspects of Byzantine Military Technology from the Sixth to the Tenth Centuries." *Byzantine and Modern Greek Studies* 1 (1975): 11–47.

———. *Warfare, State, and Society in the Byzantine World, 565–1204*. London: UCL Press, 1999.

Heather, Peter. *The Goths*. Oxford: Blackwell, 1996.

Hendy, M. *Studies in the Byzantine Monetary Economy c. 300–1450*. Cambridge: Cambridge University Press, 1985.

Hovannisian, Richard G. *The Armenian People from Ancient to Modern Times*. New York: St. Martin's Press, 1997.

Howard-Johnston, J. D. "Heraclius' Persian Campaigns and the Revival of the East Roman Empire, 622–630." *War in History* 6 (1999): 1–44.

Huxley, George L. "The Emperor Michael III and the Battle of Bishop's Meadow (A.D. 863)." *Greek, Roman, and Byzantine Studies* (1975): 443–50.

Isaac, Benjamin H. *The Limits of Empire: The Roman Army in the East*. Oxford: Clarendon Press, 1990.

James, Simon. "Evidence from Dura Europos for the Origins of Late Roman Helmets." *Syria* 63, nos. 1–2 (1986): 107–34.

———. "The Fabricae: State Arms Factories of the Later Roman Empire." In *Military Equipment and the Identity of Roman Soldiers: Proceedings of the Fourth Roman Military Equipment Conference*, edited by J. C. N. Coulston, 257–331. Oxford: British Archaeological Reports, 1988.

———. "Stratagems, Combat, and 'Chemical Warfare' in the Siege Mines of Dura-Europos." *American Journal of Archaeology* 115, no. 1 (2011): 69–101.

Jomini, Antoine Henri, baron de. *The Art of War.* Translated by G. H. Mendell and W. P. Craighill. Philadelphia: J. P. Lippincott, 1862.

Jones, A. H. M. *The Later Roman Empire, 284–602: A Social Economic and Administrative Survey.* London: Blackwell, 1964.

Kaegi, W. "Byzantine Logistics: Problems and Perspectives." In *Feeding Mars: Logistics in Western Warfare from the Middle Ages to the Present*, edited by J. A. Lynn, 39–55. Boulder: Westview Press, 1993.

———. *Byzantium and the Early Islamic Conquests.* Cambridge: Cambridge University Press, 1992.

Kamp, Norbert, and Joachim Wollasch. *Tradition als historische Kraft: interdisziplinäre Forschungen zur Geschichte des früheren Mittelalters.* Berlin: de Gruyter, 1982.

Kennedy, Hugh. *The Armies of the Caliphs.* London: Routledge, 2001.

———. *The Great Arab Conquests: How the Spread of Islam Changed the World We Live In.* Philadelphia: Da Capo, 2007.

Kolias, T. *Byzantinische Waffen: ein Beitrag zur byzantinischen Waffenkunde von den Anfängen bis zur lateinischen Eroberung.* Vienna: Verlag der Österreichischen Akademie der Wissenschaften, 1988.

Kulikowski, M. *Rome's Gothic Wars: From the Third Century to Alaric.* Cambridge: Cambridge University Press, 2007.

Kyriakidis, Savvas. *Warfare in Late Byzantium, 1204–1453.* Leiden: Brill, 2011.

Lawrence, T. E. *Seven Pillars of Wisdom.* London: Vintage, 2008.

Lecker, Michael. "Siffin." In *The Encyclopaedia of Islam*, edited by C. E. Bosworth, E. van Donzel, and W. P. Heinrichs, 552–56. Leiden: Brill, 1997.

Liddell Hart, B. H. *The Strategy of Indirect Approach.* London: Faber and Faber, 1941.

Lilie, R.-J. "Die Zweihundertjährige Reform: zu den Anfängen der Themenorganisation im 7. und 8. Jahrhundert." *Byzantinoslavica* 45 (1984): 27–39, 190–201.

Luttwak, Edward N. *The Grand Strategy of the Byzantine Empire.* Cambridge, Mass.: Harvard University Press, 2009.

Maenchen-Helfen, Otto. *The World of the Huns: Studies in Their History and Culture.* Berkeley: University of California Press, 1973.

Malaterra, Goffredo. *The Deeds of Count Roger of Calabria and Sicily and of His Brother Duke Robert Guiscard.* Ann Arbor: University of Michigan Press, 2005.

Markle, Minor M., III. "The Macedonian Sarrissa, Spear and Related Armor." *American Journal of Archaeology* 81, no. 3 (1977): 323–39.

McGeer, Eric. *Sowing the Dragon's Teeth: Byzantine Warfare in the Tenth Century.* Washington, D.C.: Dumbarton Oaks, 2008.

McLeod, W. "The Range of the Ancient Bow." *Phoenix* 19, no. 1 (1965): 1–14.

Mercier, Maurice. *Le Feu Grégeois: Les Feux de Guerre Depuis L'antiquité, la Poudre à Canon.* Paris: P. Geuthner, 1952.

Michael Psellus. *Fourteen Byzantine Rulers: The Chronographia of Michael Psellus.* Translated by E. R. A. Sewter. New York: Penguin Books, 1966.

Mitchell, Russ. "Archery Versus Mail: Experimental Archaeology and the Value of Historical Context." *Journal of Medieval Military History* 4 (2006): 18–28.

Morrisson, Cécile, and Jean-Claude Cheynet. "Prices and Wages in the Byzantine World." In *The Economic History of Byzantium: From the Seventh Through the Fifteenth Century,* edited by Angeliki E. Laiou and Charalampos Bouras, 681–96. Washington, D.C.: Dumbarton Oaks Research Library and Collection, 2002.

Nicephorus Bryennius. *Nicéphore Bryennios Histoire: Introduction, Texte, Traduction et Notes.* Translated by P. Gautier. Corpus Fontium Historiae Byzantinae. Brussels: Byzantion, 1975.

Oikonomides, A. N. "Les Premières Mentions des Thèmes dans la Chronique de Théophane." *Zbornik radova Vizantoloskog Instituta* 16 (1975): 1–8.

Parani, Maria G. *Reconstructing the Reality of Images: Byzantine Material Culture and Religious Iconography (11th–15th Centuries).* Leiden: Brill, 2003.

Parker, S. Thomas. *The Roman Frontier in Central Jordan: Final Report on the Limes Arabicus Project, 1980–1989.* Washington, D.C.: Dumbarton Oaks, 2006.

Pentz, Peter. "A Medieval Workshop for Producing 'Greek Fire' Grenades." *Antiquity* 62, no. 234 (1988): 89–93.

Perevalov, S. M. "The Sarmatian Lance and the Sarmatian Horse-Riding Posture." *Anthropology and Archeology of Eurasia* 41, no. 4 (2003): 7–21.

Pryor, John H., and Elizabeth M. Jeffreys. *The Age of the Dromon: The Byzantine Navy Ca. 500–1204.* Leiden: Brill, 2006.

Rance, Philip. "Narses and the Battle of Taginae (Busta Gallorum) 552: Procopius and Sixth-Century Warfare." *Historia: Zeitschrift für Alte Geschichte* 54, no. 4 (2005): 424–72.

Robert, Louis. "Noms Métiers dans des Documents Byzantins." In *Charisterion Eis Anastasion K. Orlandon 1*, edited by Anastasios K. Orlandos. 324–27. Athens: He en Athenais Archaiologike Hetairea, 1965.

Runciman, Steven. *The Sicilian Vespers: A History of the Mediterranean World in the Later Thirteenth Century.* 1958; Cambridge: Cambridge University Press, 1992.

Seeck, Otto. *Notitia Dignitatum: Accedunt Notitia Urbis Constantinopolitanae et Laterculi Prouinciarum.* Berlin: Weidmann, 1876.

Shepard, Jonathan. "The English and Byzantium: A Study of Their Role in the Byzantine Army in the Later Eleventh Century." *Traditio* 29 (1973): 53–92.

———. "The Uses of the Franks in Eleventh-Century Byzantium." *Anglo-Norman Studies* 15 (1993): 275–305.

Sophoulis, Panos. *Byzantium and Bulgaria, 775–831.* Leiden: Brill, 2012.

Stephenson, I. P. *Romano-Byzantine Infantry Equipment.* Stroud, Gloucester: Tempus, 2006.

Stephenson, Paul. *Byzantium's Balkan Frontier: A Political Study of the Northern Balkans, 900–1204.* Cambridge: Cambridge University Press, 2000.

Stratos, Andreas Nikolau. *Byzantium in the Seventh Century 3. 642–668.* Translated by Harry T. Hionides. Amsterdam: Hakkert, 1975.

Tarleton, N. "Pastoralem Praefixa Cuspide Myrtum (Aeneid 7.817)." *Classical Quarterly* 39, no. 1 (1989): 267–70.

Tarver, W. T. S. "The Traction Trebuchet: A Reconstruction of an Early Medieval Siege Engine." *Technology and Culture* 36, no. 1 (1995): 136–67.

Theotokis, Georgios. "The Norman Invasion of Sicily, 1061–1072: Numbers and Military Tactics." *War in History* 17, no. 4 (2010): 381–402.

Treadgold, Warren T. *The Byzantine Revival, 780–842.* Stanford, Calif.: Stanford University Press, 1988.

———. *Byzantium and Its Army, 284–1081.* Stanford, Calif.: Stanford University Press, 1995.

———. *The Early Byzantine Historians.* New York: Palgrave Macmillan, 2007.

Tsounkarakes, Demetres, and Euangelos K. Chrysos. *Byzantine Crete: From the 5th Century to the Venetian Conquest.* Athens: Historical Publications St. D. Basilopoulos, 1988.

Vagts, Alfred. *Landing Operations: Strategy, Psychology, Tactics, Politics, from Antiquity to 1945.* Harrisburg, Pa.: Military Service Publishing, 1946.

van der Veen, Marijke , and Alison Cox. *Consumption, Trade and Innovation: Exploring the Botanical Remains from the Roman and Islamic Ports at Quseir Al-Qadim, Egypt.* Frankfurt am Main: Africa Magna Verlag, 2011.

Vryonis, S. "The Byzantine Legacy and Ottoman Forms." *Dumbarton Oaks Papers* 23–24 (1969–70): 251–308.

Yahya-Ibn-Sa'id, d'Antioche, I. Kratchkovsky, and A. Vasiliev. *Histoire de Yahya-Ibn-Sa`id d'Antioche, continuateur de Sa`id-Ibn-Bitriq, Fascicule I.* Patrologia Orientalis. 3 vols. Vol. 1, Paris: Firmin-Didot, 1924.

———. *Histoire de Yahya-Ibn-Sa'id d'Antioche, continuateur de Sa'id-Ibn-Bitriq: Fascicule II.* Translated by I. Kratchkovsky and A. Vasiliev. Patrologia Orientalis, edited by René Graffin and François Nau. 2 vols. Vol. 2, Paris: Firmin-Didot, 1932.

INDEX

Leo V, 28, 79
Leo VI, 42, 77, 80, 98, 120, 128, 131-132,
    158, 223
Licinius, 2
Life of St. Germanus, "iron cavalry" and, 110
limitanei, border troops and, 7, 50, 67-68,
    71-72, 77, 84, 90, 95, 233-234
Lombards, 25, 86, 163, 165
Longshanks, Edward I, counterweight tre-
    buchets, 229
Louis VII, 199
Luttwak, Edward N., "Grand Strategy"
    and, 132

Macedonian dynasty, ix, 28, 30, 98, 117,
    131, 136, 147, 177, 230
Majorian, 180
Manfred of Sicily, 144
Maniakes, George, 33, 49, 221
Marcellinus, Ammianus, 10, 12, 109, 124
Marcian, 180
Martel, Charles, 219
Massagetae, 54, 85, 183
Master of Offices, fabricae workshops and,
    95
Masud, 199
Maurice
    army organization and, 92
    assassination of, 15, 45
    Book XII and, 151
    hybrid horse archer-lancers and, 149
    imperial armamenta and, 96
    lamellar armor and, 112
    Lombards and, 163
    maces and, 120
    practice of combined arms and, 230
    ratio of horse to foot and, 75
    sons of fallen soldiers and, 84-85
    Strategikon and, 41, 72-73, 77-78, 104-
        107, 113, 117, 121, 123, 132, 135,
        138, 146-148, 150, 154, 158, 167-
        169, 214, 221
    tactics and, 127, 136
    tagmas and, 108
McClellan, George, 231

Mehmed II, vii, 40
Merkourios, 10
Michael I, 28
Michael II, 79, 87, 209
Michael III, 25, 48
Michael, Khan Boris, 173
Michael VII, 82, 199
Michael VIII, 37, 48-49, 83, 91, 137, 144
Miracles of St. Demetrios, Avar siege and, 125
Mount Aetna, 183
Mu'awiya, 21-22, 142, 207
Muhammad, 18, 20
Mundhir, 15
Mundus, 45, 47
Muslims, *see also* Arabs
    Anatolian commanders and, 49
    attacks on Constantinople and, 22
    Basil II and, 147
    battle at Chandax and, 210-211
    battle with Heraclius's army and, 20-21
    civil war and, 142
    Constantine VII and, 191
    creation of an Arab fleet and, 142
    eastern campaigns of Nikephoros
        Phokas and, 191-195
    fortress of Babylon and, 21
    fortress of Shaizar and, 64
    "forward defense" and, 129
    Greek fire and, 224
    jihad and, 24, 63, 129, 145, 191-192
    John Tzimiskes and, 57
    Khazar khanate and, 137
    methods of warfare and, 171
    organization of armies and, 170-171
    post system and, 101
    siege of 674–78 and, 222
    spies and, 146
    sustained assaults (717-718) and, 207-
        208
    victory at Constantinople and, 40
Mygdonius River, 8-9

Nagyszentiklós
    depiction of Bulgar warrior and, 113
    treasure of, 113, 168